Books by Thomas H. Ormsbee

Early American Furniture Makers

The Story of American Furniture

If You're Going to Live in the Country
    (with Richmond Huntley)

Collecting Antiques in America

Staffordshire Pottery
    (with Josiah Wedgwood)

Antique Furniture of the Walnut Period
    (with R. W. Symonds)

A Storehouse of Antiques

Prime Antiques and Their Current Prices

Care and Repair of Antiques

Field Guide to Early American Furniture

Field Guide to American Victorian Furniture

Field Guide
TO
EARLY AMERICAN
FURNITURE

ANTIQUES IN USE

A country living room furnished with American furniture
made between 1700 and 1850. The pieces shown here are all
representative of those described and illustrated in this book.
Left to right they are wagon seat, No. 307; slat-back armchair, No. 5; American Empire tabernacle mirror, No. 285;
Hepplewhite lamp stand, No. 97; American Empire vase-
splat side chair, No. 40; William and Mary highboy, No. 201;
Sheraton pedestal table (with turn-top instead of drop-leaves)
No. 102 and Boston rocker, No. 43.

Field Guide

TO

EARLY AMERICAN FURNITURE

by

Thomas H. Ormsbee

DRAWINGS BY NORMAN B. PALMSTROM

Bonanza Books · New York

This edition published by Bonanza Books,
a division of Crown Publishers, Inc.,
by arrangement with Little, Brown and Company

G   H

PRINTED IN THE UNITED STATES OF AMERICA

To
E. L. B.
and
D. A. C.
Who plotted this book

Code Symbols
and Table of Comparative Values

X	*Under*	to	$ 25
XX	$ 25	to	$ 75
XXX	$ 75	to	$ 100
Y	$ 100	to	$ 150
YY	$ 150	to	$ 250
YYY	$ 250	to	$ 500
Z	$ 500	to	$ 750
ZZ	$ 750	to	$ 1000
ZZZ	$ 1000	to	$ 1500
Q	$ 1500	to	$ 2000
QQ	$ 2000	to	$ 3000
QQQ	*Above* $ 3000		

Contents

CONTENTS

Cabinetmakers' Language

ACANTHUS LEAF. A conventionalized carved detail.

ACORN FINIAL. So called because of its shape.

ANTHENION. The Greek honeysuckle. Used as a carving detail.

APPLIED CRESTING. A carved crest piece, done separately and attached to the top rail of a chair or sofa.

APPLIED ORNAMENT. A detail shaped or carved separately and then attached to the surface of a piece of furniture.

APRON. *See* Skirt.

ARCADED. A series of low-relief flat arches used to decorate a cornice frieze.

ARCHED MOLDING. A plain, half-round convex molding used singly or in pairs.

ARCHITECTURAL FURNITURE. Large piece in which the design includes architectural features.

ARM PAD. A stuffed and upholstered pad attached to a chair arm.

ARM STUMP. The front support of a chair arm that replaces the upward extension of a front leg. Sometimes called an *Arm Support.*

ARROW SPINDLE. A flat spindle with one end resembling an arrow, used with some Windsor chairs.

ASTRAGAL. A convex molding chiefly used to overlap the joining of double doors in secretaries and cupboards.

BAIL HANDLES. A brass pendant half-hoop with ends anchored in the attached posts, thus serving as a drawer pull.

BALL FOOT. Boldly turned in the shape of a ball and of ample proportions.

BALL LEG TIP. A small brass ball-shaped foot with cup above which fits over the end of a table or chair leg.

BALL-AND-STEEPLE FINIAL. A turned finial with a well-formed ball as the lowest element surmounted by a series of ring turnings that diminish in size.

BALUSTER TURNED. Originally one of the small columns supporting a railing. In furniture a turning that resembles such a column.

BAMBOO TURNED. Done with ringing to resemble the joints in a length of bamboo.

BANDING. A narrow border framing a drawer front, a band of contrasting inlay or a border of veneer framing the textile or leather panel on the writing surface of a desk.

BANISTER. A corruption of baluster, used chiefly to describe the split turned splats that form the back of a banister-back chair.

BASE. The element on a piece of case furniture immediately above the feet. Also the lower section of any two-part piece.

BAT'S-WING BRASSES. Those where handle plates and escutcheons resemble a bat with outstretched wings.

BATTENS. Projecting strips of wood fastened across one or more boards as cleats.

BEAD MOLDING. *See* Cock-Bead Molding.

BEARER STRIP. A narrow piece of wood at the bottom of a drawer opening and on which the front rests when drawer is closed.

BEVEL. A slanting cutting away of the edge of a board or sheet of glass to reduce thickness.

BIRD CAGE. The double block construction by which a tilt-top table top may both tilt and rotate. So named for its resemblance in outline to a cage.

BLANKET CHEST. A case piece with hinged lid, a deep well and one or two drawers beneath.

BLOCK FOOT. The projecting square end of a chair or table leg of Chippendale period. Also known as a *Marlborough Foot.*

BLOCK FRONT. A Baroque treatment wherein the front of a case piece is divided into three vertical panels, the outer ones projecting and the central one recessed.

BLUNT ARROW LEG. A Windsor chair leg terminating in a ball-like end resembling a blunted practice arrow.

BOBBIN TURNED. The bulging element of turned stretchers. So called for resemblance to a wound bobbin.

BODY CONFORMING. Shaped to the human form, such as a

chair back slightly concave instead of perpendicular.
Also called *Spooned*.

BOMBÉ BASE. Has outward swelling sides and front. Because this curve resembles that of a kettle, is sometimes referred to as a *Kettle Base*.

BONNET TOP. An enclosed broken pediment.

BOSS. A small circular or oval applied ornament.

BOW FRONT. The front of a case piece with a continuous outcurve.

BOX STRETCHER. One where the square or turned members are so placed as to form a square or rectangle.

BRACKET. A shaped support that reinforces the joining of a leg to the seat rail of a chair or to a table bed.

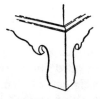

BRACKET FOOT. A simple case piece support running two ways from a mitered corner with inner edges cut in silhouette. Is of three types, plain, scrolled or molded.

BRAD. A small slender nail from a quarter to an inch long having little or no head.

BREAK-FRONT. A case piece with a projecting central section.

BROKEN PEDIMENT. A pediment where the cyma-curved or straight elements do not meet at the apex.

BUN FOOT. A ball foot slightly flattened top and bottom.

BURL VENEER. Figured, mottled or speckled veneer cut from an excrescence on a tree trunk.

BUTT HINGE. Hinge with plain rectangular leaves. Is attached on doors so that only rounded pin joint shows.

BUTT JOINT. A joining of squared edges of two members at right angles.

CABRIOLE LEG. A curved leg with outcurved knee and incurved ankle. Originated in Italy and is a conventionalized representation of the rear leg of a leaping goat.

CAMEL BACK. The double curved crest rail of some Hepplewhite chair backs, the outline of which resembles that of a single-hump camel.

CANDLE BRACKETS. A pair of pull brackets at base of upper part of a secretary, devised for candlesticks.

CANE. Long, narrow strips of rattan bark used for weaving seats and backs of chairs and settees.

CANOPY. The framework, frequently textile covered, that surmounts the tall posts of a bed. Also called a *Tester*.

CANTED. Slanting or sloping. Part of a piece of furniture that slants or slopes, such as a canted corner or leg.

CARCASE. The body of a case piece of furniture.

CARTOUCHE. An ornamental feature, carved or inlaid, in the form of an unrolled scroll or an oval tablet.

CASE PIECE. Any piece of furniture of boxlike structure.

CHAMFERED. A right-angle corner cut away to form a slight bevel.

CHEVAL GLASS. A large mirror, generally about figure length with frame, swinging on vertical posts supported by trestles.

CHIP CARVING. Simple carving done in low relief with flat chisels and semicircular gouges.

CLAW-AND-BALL FOOT. Carved to represent a bird's claw grasping a ball. Derived from the Chinese dragon's claw holding a crystal ball or jewel.

CLEAT. A strip of wood attached to a flat surface for strength, bracing or to prevent warping.

CLEATED ENDS. The strips of wood nailed or morticed and tenoned to the ends of some table tops.

COCK-BEAD MOLDING. A small half-round projecting molding.

COLONNETTE. A miniature column most frequently used in groups of four as a table pedestal.

COMB-BACK. A chair with back surmounted by a comb-piece.

COMB-PIECE. The cresting rail supported by long spindles on some Windsor chair backs. So named because of the resemblance to the high combs worn by women of the period.

COMPOSITION. A molded substitute for carving, made of plaster of Paris, rosin and size mixed with water. Also called *Compo.*

CONSOLE. From the French, meaning *bracket.* A table having only front legs and attached bracketlike to a wall.

CORNER BLOCK. A shaped triangular block used to brace the joining of legs and seat rails of chairs or sofas.

CORNER CHAIR. Seat is set on diagonal, fits into corner of room, hence the name. Also called *Roundabout Chair.*

CORNER STILES. The vertical members at the corner of a piece of wainscot furniture.

CORNICE. The top horizontal molding or group of moldings of a piece of furniture.

COURT CUPBOARD. A low cupboard mounted on an open frame. Is derived from the French *court,* meaning short.

COVE MOLDING. A large concave molding chiefly used in cornices.

CREST RAIL. The top rail of a chair back, particularly when shaped or carved.

CRESTING. The ornamental top member of a chair, settee or sofa back.

CREWELWORK. Linen embroidered with worsted, generally done in scroll and floral designs. Used for bed hangings, table covers and backs and seats of some chairs.

CROSSBANDING. Veneer border banding in which the grain runs across the banding.

CROSS MEMBER. A structural horizontal part of a piece of furniture joined to sides or uprights.

CROSS RAIL. A horizontal member in a chair back.

CROTCH GRAIN. Veneer generally cut from the main crotch of a mahogany tree.

CUP CASTER. A brass furniture roller with cup above that fits over the end of a chair or table leg.

CUPID'S BOW. Top rail of a chair back having a double ogee curve resembling a cupid's bow in outline.

CURULE CHAIR. Originally the Roman chair of office.

Later a folding chair with curved legs and, in the Sheraton period, one where the legs are replaced by two tangent semicircular segments.

CYLINDER FRONT. The quarter-round front of a desk or secretary so mounted that it pivots.

CYMA CURVE. A continuous curve, one half of which is concave, the other convex.

DIE. A rectangular block surmounting a leg or pilaster.

DOCUMENT BOXES. Narrow, vertical, open-top drawers flanking the central locker in the writing interior of a desk or secretary.

DOVETAIL. A type of joining with interlocking flaring tenons which resemble the tail feathers of a dove.

DOWEL. A circular wooden pin used to fasten two pieces of wood.

DRAKE FOOT. So carved with three toes as to resemble the contracted claw of a male duck.

DRAWING-BOOK CHAIR BACK. A design widely used by American cabinetmakers that was copied in detail from Sheraton's *The Cabinet-Maker and Upholsterer's Drawing-Book*.

DUST BOARD. Board separating a drawer space from that above or below it.

DUTCH FOOT. A plain, slightly curved foot that terminates the early cabriole leg. Sometimes called a *Pad Foot*.

EBONIZED. Wood stained or painted to simulate ebony.

ESCUTCHEON. A brass keyhole plate.

FALL-FRONT. Writing flap of a desk or secretary which hinges from the upright to the horizontal.

FESTOON. A carved, inlaid or painted decoration reproducing the line of a garland or drapery hanging done in a series of scalloplike loops.

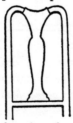

FIDDLE-BACK. The single splat of a chair back which resembles the outline of a violin.

FIELD BED. A tall post bed with an arched canopy. Sometimes called a *Tent Bed* from its resemblance in outline to an army officer's tent of the eighteenth century.

FIELDED PANEL. A panel with plain surface framed by molding, beveling or grooving or a panel composed of smaller panels.

FILIGREE. Ornament done with gold or silver wire. In furniture gilded wirework in delicate ornamental patterns.

FINIAL. Decorative finish at top of back uprights of a chair or corners and center of a pediment. Generally turned or carved in urn, flame or steeple form.

FLARE. Outward spread, as with a chair seat that is wider at the front than at the back.

FLEMISH SCROLL. A Baroque scroll with curve broken by an angle.

FLUSH. Even or level with the surrounding surface.

FLUTING. A series of rounded furrows or channels cut vertically on a column, shaft, pilaster, leg or frieze. Is reverse of *Reeding.*

FREE-STANDING COLUMN. A column with open space behind it. Frequently when vase-shaped and reeded, forms the upper extension of the front corner legs on Sheraton sofas and settees.

FRENCH FOOT. A slightly outswept bracket foot always combined with a valanced skirt.

FRET CARVING. An outline done with a fret saw in balancing scrolls.

FRETWORK or FRETTED. An interlaced ornamental pattern either in silhouette and pierced or carved in low relief. Frequently done in geometric motifs.

FRIEZE. The flat surface beneath a cornice molding.

FRIEZE DRAWER. An overhanging top drawer in a chest of drawers, generally supported by columns or pilasters.

GADROONING. Ornamental carving of an edge or of a wide molding with repeated curved and fluted elements as the pattern.

GALLERY. A railing of brass or wood or a raised rim.

GARLAND. A carved floral wreath.

GATE-LEG. A swinging leg that supports a table leaf. Resembles a fence gate in outline, hence the name.

GEOMETRIC. An abstract pattern evolved of interlacing squares, triangles, circles or arcs.

GESSO. A mixture of plaster of Paris, glue and water applied to wood surfaces to fill pores and obtain a glasslike smoothness. Used where surface is to be gold-leafed or painted to simulate veneer.

GIRANDOLE. French for a branched candlestick. In America, the name of a circular mirror with scrolled candle arms and a convex glass.

GOOSENECKS. The balancing double curved elements in an arched pediment. So named for their resemblance to the projected neck of a hissing goose. When the direction of the double curve is nearly vertical, it is sometimes called a *Swan's Neck*.

GUINEA POCKETS. The four saucerlike depressions carved into the top of a gaming table to hold coins or chips during a game played for stakes.

HALF-COLUMN. A split column mounted against a flat surface. Also called a *Rounded Pilaster*.

HERRINGBONE. Inlay done with slanting pieces of wood of contrasting colors.

HOODED TOP. *See* Bonnet Top.

HUSK. An ornamental detail, generally as a pendant, of conventionalized foliage, either inlaid or carved in low relief.

INCISED CARVING. Cut into the surface ornamented.

INLAY. Wood of contrasting color or texture inset into a surface for decoration. Done in geometric, floral or other designs. When done as straight lines is called *Stringing*.

INSET PILASTER. A pilaster inset in a flat surface. Most frequently at the front corners of a case piece.

INTAGLIO CARVED. So done that the design is slightly lower than the surrounding surface.

JACOBEAN. From the Latin *Jacobus* for James I. The general designation for English furniture design, 1603 to 1688, interrupted 1649 to 1660 by the Cromwellian. The later Jacobean is sometimes known as *Restoration* or *Carolean*.

JOINT. With furniture the joining of two members in the structure of a piece

KETTLE BASE. *See* Bombé Base.

KEYHOLE ESCUTCHEON. A decorative brass plate with centered keyhole.

KEYHOLE SURROUND. Cast metal inset of keyhole shape used instead of an escutcheon.

KNEE. The outcurved upper portion of a cabriole leg.

KNOB-AND-RING FINIAL. A turned finial with knob shaping above one or two elements of ring turning.

KNOB TURNING. Turning done in a series of knobs.

KNUCKLE CARVED. Carving that resembles the knuckle of the human hand.

LACQUERED. A finish done in imitation of the Chinese in gilt and colors on a single color background.

LADDER-BACK. A chair of Chippendale design with shaped and sometimes pierced horizontal back and splats, resembling a section of a ladder.

LAMINATED WOOD. Made of thin layers of wood glued together with grain of each layer at right angles to that above and below.

LAP JOINT. A joint where the two pieces are cut to half thickness and lapped one over the other.

LATTICEWORK. A crisscross pattern formed by narrow bars either carved from one piece of wood or assembled and joined.

LIP MOLDING. *See* Thumb Molding.

LOCKER. The central miniature cupboard in a desk or secretary writing interior.

LOOSE SEAT. *See* Slip Seat.

LOW RELIEF. Carving in which the design is close to background.

LOZENGE. Diamond shape.

LUNETTE. A semicircular or half-moon element in a decorative design, either carved or done with lines of inlay.

LYRE. A decorative design based on the classic Greek form of the harp.

MARQUETRY. A decorative design done in inlay with woods of contrasting colors set into a veneer background.

MELON-TURNED. Turning done in melon shape with characteristic vertical ribbing.

MITERED JOINT. A joint cut at an angle, generally 45 degrees.

MOLDED BASE. The base of a case piece formed with molded elements.

MOLDED BRACKET FOOT. A case piece support running two ways from a mitered support where the faces are molded in a cyma curve.

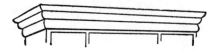

MOLDED CORNICE. A cornice formed of molded elements.

MOLDING. A narrow continuous surface, projecting or incised, used for decoration.

MORTICE. A slot cut into a wooden member, generally half of a mortice and tenon joint.

MOUNTS. The brass handles, escutcheons and other decorative details applied to pieces of furniture. Also pressed glass and turned wooden knobs.

MUNTINS. The wooden separations that retain the panes of glass in a glazed door.

MUSHROOM-TURNED KNOBS. Circular wooden knobs with fronts flatly curved, resembling a mushroom cap.

NESTED TABLES. Tables three or four in number of graduated sizes fitting one inside the other.

OGEE. A molding with a single or double cyma curve.

ORMOLU MOUNTS. Made of a special alloy of copper and zinc in elaborate Directoire designs.

OPEN BACK. A chair back formed of the framing and splat or splats and not covered by upholstery.

OUTROUNDED CORNERS. The corners of square or rectangular table tops where a semicircular curve replaces a right angle.

PAD FOOT. *See* Dutch Foot.

PANEL. A square or rectangular board held in place by stile and rails.

PARCEL GILDING. Ornamental gilding frequently stencil applied.

PATERA. Small round or oval ornaments, either carved or inlaid, with equally spaced lines radiating from the center. Used also as halves and quarters. Sometimes called *Sunbursts*.

PATINA. The mellow quality of color and texture that furniture surfaces, finished and unfinished, acquire with age.

PAW FOOT. A foot carved to resemble an animal's paw, most frequently that of a lion. Above it there is generally carved leafage.

PEDESTAL TABLE. Having a central pedestal instead of legs.

PEDIMENT. The ornamental top surmounting a tall piece of furniture. Frequently has a scrolled or straight triangular profile broken at the center. Is an adaptation of the triangular space forming the gable end of a roof in classic Greek and Roman architecture.

PEG. A rounded wooden pin or dowel that passes through both parts of a mortice and tenon joint to secure it.

Very small wooden pegs sometimes used instead of nails to join parts of pigeonhole drawers.

PEG FOOT. A small, short turned foot set canted in the base of a simple candlestand.

PEMBROKE TABLE. A drop-leaf table where central fixed leaf is about twice as wide as the drop leaves.

PENDENT BELLFLOWER. An ornamental detail, inlaid or painted, resembling a bell-shaped flower.

PENDENT FINIAL. A downward projecting finial.

PENDENT HUSKS. An ornamental detail, inlaid or painted, resembling the cornflower, hanging down and arranged in a diminishing series.

PENDENT SPHERES. Turned wooden spheres used for ornament and attached to the lower edge of a skirt or cross member.

PIECRUST TABLE. A circular tilt-top table with raised carved rim.

PIER GLASS. A narrow tall mirror designed to be hung on a wall between windows.

PIER TABLE. A table originally designed to stand in front of a wall space between windows.

PIERCED SPLAT. The back splat of a chair in which details of the design are openwork generally done with a fret saw.

PILASTER. A rectangular or half-round attached or engaged column.

PLAQUETTE. A square or rectangular detail of contrasting veneer with a centered inlaid detail such as an urn or spread eagle.

PLINTH. The base of a column, pilaster, pedestal or finial.

PLYWOOD. Sheets or panels of wood made of several thin layers glued together. Modern, dates after 1900.

POLYCHROME. Multicolored.

PRESS CUPBOARD. A low recessed cupboard resting on a case containing drawers or cupboard space.

PRINCE OF WALES FEATHERS. A decorative motif derived from the three plumes in the Prince of Wales crest.

PULL BRACKETS. Located on either side of the top drawer of a desk or secretary and pulled out to support the writing flap.

PUNCH WORK. Fine stipple carving of background done with a pointed steel punch.

QUADRANT BRACKETS. Quarter circle cast brass brackets which support the fall-front of a desk or secretary.

QUARTER-ROUND PILASTER. Is one quarter of circular column, generally reeded but may be plain.

RAIL. A horizontal connecting member in furniture construction.

RAKE. The slant or angle of a chair leg or back.

RAM'S-HORN STUMPS. Arm supports with double curve resembling those of a ram's horn.

RAT-TAIL HINGE. A hinge in which the anchor leaf is replaced by a cyma-curved round tapering member with flattened tip resembling a rat's tail.

REBATE. A rectangular slot or groove.

REBATE JOINT. A joint where the two parts have matching slots.

RECESSED STRETCHER. Box stretcher of a chair with front member located a little behind the front legs to make room for the sitter's heels.

RED FILLER. A finish used on country-made pieces as late as 1835. The pigment, Spanish brown, is mixed with raw linseed oil and thinned with turpentine.

REEDING. A series of rounded, continuous, closely set beading done in parallel lines. The opposite of *Fluting*.

RETURNS. An architectural term used to designate the horizontal moldings on the sides of cupboards.

REVERSE SERPENTINE. The opposite of a simple serpentine curve.

RING-AND-BALL. Turning composed of ring and ball elements. With a stretcher there are generally two ball elements flanking the ring element. With a finial a single ball element surmounts the ring.

RING TURNING. A turning in which one or more narrow rings provide the decorative treatment.

ROCKERY. Carving on some gilded mirror frames that simulates naturalistic rock-work.

ROCOCO. Elaborate ornamentation with many curves combined with shells, rocks and other conventionalized rustic details. Is derived from a combination of two French words, *rocaille* (rock-work) and *coquille* (shell).

ROLLED ARM. A sofa or chair arm with an outward curve or roll from the perpendicular.

ROSETTE. A circular ornamental detail with flower or foliage carving.

RULE JOINT. Resembles the central joint of a carpenter's or cabinetmaker's folding rule. Also known as a *Knuckle Joint*.

RUNNERS. The wooden strips attached to the inner sides of a case piece on which the drawer sides slide.

RUSH SEAT. A chair or settee seat tightly woven of twisted rush. In America sometimes called *Flag Seat* from the kind of rush used. Such seat work dates back to the ancient Egyptians.

SABER LEG. A front chair leg with a perpendicular curve like that of a saber.

SADDLE SEAT. A solid wooden chair seat with a central ridge at the front resembling the pommel of a saddle

and the central portion hollowed to be body conforming.

SALTIRE. An X-shaped stretcher.

SAUSAGE TURNING. A turning that resembles a length of
short plump sausages.

SCALLOP SHELL. A carved decoration inspired by the scallop shell.

SCRATCH CARVING. Crude carving done with a coarse
V-shaped chisel.

SCROLL SAW CUT. An outline of curves and scrolls or
pierced openings done with a scroll saw.

SERPENTINE FRONT. The front of a case piece, chair or sofa
having a balanced wavy curve that is convex at center
and ends and concave between.

SETTEE. A light open seat, for two to six persons, with a
low back and arms.

SETTLE. A wooden bench with enclosed back and arms.

SHAPED PEDIMENT. A pediment in which the plinths of the
central and corner finials are connected by two members, the upper edges of which are concave, convex or
cyma curved. Made fixed or removable.

SHELL CARVED. Ornamented with shell motif carved in relief or incised. Generally resembles the scallop shell in
form and outline.

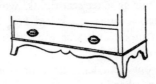

SKIRT. A cross member, frequently valanced, found on
case pieces at bottom of carcase, on tables under top

connecting legs and under seat of chairs. Also called
Apron.

SLIP SEAT. A removable upholstered seat.

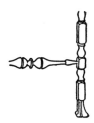

SPANISH FOOT. A curved foot, not fully articulated, surmounted by a turned and blocked leg. Used on some
chairs and tables of the William and Mary and Queen
Anne periods.

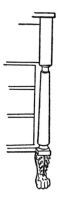

SUPPORTING COLUMN. A column at front corners of a case
piece which supports an overhanging frieze drawer.
Used chiefly on American Empire chests of drawers
and sideboards.

TAMBOUR. A flexible sliding shutter made of thin strips of wood glued to a coarse textile backing.

TANG. Wirelike strips of wrought iron bent double. Used to attach teardrop and early bail handles.

TAVERN TABLE. A table with leafless rectangular top supported by square or turned legs, frequently stretcher-braced. Originally a utilitarian table designed for tavern use.

TEARDROP BRASSES. Furniture mounts with pendent handles similar in shape to a teardrop.

TENON. A thin projecting tongue that fits into a corresponding groove or mortice.

TENT BED. *See* Field Bed.

TESTER. *See* Canopy.

THREE-QUARTER ROUND PILASTER. A projecting pilaster three-quarter round in cross section. May be either reeded or ring turned.

THUMB MOLDING. A convex with flattened curve. Also called *Lip Molding*.

TILL. A covered compartment for valuables. Found in some chests at one end of the well close to the top.

TILT-TOP TABLE. A tripod table with circular, square or octagon top, hinged to tilt to the perpendicular.

TONGUE AND GROOVE JOINT. Used for joining two boards. On the side of one is a continuous beadlike molding and on the other a continuous channel into which the former fits.

TOP RAIL. The top horizontal rail of a chair or sofa back.

TORUS MOLDING. A bold convex molding usually semi-circular but sometimes slightly flattened.

TRAY-TOP. A table top with raised molded edge resembling a tray.

TRESTLE TABLE. One with fixed leaf supported by two or three trestles instead of legs.

TRESTLES. Postlike uprights supporting a table top. Are generally mounted on block or shoe feet.

TRIPOD TABLE. A table with pedestal supported by three outcurved legs.

TRUMPET LEG. A turned leg that resembles an upturned trumpet in outline.

TRUNDLE BED. A low small bed designed to roll under a full-size four-poster. Used for children.

TUCKAWAY TABLE. A table with very narrow fixed leaf, two drop leaves and pivoting legs. Occupies very little space when closed or folded, hence the name.

TURN BUTTON. A small oblong wooden button mounted loosely with screw or nail as substitute for latch.

TURNED-DOWN POSTS. Bedposts that have been re-turned on a lathe to reduce thickness.

TURNING. Shaping of wood on a lathe, done with turning chisels.

TURNIP FOOT. A variation of the ball foot; has a collar at the base and resembles a turnip in outline.

UPRIGHTS. The vertical members of a chair frame.

URN. A turned decorative detail largely used as a finial.

VALANCE. Decorative shaping done in balancing scrolls on lower edge of a cross member. Is a conventionalized representation of drapery.

VASE-AND-CYLINDER TURNED. Turning which combines vase and cylinder shaped elements.

VASE-AND-RING TURNED. Turning that combines vase and ring shaped elements.

VASE-SHAPED SPLAT. A chair back splat with vase outline

VASE TURNED. Turning where the principal elements have a vase shaping.

VENEER. Any thin layer of wood glued on a base wood for decorative effect of grain or contrasting color.

VOLUTE. A spiral ornamental scroll.

VOLUTED. Having a spirally scrolled end.

WAINSCOT. Wooden wall covering where stiles and rails frame large or small panels.

WATER LEAF. An ornamental detail derived from an elongated laurel leaf, generally carved in low relief.

WEB FOOT. *See* Drake Foot.

WHATNOT. An open tier of shelves with slender turned or scrolled supports. Used for display of curios in Victorian period.

WHEAT EARS. An ornamental detail showing several ears of wheat carved in low relief.

WILLOW BRASSES. Furniture mounts with plates that are Baroque scrolled in outline.

WINGED PAW. An animal foot, wing-carved on knee.

WREATH. An ornamental carved detail derived from the Classic Roman.

WRITING ARM. A wide wooden tablet attached to right arm of a Windsor chair.

Field Guide
TO
EARLY AMERICAN
FURNITURE

Section I

How to Use

During the past seventy years, close to two hundred books about American antique furniture have appeared. Through them the two centuries of cabinetmaking in this country have been presented in various ways. There have been authoritative volumes; there have been chatty little books in which nuggets of fact were sugar-coated with romance, comments on quaintness or adventures in acquiring that made easy reading. In one way or another they have served their purpose of giving us insight as to how the early Americans lived and what kind of furniture they used. They are valuable and important reading for that reason and as a background for knowing antique furniture.

But up to now, when a collector found a piece of furniture unfamiliar to him, he frequently found such holes in that background that he was apt to misdate it or even pass it by as some sort of maverick. His friends with enthusiasms for wild life, winged or footed, had the advantage of well-organized manuals for their delvings into the ways of Nature that were compact, explicit and easy to thumb through. They had to be, for birds and beasts are on the go. They don't hold poses as studio models do.

Having learned about antique furniture the hard way, by trial and more errors than it is comfortable to recall, I follow in this book a radically different plan from the books I have written previously or any that I have read. This first field handbook for antique furniture is intended to do for collectors what the Nature handbooks have long done for bird and animal enthusiasts.

There is no stimulus in it for daydreaming about that wonderful comb-back Windsor writing chair that might be found in a farmhouse attic for next to nothing, for things like that mostly stopped happening with the Coolidge era, but there is brief and factual information as to what such a chair looks like, how, where and when it was made and its comparative value. American furniture is here reduced to its ten most important forms, with text and line drawings arranged to make the book a usable tool for the furniture collector — one that can be carried about and thumbed through readily for information and advice as need arises.

First Step in General Preparation

But before going on an antiques hunt or trying to identify a specific piece, it is advisable to read and digest the two sections that follow this one. They are "Periods of American Furniture" and "Detecting Genuine Pieces." Section II gives one a quick look at the eight style periods, tells the outstanding characteristics of each, the principal pieces of furniture made and the woods of which they were most frequently fabricated. In ten to twenty minutes' reading, for the accounts of each period are brief, will be found the essentials of all these periods from the Puritan Span through the Early Victorian, a sweep that took two centuries or about six generations of forebears. Further, the chief characteristics of each of the eight periods are reduced to five prime essentials, phrased like newspaper headlines. Refer to this section often. Get to know these characteristics as you do the lines of the leading makes of automobiles. This will be of material aid in placing the antiques you see as to kind and time without having to ask questions or read labels. To be able to recognize the characteristics of any period from Puritan Span to Early Victorian gives you a sureness that is worth the time and effort taken to acquire it.

Second Step in General Preparation

In Section III, "Detecting Genuine Pieces," will be found the fundamental points by which any piece may be appraised for authenticity. There are seven of them — patina, normal signs of wear, tool marks, construction, dimensions, varieties of woods used and condition. These can well be regarded as clinical notes. As such they should be thoroughly studied and referred to, preferably with some actual pieces at hand for direct examination.

Of course becoming an expert on anything is not accomplished overnight, but with a little practice and patience you soon begin to recognize such things as the rich and mellow glow of old wood, both finished and in the raw, the worn stretcher, the marks of the jack plane, the size and shaping of hand-done dovetails and so forth. Gradually a remembered background is assembled of what is right and what is wrong. Knowing what one may expect to find when the piece under consideration is authentic is every bit as important as recognizing badly done restoring or outright counterfeiting.

With this as a briefing, you are now ready for a little field work. For example, you spot a piece of antique furniture of a kind or design that is new to you. It may be in a shop window, at an auction or in an antiques show. You are interested but somewhat at a loss as to what it is or when or where it was made. The same with value. Since you have your copy of the *Field Guide* in pocket or purse, you thumb it through until you find a picture similar to the piece in question among the numbered line drawings. On the same page or one preceding or following this picture will be a description with the same number.

As you read, compare it with the actual piece you have just seen, for in that short description the typical example of that particular piece is named and its essential characteristics are set forth. If it is a case piece, the proper sort of handles for the drawers are stated. These specifications also include the kind of wood, mention special finish, tell whether the piece was made generally or in some particular section of the country, give approximate years when it was made and conclude with its comparative value.

For a specific demonstration, let us select an uncommon but not rare piece, a small settee on rockers with solid wooden seat and removable spindle frame mounted at the front of the seat. You turn to the "Day Beds, Sofas and Settees" section and toward the end find a line drawing of just such a piece. Its number is 262. Beneath it the description of like number reads:

262. Hitchcock Settee Cradle

Construction and lines are the same as the foregoing. The back always has a wide top rail and about twelve slender spindles. The arms are like those of a Boston rocker (*see*

No. 43). The solid seat is of pine and slightly body conforming. At right, the front of the seat has two one-inch
holes into which fit the ends of the cradle fence which consists of two turned uprights and two flat horizontal slats.
Settee has four turned legs, the front ones vase-and-ball
turned and the rear ones plain, mounted on short narrow
rockers. Legs are braced by a box stretcher with front and
back members flat strips and end ones turned.

Piece was designed so that an adult could sit at one end
while the infant slept behind the protecting fence. Occasionally a settee cradle is found with fences at both ends
to accommodate twins. Length varies from 48 to 56 inches.

Made of maple with pine seat by Hitchcock and other
chair makers. Painted black or other dark color and striped
in yellow or gilt. *Ca. 1830–1840.* XX to Y

The capital letters at the end are part of a four-letter
code which gives the *comparative value* for any piece
and is explained later in this section. Translated into
dollars, XX to Y runs from a low of $25 to $75 for a
cradle in the rough, depending on how much repair and
refinishing it requires, to a high of $100 to $150 for one
in fine condition, possibly with the Lambert Hitchcock
label.

With very little practice anyone can duplicate this
identification for the rest of the 309 pieces of furniture
that are illustrated in this handbook. In addition, there
are 21 more that are described but not pictured since
they closely resemble others that are illustrated and placed
immediately preceding them. Of these unillustrated pieces
a considerable number are referred to as *survivals.*

As the name indicates, a survival example is a piece of
furniture made in an earlier style than the one current

at the time of its production. Generally the work of a country cabinetmaker, its design may date fifty to a hundred years earlier than its actual date of making but it is still a genuine antique of its kind and type. It is always simpler in ornamental detail and its lines and construction may be more direct than those of its sophisticated ancestor. Further, a good proportion of the antique furniture that the average collector is apt to acquire is either of the survival or of the less ornate country-made type.

As a concrete example of a survival piece, look at Nos. 68, 69, 70 and 73 in Section VI. All are tavern tables. The first three were made between 1700 and 1775, but No. 73 was made between 1800 and 1830. This survival of an early eighteenth-century design adheres to the same construction details but in simplified form. In fact, sturdy simplicity is the earmark of any survival piece whether it is a chair, table, chest of drawers or a desk.

In Sections IV to XVII, the ten main furniture forms are treated, as are special developments or types, such as Windsor chairs, block-front and bombé pieces, Pennsylvania Dutch, Shaker and primitive furniture. Placing these in separate sections highlights their distinctiveness. Examples of each furniture form are presented chronologically by style periods except for some special instances. Outstanding are the slat-back chair, the corner chair and the tavern table. With these the survival examples of each of these pieces are inserted immediately after those of the prototype. This has been done to make it clear how these pieces in their survival form adhered basically to the original design and were affected only slightly by succeeding stylistic trends.

Section XV, "Mirrors," is of necessity presented in a slightly different manner than the other furniture forms. Not only were the early ones imported from England, frame and all, but long after many of the frames were produced here, American frame makers, who were also importers, put their labels on both the domestic and imported mirrors. Consequently even experts have to be content to say, "English or possibly American."

In selecting the typical pieces to be illustrated and described, I have intentionally given preference to good forthright examples of the sort most frequently seen in dealers' shops, the kind that you and I can afford. Of course certain pieces essential to the whole story but found only in museums or private collections of the same quality have been included, not only because they are necessary to a well-rounded whole but because such rarities have been known to crop up sometimes in unusual places and it is therefore well to know what they are and be able to recognize them.

Every description is complete in itself as to identification, but to show how it fits into its group, each of the sections begins with a brief account of the particular furniture form, tells how it began and what changes occurred in its design during the time it was made by American cabinetmakers. Immediately following and of considerable importance as an aid to judging the genuineness of a piece are a number of brief notes under the heading of "Special Comments." They include explanations of construction methods which the old cabinetmakers used consistently in their work, as applied to that one form, as well as descriptions of special features, such as those fascinating but elusive secret drawers and hidden

compartments in desks and secretaries. The specific points
for judging the quality and originality of pieces of that
form are also named and explained.

Those not mechanically minded may find reading
these comments stiff going, but if they will persevere, I
believe they will be equipped to make wiser purchases
and be saved from acquiring pieces of doubtful merit. By
that I mean pieces that have been butchered through
ignorant restoration or deliberately glorified or rebuilt in
an effort to enhance the flash appeal if not the worth of
inferior or damaged antiques. Never forget that every
piece of American antique furniture has characteristics
and clues that certify to its genuineness. What they are
and where to look for them are included in these comments. They are what you need to know if you are to be
proficient in judging a piece.

The section on "Detecting Genuine Pieces" stresses the
seven major points to be observed in judging any piece
of antique furniture. The importance of knowing these
cannot be overemphasized. Therefore this section should
be repeatedly consulted in using this handbook until it
and the details it describes have become stored knowledge.

In this detecting I have found it worth while to have
with me what I call my scout's kit. Nothing elaborate or
a trouble to carry around. It includes a pocket flashlight
for examining the interior or underside of a piece; a
jackknife with its largest blade sharp enough to serve
as a scraper for use on pieces where the wood is concealed by later coats of paint; a powerful pocket reading
glass for inspecting inlay or other details and a small
screw driver for occasionally removing a few screws to

determine whether they are the original hand-filed ones described in Section XVIII, "Hardware."

Take plenty of time in judging a piece. Not too long ago, I was shown a small Hepplewhite secretary made of mahogany and satinwood, the kind all collectors dream of finding. Design, patina, workmanship and condition looked to be of the best. Although old enough to know better, I accepted it as original without sufficient examination. Later a more impervious judge also feasted his eyes on it and then turned it upside down. Everywhere, the concealed parts, although of old wood, were covered with the circular marks of the modern buzz saw. They stood out like headline type. A lovely piece in superb condition but a fake. Ten minutes more spent in making a detailed examination of it would have saved me considerable chagrin.

In Section XIX, the various woods used by American cabinetmakers are briefly discussed and any special use mentioned, together with the time when any one of them was especially popular. Details about handles and other hardware used on furniture are set forth in the preceding section mainly as a guide to the proper kind and design that should be selected for a piece that has either lost its original mounts or has been fitted with the wrong kind.

Pieces of extreme rarity or of little interest to collectors have been purposely omitted from this handbook. The omissions include the flat-top desk, the chest-on-chest-on-frame, the china closet, the Baltimore mixing table, the cupboard-top highboy, the window seat, the backless and armless settee, the cheval mirror, the cradle and trundle bed. They are all obvious variations of furniture forms that are described in detail and have the same general construction.

In writing this *Field Guide* over a hundred illustrated catalogues of auctions of important collections were studied and referred to frequently. These dated back as far as the Jacob Paxson Temple sale in 1922 which was outstanding for its Pennsylvania Dutch pieces and the Alexander M. Hudnut sale of 1927 when the first sizable group of Duncan Phyfe pieces was put on the auction block.

In the course of reviewing these auction catalogues, I had several surprises. Not over six antique American window seats turned up during a period of over twenty-five years. Also only one flat-top desk, although George Washington used one when he was President of the United States, three cheval mirrors and two chests-on-chests-on-frame, although this piece is nothing more than a further development of the chest-on-frame which is illustrated and described. I found no examples of the Baltimore mixing table or the cupboard-top highboy.

But collecting antiques is always full of surprises. Finding a window seat, a chest-on-chest-on-frame or a cheval mirror could be the surprise of your life so I mention them as pieces that exist.

Cradles and trundle beds are not especially scarce but no one but a museum curator who happened to be arranging a period bedroom would want either. The same goes for the Sheraton and American Empire washstands with the large hole in the top where the china washbowl was placed. There is little you can do with such a piece except be thankful for modern plumbing.

As for value, prices for American antique furniture are

not like those of standard commodities. They are determined individually and a number of factors are involved, such as age, rarity, design, craftsmanship, condition and collector demand.

On the other hand, there is a schedule of comparative values which is recognized and understood by experienced dealers and collectors. It applies year in and year out with the ratios between the various price levels for different grades remaining fairly constant. Relative values for antiques of finer quality stay more or less the same through lean or boom years. Run-of-the-mill pieces are more readily affected. Their prices rise faster during inflation periods and decline with equal speed when a recession threatens.

Other factors that influence actual prices temporarily, but have little effect on comparative values, are passing fads or special interests on the part of collectors. For instance, some years ago a clamor arose for maple furniture. It became widespread and lasted for some time. During it any maple piece, because it was maple, was priced at from one and a half to twice that of essentially the same piece in another hardwood. When this special demand ceased, prices for maple pieces quickly returned to normal and the long-range comparative values had not been much affected by the "maple craze."

As a demonstration of how these comparative values apply, take as a common denominator a chest of drawers. It is made of one of the native hardwoods, has four drawers, simple bracket feet, is about 38 inches wide by 34 inches high and 20 inches deep and dates between 1790 and 1820. It is without special carving, inlay or other features that would place it definitely as belonging to a particular period. It is just a plain little piece of the sort frequently offered to antiques dealers and most frequently requested by their customers.

We will give it an arbitrary price of $100, which is in the neighborhood of its cost in most shops. Now compare this price with that of some other pieces, some contemporary, some made earlier, but all average examples of kind and type. A similar chest of drawers made of mahogany would be worth half as much again. A four-legged drop-leaf table would cost from one and a half to twice as much; a slant-top desk from two to three times as much; a plain, flat-topped highboy four to six times as much; an average comb-back Windsor armchair, two to four times as much; and a matched set of rush-seated Hitchcock-type chairs, repainted but not stenciled, would be worth about three times as much.

This simple comparison has been given to show how prices for other pieces are related to that of the chest of drawers. The same relation exists throughout the entire gamut of American antique furniture. The value of any piece, except for an extremely fine one or one so excessively rare that only a few examples are known, is directly related to that of an average simple piece of its kind. It forms what is known as a standard of comparative values.

This should not be confused with actual prices of specific pieces. It is merely a gauge against which individual prices may be checked for an average of several years under normal, *uninflated* price levels. As such it is intended to serve as an indication as to whether the price asked for a specific piece is high, low or average.

It is a composite of average fair prices for pieces of

the same sort and period that could be bought in good refinished condition from established dealers of reputation. Added refinements would increase their values and crudities or excessive replacements would decrease them.

For the convenience of the reader, a simple four-letter code of *comparative values* has been devised. It aims to reflect average prices the country over and is divided into twelve groups. The code symbols appear after the descriptions of all the typical pieces of each furniture form discussed elsewhere in this book.

These code symbols of *comparative* worth are all given with a considerable range from low to high. The low indicated is for a simple example of a specific piece that is in the rough and will need refinishing and possibly some minor repairs. The high price is for an example with fine detail and so well preserved that it requires no refinishing or restoration. The reason for the spread is obvious.

Code Letters and Table of Comparative Values

X	Under $25
XX	$25 to $75
XXX	$75 to $100
Y	$100 to $150
YY	$150 to $250
YYY	$250 to $500
Z	$500 to $750
ZZ	$750 to $1000
ZZZ	$1000 to $1500
Q	$1500 to $2000
QQ	$2000 to $3000
QQQ	Above $3000

Periods of American Furniture

WHAT the first American colonists used for furniture during the years immediately following their various landings on the shores of our Atlantic seaboard is not known. From all accounts their first homes were the crudest of rude shelters and their few furnishings must have been makeshifts that were discarded as more substantial furniture became available for not a stick of it has survived.

But by 1650, things were on a firmer footing. Six of the Thirteen Colonies had been established; the standard of living had risen and there were better homes. Among the Englishmen who came in increasing numbers as time wore on were many trained cabinetmakers who worked according to the fashions current in England. Due to slow transportation and a tendency on the part of most colonists to be conservative in accepting a new fashion and equally so in relinquishing the old, there was a definite lag between style changes in England and those in America. Ten to twenty years was not unusual.

Consequently there was considerable overlapping. Eight styles found acceptance in America during the two hundred years when furniture making was a craft. With all, English influence predominated. Save for the English provincial pieces, American-made furniture was always simpler and less ornate. Our cabinetmakers not only adapted the various styles to the simpler tastes of their clients but added a few touches of their own and so produced typically American pieces.

The eight styles with their approximate years are:

PURITAN SPAN	1650–1690
WILLIAM AND MARY	1690–1720
QUEEN ANNE	1720–1750
CHIPPENDALE	1750–1775
(Hiatus due to American Revolution)	
HEPPLEWHITE	1785–1800
SHERATON	1800–1820
AMERICAN EMPIRE	1820–1840
EARLY VICTORIAN	1840–1865

PURITAN SPAN
1650–1690

Wood — oak combined with pine
Construction — wainscot
Decoration — flat carving, applied moldings and turnings
Handles — elongated wooden knobs
Size — massive and architectural

A memory version of the Jacobean style, produced by cabinetmakers trained in the mother country, this furniture is mostly of wainscot type with stile and rail framing and inset panels. Case pieces are without shaped legs or feet. Ornamentation includes flat carving done in flower motifs or chip carving of conventionalized lunettes, scrolls, leafage and geometric details; applied moldings arranged in geometric patterns and ebonized split banister turnings and bosses.

Principal pieces made are court and press cupboards, dower chests, Bible boxes, wainscot and turned arm-chairs, such as Brewster, Carver and slat-back, joined stools, trestle tables and table-chairs.

WILLIAM AND MARY
1690–1720

Wood — walnut or maple

Construction — turned trumpet legs, large ball feet

Decoration — burl and fancy-grain veneer

Handles — teardrop brasses or wooden knobs

Size — many pieces small and delicately proportioned

A complete break with earlier furniture construction, it is characterized by plain unpaneled surfaces with dove-tail joinings. Decoration is achieved by use of fancy-grained wood, such as burl walnut. Case pieces have bulbous ball, bun or turnip-shaped feet and brass tear-drop drawer handles. Legs on carcase pieces some twenty inches from floor are spirally or trumpet-turned and braced with flat stretchers. Highboys are flat-topped and finished with molded cornices. Table legs are turned in ball, ball-and-ring, spool-and-vase shapes and end in small knob-turned feet. Stretchers are either turned or square. The carved Flemish scroll, known as the Spanish foot, is found on some chairs and tables. Chair backs some-times have a slight body-conforming or "spooned" curve.

New pieces are highboy, lowboy, carved high-back chair with cane back-panel and seat, day bed, slant-top desk, gate-leg, butterfly and tavern tables. Next to walnut, maple is most favored wood. Start of lacquering maple pieces in the Chinese manner occurs in this period.

QUEEN ANNE
1720–1750

Wood — walnut, maple or sometimes cherry

Construction — cabriole leg with Dutch foot — scrolled bracket foot — valanced skirt — vase-shaped chair back splat — broken pediment top with urn or flame finials on tall case pieces

Decoration — carved shell, sunburst or fan motifs

Handles — bat's-wing brasses with bails

Size — many pieces small — all delicately proportioned

Is an amplification of preceding period with trend to lightness and use of curves accentuated. One of the obvious changes is the substitution of the cabriole for the turned leg with chairs, tables and some case pieces. With it three kinds of foot are used — pad or Dutch, drake and Spanish — the latter a holdover from preceding period and chiefly found on early pieces. Many chests of drawers and similar case pieces have valanced skirt and scrolled bracket feet.

The corner cupboard, sofa, secretary, gaming table, Windsor, banister-back, fiddle-back, corner and wing chairs make first appearance. Ornamentation is achieved by carving, with characteristic motif the scallop shell, done in relief on knees of cabriole legs. Fan and sunburst carvings are used on small central drawers of highboys and lowboys. Broken pediment top is found on some tall case pieces; others have the flat cornice top. Cabinet brasses are scrolled plates of bat's-wing and willow type for drawer handles and H-hinges set on front surfaces of paneled doors.

CHIPPENDALE
1750–1775

Wood — mahogany or sometimes walnut

Construction — cabriole leg with claw-and-ball foot — straight molded leg — molded bracket foot — pierced chair back splat — serpentine or bowed carcase fronts — fluting and inset reeded pilasters

Decoration — elaborate shell, scroll, foliage or gadroon carving — Chinese fretwork

Handles — willow brasses with bails or rosettes-and-bails

Size — ample scale for all pieces

Takes its name from Thomas Chippendale, London master cabinetmaker and furniture designer. His book, *The Gentleman and Cabinet-Maker's Director,* published in 1754 and enlarged and reprinted in 1759 and 1762, was well known to leading American cabinet-makers. Its plates inspired much of the finest work done in the colonies.

This style is a further development of the Queen Anne with rococo embellishments. It also includes motifs, details and forms borrowed from French, Gothic and Chinese sources. Carving includes balanced scrolls framing incised scallop shells on fronts of highboys and lowboys, carved and pierced back splats in strapwork, lozenge and ribbon designs for side and armchairs. Two kinds of legs are characteristic — a boldly curved cabriole, ending in deeply carved claw-and-ball foot, and a straight square leg, fluted or reeded on outer sides with chamfered inner edge, sometimes terminating in a square foot known as Marlborough. Broken pediment tops on tall case pieces are more ornate than in the preceding period. Cabinet brasses are of the willow type with scrolled outlines and are larger and heavier than earlier ones. Drawer handles are all of bail type.

New pieces include chest-on-chest, linen press, tilt-top table with plain, dish or piecrust top, knee-hole writing table, sideboard table, block-front and bombé or kettle-base furniture. Mahogany is most favored wood but walnut is found with some of the early pieces and those of New England provenance are often cherry.

HEPPLEWHITE
1785–1800

Wood — mahogany, frequently with satinwood veneer and box or holly stringing

Construction — square tapering legs, sometimes with spade feet — outcurved French feet with connecting valanced skirt — shield-shaped, entwined heart or oval chair backs — shaped pediment top on tall case pieces — geometrically glazed cupboard doors

Decoration — carving of drapery festoons, Prince of Wales feathers — inlaid oval panels of satinwood, etc. — medallions of eagle

or classic figures — stringing outlines —
checkered fillets

Handles — oval stamped brass plates with bails
Size — all pieces slender and delicate

Straight perpendicular lines, horizontal curves, color-
ful use of contrasting inlay and veneer and restrained
elegance are characteristics of the style named for the
London cabinetmaker George Hepplewhite. In his book,
The Cabinet-Maker and Upholsterer's Guide of 1788,
1789 and 1794, the designs are based on the classic style
of the Brothers Adam but modified by the French style
of Louis XVI.

Slender tapering legs are the outstanding structural
characteristic of this period. They are usually square and
terminate in small spade feet on the finer pieces. Slightly
outswept French feet, connected by a deeply valanced
apron, occur on chests of drawers and other case pieces.
Carving is absent except on chair backs where the motifs
include urns, Prince of Wales feathers, heads of wheat
and drapery festoons. Inlay, shaped veneer panels and
banding of satinwood, fancy-grain maple or crotch-grain
mahogany furnish the ornamentation of other pieces of
furniture. Inlay motifs most favored are sunburst, spread-
eagle and conch-shell medallions. Glazed doors appear
on many secretaries and cupboards with muntins arranged to form geometric patterns. Brass drawer handles
and keyhole escutcheons are oval in shape. The handles
have bail drops and plates die-stamped in relief, with
or without classic motifs in center.

New pieces are sideboard, two- and three-part dining
table, half-round card table, sewing table, tambour desk,

PERIODS OF AMERICAN FURNITURE   23

break-front secretary and field bed. Mahogany continues as favored wood with cherry sometimes substituted in New England.

SHERATON
1800–1820

Wood — mahogany with satinwood or crotch-grain veneer, cherry with fancy-grain maple veneer, plain or curly maple

Construction — turned and reeded legs — interlacing rectangle, tripod and lyre-shaped chair backs — vase and lyre-shaped table pedestals — three-quarter round reeded pilasters with vase-and-ring turned legs for case pieces — legs and feet generally castered

Decoration — shaped panels of satinwood, crotch-grain mahogany or fancy-grain maple — low-relief carving of drapery festoons, bowknotted wheat ears, thunderbolts or foliage sprays, water-leaf carving — rosettes

Handles — oblong stamped brass plates with bails — brass rosette knobs — lion's-heads with pendent rings

Size — general appearance of lightness but not as delicate as Hepplewhite style

Is named for Thomas Sheraton of London who published two books of furniture design, *The Cabinet-Maker and Upholsterer's Drawing-Book,* 1791–1794, and *Designs for Household Furniture,* 1812. The main differences between Hepplewhite and early Sheraton styles are a predominance of straight lines, prevailing use of slender turned and reeded legs and of delicate carving done in low relief with punch-marked background. Chests of drawers and similar case pieces have reeded columns projecting beyond the plane of straight or slightly bowed fronts. Square chair backs with cresting and lower cross rails connected by either carved and pierced urn-shaped splats or by reeded vertical rods are also characteristic.

The French Directoire style, introduced by his later book, uses the lyre motif, acanthus-leaf carving and either carved or brass paw feet. Pedestal table bases are also characteristic as well as sofas with long curving bodies supported on cornucopia-shaped feet or carved animal feet with eagle wings above.

New pieces are the painted fancy chair and the chest of drawers with attached mirror. Brass drawer handles are of three types — oblong, stamped plates with bails, rosette knobs and lion's-heads with pendent rings. Wood most frequently used is mahogany with satinwood and fancy-grained maple for contrast.

AMERICAN EMPIRE
1820–1840

Wood — mahogany with crotch-grain veneer, cherry with or without fancy-grain veneer, curly maple and maple or other woods finished in red filler

Construction — turned legs, spirally reeded or acanthus-leaf carved — long square section

on some later pieces — saber legs, solid
vase-shaped chair-back splat — veneer-faced
table columns, circular or octagonal, resting on shaped plinth, supported by heavy
scrolled or flattened ball feet, castered

Decoration — wide ogee molding faced with
crotch-grain veneer for drawer fronts,
cornices, skirts and mirror frames — boldly
done carving — stencil gilding

Handles — brass rosettes, mushroom-turned
wooden or pressed glass knobs

Size — ponderous proportions and heavy lines

Is a continuation of late Sheraton with French design
details inspired by the classic Roman. Main characteristics are bulk, boldly cut carving in acanthus-leaf, pine-
apple and horn-of-plenty motifs, lavish application of
crotch-grain mahogany veneer and use of ogee molding.

New pieces are the sleigh bed, Récamier or Grecian
sofa, Boston rocker and Hitchcock chair. New drawer
handles are turned wooden knobs in mushroom shape
and pressed glass knobs, clear or iridescent. Case pieces
of cherry with curly or bird's-eye maple are among pleasing works of country cabinetmakers.

EARLY VICTORIAN
1840–1865

Wood — rosewood and black walnut

Construction — balancing scrolls — cabriole leg
terminating in rudimentary foot — white
marble tops for tables and case pieces

Decoration — crestings and cartouche-shaped medallions of carved flowers and fruits with foliage boldly done and framed with applied moldings

Handles — carved wooden pulls with finger grips on underside

Size — large and ponderous except for side chairs

Combines Gothic simplicity with Gallic ornateness and is characterized by undulating curves and realistic carvings of leaves, flowers and fruits done in high relief. Marble tops for tables, chests of drawers and sideboards predominate.

Rosewood and, later, black walnut are favored woods. Some early examples are of mahogany and occasionally satinwood trimmed with applied rosewood moldings and handles for sophisticated parlor and bedroom suites which appear for first time. Other newcomers are the extension table with removable leaves, papier-mâché table with mother-of-pearl insets, whatnot, oversize footstool or ottoman, spool bed and modern bedstead. Side chairs of this period are often graceful and pleasing in outline and design.

Detecting Genuine Pieces

To BECOME proficient in judging a piece of furniture requires three things — an open mind, willingness to observe a variety of details that at first may seem unimportant, and practice. Given these, a piece will speak for itself and can be placed as genuine, reconstructed, a modern copy or a deliberate fake.

Assuming that it is an antique until proved otherwise, examine the evidence. In doing so the following points should be observed. They are (1) patina, (2) normal signs of wear, (3) tool marks, (4) construction, (5) dimensions, (6) varieties of woods and (7) condition.

PATINA

Patina is just another name for the complexion that cabinetwood surfaces acquire through age and usage. It cannot be imitated or hurried. Dyeing or staining new wood only results in a pancake make-up that nowise resembles the clear glow that years of wear and care create.

The tone of patina varies with different woods, such as the brownish-red of mahogany, the reddish-brown of eighteenth-century walnut and the honey-yellow of maple, but the bloom of age is still there. The finish on the old piece, while still transparent, has deepened and become richer in color. Also the parts originally left raw or "in the white," as the old cabinetmakers called it, have acquired a different but just as easily recognized complexion or patina. This can be seen on backboards and drawer parts of case pieces, on the undersides of table tops and on the backs of mirror frames.

Most of these parts are made of native softwoods. Backboards and other surfaces that have been exposed to years of dust and dirt are naturally much darker than the protected inside surfaces of the same boards, but even there the mellow tone is apparent. One of the small pigeonhole drawers of an old desk or secretary offers the best opportunity to observe the special patina of un-varnished wood. Looked at in bright sunlight, surfaces of sides, back and bottom vary, according to the wood of which they were made, from a honey-yellow to the brown of old parchment.

A different patina tone is found with the tops of utilitarian pieces that were scrubbed almost daily with harsh soap and water. There is a grayness that only these repeated washings could produce. This is best seen on the tops of tavern, gate-leg and kitchen-used drop-leaf tables.

Patina of old painted pieces is distinctly darker and richer than that of new ones. It is especially apparent with Windsors, Hitchcock chairs, Boston rockers and old chests. If there is gilt and colored stenciling or other decorative design, the tones of these are also mellow and subdued.

Where an antique has been so scraped and sandpapered in the process of refinishing as to remove the thin "skin" of the wood surfaces, the patina is practically destroyed. In such a case, the piece must be judged by the appearance of interior surfaces and indications of old workmanship. If it is all right otherwise, it need not be ruled out.

It is still an antique and will eventually acquire a good patina.

NORMAL SIGNS OF WEAR

Except for furnishings of parlors kept tightly closed year after year and only opened for weddings and funerals, practically all of our antique furniture has been used daily by three or four generations. Consequently it bears normal signs of wear. These vary from scarcely noticeable ones on handsome, cherished pieces to marks of use and abuse on others that, being out of fashion, were banished to kitchen, cellar, workshop or even barn.

Antique dealers classify furniture as "original finish," "in the rough," and "refinished." The first means that only polishing and a few minor repairs are needed. These are the most desirable pieces and hardest to find. But even they bear signs of wear. Close inspection, either in a strong light or with a reading glass, of the varnished surfaces will reveal a network of fine scratches, the result of years of frequent contact with the household dustcloth. Minute particles of grit which were part of the dust made these nearly invisible marks. Sometimes, too, small scars can be seen, caused by minor, long-ago mishaps.

Next, look at the edges of the piece. Those that were sharp right angles originally will have become slightly rounded and along these same edges slight dents will be found. Both are indications of years of use. If the piece has any carving, the sharpness of its edges will have been dulled. This can be more readily felt with the fingers than seen by the eye. Compare a piece of new carving with a like piece of old work. There will be a difference in the feel of the two. Also with old carving there may be slight minor defects, such as small breaks and little spots that have chipped off during the passage of time. In the same way sections of overlapping moldings on drawer fronts and slanting desk lids may be broken, missing or skillfully repaired.

If a piece has inlay, it is not uncommon to find some small part missing, such as a short length of hair-line striping. With veneered pieces, cracks are frequently seen. Some of them are so slight as to look like fine tears. These have been caused by the gradual drying and shrinking of the base wood. Duncan Phyfe consistently used pine as base wood for the veneered tops of his clover-leaf card tables. To prevent warping beneath veneer at each end he inset a diagonal crosspiece. As a result, the veneer always has cracks or tears above the lines of these diagonals which are indications of Phyfe work.

Warping is usual with table leaves made of single boards. The wider the leaf, the more noticeable it is, and it is shown by an upward curl with edges higher than the center. A variation of as much as a quarter of an inch can be observed by laying a ruler across a leaf. Also, the circular top of an old tilt-top table will measure half to three quarters of an inch less across the grain than with it because of gradual shrinkage over the years. This takes place with all wood *across* but never with the grain.

It is well to look at the legs and feet of a piece for signs of wear. Being close to the floor, such parts bear slight dents and bruises where they were hit by the feet of former owners or by house-cleaning implements. One sign of wear on slat-back chairs indicates how our ancestors managed to read or work after sundown during the candlelight era. A pair of wrought-iron candlesticks hung by the lip on the top slat furnished a fair light but sometimes the candle flames flared and charred the finials above them. Tilt-top tables that doubled as candlestands are sometimes found with similar charring on the underside of the top.

Chair and table stretchers show signs of wear on their upper sides which will be worn away noticeably because of the feet that rested on them daily for generations. The wear shows to a marked degree on the front stretcher of a chair. In fact, the upper side of it may be worn practically flat. In the same way, stretchers of a tavern table that has seen service for over a century are often reduced to nearly half their original thickness. Beginning where they are morticed into the legs, the upper sides have a series of undulating curves that show where people sat at mealtimes during the course of a hundred years or more.

Drawers of case pieces and tables are sure places to find signs of wear. Here the lower edges of drawer sides have a shallow curve that is deepest near the front. Sometimes the sides are so worn that the drawer tilts downward about two inches when half opened. Take out the drawer and the upper surface of the runners will show grooves slightly wider than the sidepieces. Turn the drawer over and the bottom will be as smooth in spots as if it had been sandpapered, due to rubbing against the cross member or bearer strip.

Another test for genuineness at this point is to replace the drawer upside down. Unless the runners are badly worn, it will move back and forth as readily in that position as right side up. This is because the old cabinetmakers were precise workmen and made both drawer and opening exactly square. If a drawer so tested binds, sticks or won't fit, it usually means that it has been rebuilt by a repairman who was satisfied if it fitted in its normal position. This test is particularly satisfactory with desk and secretary pigeonhole drawers which often have to be replaced or rebuilt.

Quite often handles or knobs on case pieces are of a later period. Usually this is the result of former owners wanting to bring the piece up to date. Clues to such refurbishing may be seen by neatly plugged holes on the drawer fronts where the original mountings were attached.

TOOL MARKS

The track of the jack plane is one of the marks most often seen on interior parts and undersides of antique furniture. The cutting edge of its wide blade was always given a slight arc with the center about an eighth of an inch higher than the corners. Consequently boards smoothed with it have an irregular series of slight ridges and hollows that follow the grain of the wood and vary according to the size of the plane and the effort taken in planing individual boards. With some, the ridges and hollows can be seen with the naked eye as one looks across a board toward the light. When less pronounced, their presence can be felt by passing one's finger tips lightly over the surface. Such marks can also be found on the underside of table tops, on the back of four-poster headboards and on the underside of Windsor chair and settee seats.

Another jack plane mark, with the ridges not as

clearly marked, is to be seen on the beveled ends of back-boards, drawer bottoms and the like. This beveling, done to reduce thickness at sides and ends, can also be found on backs of panels in seventeenth-century dower chests, doors of cupboards and some secretaries where stile and rail construction was used.

Next to those of the hand planes, saw marks are easiest to observe. The primary saws used by the old cabinetmakers were straight, hand-operated ones with coarse teeth. Some were five feet or longer and were operated by two men working in a saw pit. As the boards were sliced from the side of a log, the coarse ripsaw teeth left a clear pattern of straight parallel scratches. Since interior and other unseen parts were consistently left roughly finished, these saw marks may be found on backboards, drawer backs and the thin boards behind the glass in mirror frames.

The crosscut saws, used to cut off lengths of boards and square their ends, leave the same parallel, slightly slanting scratches but they are less pronounced. They are found on the ends of backboards and some structural parts.

The circular or buzz saw, always power-driven, was first introduced in the United States about 1825 but its general use in furniture shops took some years. As a result, buzz saw marks appear on the interior parts of some pieces of American Empire furniture in original condition; others have only those of the straight saw. Victorian pieces consistently show buzz saw marks.

Compare the mark of the straight saw with that of the buzz saw. With the one you have a series of straight scratches, either perpendicular or at a slight angle across the face of the wood; with the other and later saw, a series of concentric arclike scratches that form part of a circle six to eighteen inches in diameter. Also the rotary plane that came into use during the Victorian years was power-driven. The smoothness of this machine planing has a mechanical perfection far different from that of handwork. This may be seen by comparing the interior of a drawer from an earlier piece with one from a Victorian chest of drawers.

Other tool marks are those of the flat and the curved gouging chisels. Taking the underside of a table, on the side and end pieces of the bed will be four or more semicircular gouges for the screws that hold the top in place. Done freehand with a curved gouging chisel, they are from three quarters to over an inch across and taper away from the screw head. If the table has leaves, a look at the places where the hinges are attached will usually reveal traces of the wide flat chisel used to make the cuts for countersinking the hinge leaves. The same chisel marks are to be found on the softwood framework of sofas and upholstered chairs that have been stripped of all covering material.

A special type of chisel marking was used on chairs with removable seats and on four-post beds. It was Roman numbering, done with a flat chisel from half an inch to an inch wide, by which matching frame and seats were marked and generally ran from I to VI, though sometimes as high as XII. They appear on the front cross rail of the frame and on the underside of the front piece of the slip seat. For a frame and seat made by the same man, the numbering should be of the same size and as similar as handwriting. Numbering of bedposts and rails runs from I to VIII and occurs on the posts just above or below the mortices into which the tenons of the side and end rails fit and on the upper surface of the rails just back of the tenons.

Light scribings with the sharp edge of a turning chisel are found on turned parts of such chairs as slat-backs, banister-backs, simple Queen Anne vase-splats and Windsors. Done while these parts were still in the lathe, they mark the position at which mortices were to be cut so that back slats and other cross members could be inserted, also the position of holes to be bored in the legs for stretchers. Sometimes these scribings are distinct enough to be seen through a painted finish. They are still more apparent on varnished chairs.

Another tool mark consistently found on antique furniture is that of the scribing awl, which was used like a lead pencil to lay out work to be done. Dovetail joints are thus outlined on drawers, mortice and tenon joints on table legs and beds and on posts and rails of beds, as well as cuts to be made for seating drawer and door locks and countersinking hinges on drop-leaf tables. Where dovetail and other joints are part of new work such scratch marks are seldom seen.

CONSTRUCTION

Construction details of all the furniture forms show that the old cabinetmakers adhered to certain standard ways. The most readily recognized and most important are the types of joinings, especially the mortice and tenon and dovetail joints. With both the quality of workmanship varied. Prior to the use of glue, the parts of the individual joints were large and not too snugly fitted. After gluing joints became a standard practice, about 1725, the parts were made smaller and were fitted with great precision.

Accordingly, mortice and tenon joints on seventeenth- and early eighteenth-century pieces have tenons that are from two to four inches wide and are fastened with two and sometimes three wooden pegs driven into holes bored through the assembled joint. After the introduction of glue, the tenons became narrower and pinning with pegs was frequently omitted. The exceptions were joints of upright and cross members of secretary, linen press and cupboard doors, some tables, notably those of the tavern sort, and chairs. With the latter, legs and seat rail joints will be found pinned with two visible pegs until the end of the Chippendale period. Mortice and tenon joints in chairs made after that are usually only glued.

The dovetail joint, so named because of the shape of the flaring tenon, was sometimes used for joining sides, tops and bottoms of case pieces. It was always used in drawer construction and for the corner joints of chests of all sizes.

With a drawer made during the Puritan Span, the dovetail joints consist of a single flaring tenon from three to four inches wide which fits into a corresponding open mortice. Those of a drawer in a William and Mary or early Queen Anne piece are in pairs from two to two and a half inches wide and about half an inch long. From the middle of the Queen Anne through the Early Victorian period, the dovetails are consistently cut from three quarters of an inch to an inch wide at their outer ends and are from four to six in number on a drawer side.

With some, the angle of flare is more pronounced and the open mortices are narrower, reflecting the individual cabinetmaker's preference.

In general, New England cabinetmakers seem to have made less flaring dovetail joints than the craftsmen working in New York, New Jersey and Pennsylvania. Also, some outstanding master workmen, like the Townsends and Goddards of Newport, Rhode Island, added to the regularly cut and spaced dovetails of a drawer side an extra joint about half as wide as, and longer than, the others. This refinement was one of special preference and not a characteristic of the work of a region. Its use by individual cabinetmakers persisted into the Early Victorian period. On the other hand, dovetails on Phyfe furniture are all of the same size, finely cut and with a distinct flare.

Dovetails on drawers of factory-made pieces vary from six to eight in number, are small and have the regularity of machine work. Further, there is never the mark of the scribing awl with which hand-cut dovetails were laid out.

DIMENSIONS

There is a surprising uniformity of measurements and proportions in the furniture of Early American cabinetmakers. Knowledge of this can keep the collector from unwittingly acquiring chairs or tables with shortened legs, chests of drawers or desks where, because one foot was broken, the others were cut to correspond, highboy bases masquerading as lowboys, beds with "turned-down" posts, cut-down sofas and sideboards, and so on. An occasional piece may be found with dimensions greater or less but it will be the exception, probably made for some special use or location. Its genuineness will be determined by the six other tests.

Seats of chairs should be from 16 to 18 inches from the floor. Those measuring less indicate that the legs have been shortened for rockers, casters or other reason. There are two exceptions, the slipper chair where the seat may be from 12 to 14 inches high and the early Victorian side chair with seat about 14 or 15 inches from the floor. Rocking chairs are generally from 14 to 16 inches with Victorian ones as low as 12 inches.

Table tops are from 27 to 30 inches high. Tilt-tops are practically never less than 28 inches and can vary from 24 to 36 inches in diameter. Drop-leaf tables are about 36 inches wide. Component sections of two- and three-part dining tables measure 27 to 29 inches high, are from 42 to 48 inches wide with a total extended length of six to eight feet for the two-part and of nine to eleven feet for the three-part. Earlier and more primitive tavern and sawbuck tables are from 24 to 30 inches wide and from four to eight feet long.

Low occasional tables are almost never found in American antique furniture. The nearest approach to one of modern coffee table height is the butterfly which varies from 22 to 26 inches. Its top, oval, square or round, runs 34 to 36 inches long by 40 to 44 inches wide.

Chests of drawers divide into two groups, low ones with three or four full-width drawers and high ones with five to seven tiers. The low type are 30 to 40 inches high by 34 to 44 inches wide and 17 to 20 inches deep. The tall group run 48 to 66 inches high by 36 to 46 inches wide and 20 to 22 inches deep.

Feet of case pieces include the plain and molded

bracket type which should be from six to eight inches
high, with the majority seven inches; the short cabriole
legs, eight inches; the flaring French foot, eight to ten
inches; and the slender turned Sheraton leg, 10 to 12
inches. There are also the carved or turned American

Empire feet that measure not over 10 inches in height
and the bracket or carved Victorian feet which average
six to eight inches in height. Where the total height of
a case piece is below average, its feet should be inspected
for indications that two to four inches may have been
cut off.

Lowboys are consistently about a fifth smaller than

the highboy bases which they resemble in design and ornamental detail. A converted highboy base will be from 36 to 38 inches high with width and depth in proportion as against a genuine lowboy 29 to 32 inches high. An upper section of a highboy converted to a chest of drawers will generally have feet two or three inches shorter than normal.

Sideboards fall into three groups. The large type is from five and a half to seven feet wide by 39 to 54 inches high and not over 24 inches deep. The small New England type is 39 to 54 inches wide by 36 to 44 inches high and 20 inches deep. The southern hunt board is four to six feet wide by 44 to 48 inches high with a depth of 18 to 20 inches.

Sofas are nearly always too long by present-day standards, especially those of the Hepplewhite, Sheraton and American Empire periods. The smallest are six feet long and those of seven and eight feet are not uncommon. Early Victorian sofas run from five to six feet in length and some of the love-seat type measure only four feet.

Four-post beds in original condition should measure six to six feet, four inches long by three feet, six inches to four feet, two inches wide. These are over-all dimensions. Rails of high posters run from 25 to 32 inches from the floor and have posts from six to eight feet tall. Low poster rails are 24 to 26 inches from the floor with posts from four to four and a half feet tall. Under-eaves beds have head posts 32 to 36 inches high and foot posts level with the rails, which measure 20 to 22 inches from the floor.

VARIETIES OF WOODS

The fact that a piece is made of two or more different woods does not disqualify it as a desirable antique but may be an indication of genuineness. Turned chairs were consistently made of an assortment of woods selected for various parts because of strength or because they were easier to work.

With Windsor chairs, the seats were always made of such softwoods as pine, whitewood or basswood; the spindles of hickory, ash or white oak; legs and stretchers of maple, yellow birch or beech; arms and comb pieces of maple, ash, oak, hickory or beech. Maple was favored for uprights and stretchers of slat-back chairs and slats were of hickory, ash, oak, maple or sometimes birch. Pine was used for seats of Boston rockers, maple for spindles, arm supports, stretchers and crest rail, and cherry for the unpainted arms. The rockers could be of maple, ash or even chestnut.

Where New England red filler served as finish for the simpler country-made pieces, the old cabinetmakers used whatever wood happened to be around. It is not uncommon to find a mixture of native hardwood in such a piece. A drop-leaf table, for instance, could have two legs of yellow birch, two of maple and a top of cherry with possibly one leaf of some other hardwood.

The base wood for veneered furniture of American provenance is usually white pine, though other softwoods are found. Further, some eighteenth-century pieces are burl-veneered on straight-grain walnut and there are sophisticated Hepplewhite and Sheraton examples with a base wood of straight-grain mahogany beneath the crotch-grain veneering. Seymour of Boston was partial to this veneering of mahogany on mahogany and even used the same wood for structural members and drawer parts in some of his tables.

But if *oak* is found as the base wood, it is a clear indication that the piece, though antique, is of English or Continental provenance since the use of oak and occasionally beech was standard with European cabinetmakers. American craftsmen used neither.

Practically any available native softwood or even chestnut was used for backboards and interior parts of American furniture. Two or three different ones may be found in a single piece and pigeonhole drawers of some desks and secretaries may be of cedar.

But when sheets of plywood appear on backboards or drawer bottoms, it is clear evidence of slapdash repairing and a danger signal. Plywood is a twentieth-century product.

CONDITION

A genuine piece in good condition presents no problem. But for one such there are many more that have passed beyond the slight imperfections of normal wear and are classed as "in the rough." The extent of damage can range from a cracked leg or missing hardware to where little is left except the main structure. To be worth putting in usable condition, a piece in the rough should be at least three-quarters complete. Otherwise one ends with a rebuilt article instead of an antique.

With a restored piece, inspection of interior parts may bring to light marks of the circular saw or the smoothness characteristic of a rotary plane. These show that the piece has been restored by a repairman who was not willing to take the time to make the replacement parts with hand tools even though the wood used was old. It further shows that the work must have been done within the past forty years since power tools were not part of repair shop equipment until after 1910. The amount of machine-worked replacement parts will indicate how extensive a job of restoration has been done.

If there are only one or two minor replacements, such as a drawer back or two or three backboards, *provided the piece bears other marks of genuineness,* it need not be rejected. But if modern machine marks predominate, the chances are that it is either a fake, rebuilt from old wood, or a factory-made copy, ten to thirty years old, which time and use have given somewhat the appearance of an antique.

Among antique dealers, any piece that has been reworked in an effort to enhance its value is known as a "monkey." The reworking may have been done recently or could have occurred years ago and have aged enough to be difficult, though not impossible, to detect. It was a fairly common practice thirty or forty years ago to glorify simple country pieces with carving, reeding or inlay normally used on finer, more sophisticated urban furniture. Some of it was very well done, but the new work can be detected generally by the edges of the carved or reeded detail which will be sharper than those of the rest of the piece. Also the new inlay work, usually a medallion, is apt to be obvious. These medallions used for dressing up plain country pieces were made in quantity by manufacturers specializing in them for the new furniture trade and were not as well done as those used by the cabinetmakers who worked from 1790 to 1820, the period when inlay decoration was in vogue.

Other forms of glorification include re-turning bed-posts, especially those of the low-post type, to make them more delicate. Original posts should measure three inches in diameter at the square parts where the rails are inserted. The "turned-down" ones are about two inches. In refinishing secretaries that have solid doors, the glori-fier likes to substitute a geometric pattern of glazing for the wooden panels. This can be recognized by the perfect condition of the muntins that frame the panes as well as by the putty on the inside which will be uniform and have no indications of having been redone when indi-vidual panes had to be replaced.

Signs of rebuilding should also be looked for in judg-ing condition. This includes pieces that have been recon-structed of parts or materials salvaged from other pieces beyond repair; those that were too large for modern use and have been cut down; and the two-part piece made of odd sections that have been matched by cutting one down to fit the other. Highboys, secretaries and two- or three-part dining tables are the pieces most often sub-jected to this kind of rebuilding.

It can be recognized in most instances. There is apt to be a noticeable difference in the wood texture of the parts. Construction details may vary or the structural parts be of sufficiently different softwoods to indicate that base and top did not start out together. For instance in a "married" secretary or highboy, pine and poplar might be found in the lower part and spruce and chest-nut in the upper. This would be too wide a variance. Further scrutiny can also detect traces of too much recent work or too many structural parts made of new wood.

The intentional fake is rarer than either the glorified or the rebuilt piece and, like other forms of counterfeiting, always contains some trace of the spurious. Spotting it is mainly a matter of close observation of the seven points just discussed and familiarity with genuine examples.

Section IV
Chairs

AMERICAN cabinetmakers started in the mid-seventeenth century with a three-legged, triangular-seated chair and during the two hundred years that followed produced over fifty different types and styles. The chair of turned parts came earliest and stayed longest. It varied in form from the early spindle or Carver type to the slat-back, a practical and easily made chair with a distinct American flavor. Practically uninfluenced by changing furniture fashions, it held its own for nearly two centuries.

Chairs directly concerned with current styles began with the wainscot, an architectural, archiepiscopal armchair with paneled back and hard seat, and progressed through the seven furniture periods that followed to arm and side chairs of varying degrees of elegance and comfort. Except for one chair, the designs were all of English or Continental origin, but American cabinetmakers so developed or simplified them, according to public or individual taste, that they are not hard to identify today as distinctly different. The one chair for which there was no European prototype was the Boston rocker, first made in New England about 1820.

Special Comments on Chairs and Their Construction

By construction, chairs fall into two groups — the turned and the shaped.

Turned chairs are of two types, the spindle-back and

the slat-back. With both the turned uprights are of the same diameter and about twice the size of stretchers, seat rails and arms. Only socket joints are found in the spindle-back chair. With the slat-back, the ends of the flat back-slats form mortices that fit into tenons cut in the back turned uprights. The joints are pegged from the rear with small wooden pins which are visible on close inspection. All other joints are socketed. If the chair has shaped arms, the outer ends are socketed and pinned onto the ends of the front uprights.

With the shaped chair, mortice and tenon, dowel, socket, lap, and sometimes dovetail joints are used variously. Mortice and tenon joints are always used to join seat rails to back uprights and front legs. These joints are dowel-pinned and the ends are visible. When seat is shield shaped, the front legs have nearly square vertical tenons that fit in mortices cut in the seat frame just behind the rounded corners.

Mortice and tenon joints are also used in the open backs. If there is a wide vertical back splat or three to five narrower ones, the ends fit into mortices cut in the lower edge of the top rail and the upper edge of the seat rail or a lower cross rail when present. With a ladder-back chair the horizontal crossbars fit into mortices in the sides of the back uprights. With shield, oval or heart-shaped backs, the ends of splats are morticed into these shaped frames.

Mortice and tenon joints are found with flat stretcher parts. Here the ends of members fit into mortices cut in the legs. With an H-shaped stretcher or the recessed front of a box stretcher, the ends of the cross members are dovetailed to the side ones.

Dowel joints are used to attach the back top rail to the uprights. If the top rail is on the front of the uprights, it is lap-joined and secured by dowels or countersunk screws. The shaped members forming shield, oval or heart-shaped backs are also dowel-joined, as are the outer ends of arms to front legs or arm stumps. The lower ends of the latter are lap-joined to the sides of the seat frame behind the front legs and secured by dowels or countersunk screws.

Dovetail or lap-joinings are used at the curved outer corners of shield-shaped seats.

Seat frames are strengthened by corner blocks glued and screwed in place. Their replacement does not affect the original condition of a chair since, through time and normal use, they become loose or split.

Chair seats are consistently from 16 to 18 inches from the floor except for seats of rocking chairs which are 14 to 16 inches high. Lower seats indicate that legs have been shortened to add rockers or casters or for conversion to a low slipper chair.

Structural parts of shaped chairs with open backs are always of hardwood and usually all of the same wood. Upholstery may cover only the seat or may include an upholstered back panel.

When the entire framework is covered by upholstery, as with the wing chair, the seat frame is of hardwood, morticed and tenoned or dovetailed at the corners. The rest is generally of pine or other softwood, left roughly finished. Where strength does not require fitted joints, plain butt joints held by dowels, nails or screws are usual.

PURITAN SPAN

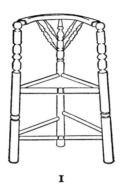

I

1. Three-Legged Chair

Has three stocky turned posts with ring-and-ball turnings above seat level. Front ones are plain or have ball-shaped finials just above U-shaped arm that surmounts back upright. Has triangular wooden seat with rounded or molded edges which rests on plain turned or square seat rails. Legs are braced by a triangular stretcher formed of turned or square members. Made in New England of oak and other native hardwoods. The few known examples are mostly in museum collections. *Ca. 1650–1670.* Z to Q

2. Wainscot Chair

Has turned front uprights and square rear ones which support a plain or carved paneled back. The heavy shaped arms are downcurved and are supported by the front uprights. The back has either a straight top rail or a carved and arched cresting above a large plain or carved panel. When this and the front seat rail are carved, the design is geometric and done in low relief. The rectangular wooden seat is slightly overhanging with molded edge. The legs are braced by a heavy box stretcher, with bead-molded edges. The front mem-

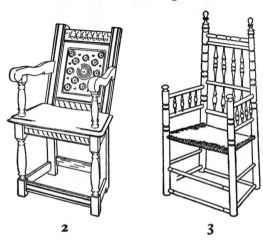

2   3

ber is sometimes ring-turned. Some examples have turned ball feet. Made in New England of native white oak. Excessively rare. Most known examples are in museum collections or are owned by colleges and used as the president's chair on ceremonial occasions. *Ca. 1650–1680.* Q

3. Turned Spindle Chair

Has postlike turned uprights with back ones terminating in steeple-turned finials. Back is formed by one or two rows of short spindles between turned cross rails. The plain turned arms are socketed into front and back uprights and sometimes there is a row of spindles beneath each arm. Has a rectangular rush or splint seat and legs are braced by a box stretcher of simple ring-turned members. A Brewster chair has a double row of spindles; a Carver chair a single row. Later examples of the Carver were sometimes made as side chairs. Made chiefly in New England of maple and ash or other close-grained native hardwoods. Not numerous. *Ca. 1650–1675.* Y to YY

4

4. Puritan Slat-Back Chair

Front and rear turned uprights are noticeably heavy, from three to four inches in diameter, and have well-executed ring turnings above the seat. The rear uprights terminate in steeple, ball or knob-and-ring finials; the front ones are plain or have flattened knob finials. The back is formed by three wide concave slats, each with bold quarter-circle cuts at the ends which reduce

them to tenons of about half-width. The arms are plain
turnings, with ends socketed into the uprights. The rectangular seat, from 22 to 26 inches wide, is of rush or
splint. The legs are braced by a box stretcher with plain
turned members.

Made mostly in New England of assorted native hardwoods. Uprights are of maple; slats, arms and stretcher
parts of ash, oak or beech. *Ca. 1670–1700.* XXX to YY

5   6

5. Four- to Six-Slat Chair

Front and rear uprights are an inch and a half to
two inches in diameter with ring, sausage or sausage-
and-ring turnings above and below the seat. Front ones
are sometimes slightly vase-shaped from seat to arms
and may have ball, knob or large button finials. Back
uprights terminate in urn-shaped or elongated ball
finials. Back is formed by four to six graduated slats
with upper edges slightly curved, arch-shaped or occa-

sionally scrolled. The arms are turned with central ring turnings or are flat-shaped, slightly flaring, and terminate in handgrips. The rectangular flaring seat, from 20 to 22 inches wide and from 16 to 18 inches deep, is of rush or splint. The legs are braced by a box stretcher with front member boldly ring-and-ball turned. Front legs generally have small ball or knob feet.

Made with and without arms and frequently in miniature as a child's chair. Produced in all sections of assorted native hardwoods. Uprights are most frequently of maple or birch; slats, stretcher parts and arms of oak, ash, beech or hickory. Shaped arms are sometimes of curly maple or cherry. *Ca. 1700–1800.* XX to YY

Survival Example

Has lighter uprights, with back ones ending in urn or spool finials, and lacks ring turnings. Back has plainer, narrower and less concave slats. Arms are turned or flat and simply shaped. Flaring seat is 18 to 20 inches wide. The box stretcher is of plain turned members. Made with and without arms of assorted hardwoods in rural sections, usually by untrained craftsmen and farmers as far west as Illinois and Western Tennessee. *Dates as late as 1860.* X to XX

6. Joined Stool

So named because parts are joined by mortice and tenon joints. Oblong top, about 18 inches wide with simply rounded edges, is attached to plain square upper rails. Is supported by four ring-and-vase turned flaring legs that terminate in small ball or knob feet. Legs are braced by plain box stretcher placed just above feet. Made chiefly in New England. Top of pine; legs, rails and stretcher of oak. Rare. *Ca. 1650–1690.* XXX to Y

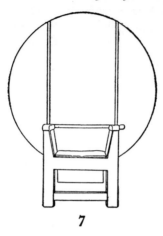

7

7. Table-Chair

Serves as chair when top is raised and as table when lowered. Base has square or turned and blocked uprights. These are surmounted by flat square arms to which top is attached by turned wooden pins inserted through holes in the two full-width scrolled cleats on the underside of top and corresponding ones in the arms. Top is square, round or oblong and generally made of two boards. Base has square overhanging seat, with rounded or molded edges, above plain or molded wide seat rails that are morticed into uprights. Legs are braced by a box stretcher with plain or bead-molded edges. Made chiefly in New England with pine top and base of oak. Not numerous. *Ca. 1675–1700.* Y to YY

Survival Example

Has slender square uprights, with or without a plain box stretcher. Pine top is generally round; seat and rest of base are of maple or other native hardwood. Generally is a simple country piece, lacking ornamental details. Made in all sections. *Ca. 1700–1825.* X to XX

8

8. Cromwellian Chair

Has square uprights, plain, knob or sausage-turned. Rear ones extend upward and support low stuffed back of fabric or leather. Square seat upholstered to match. Upholstery covers seat rails. Legs braced by turned stretcher at front, placed halfway from floor, and plain square ones at side and back placed close to floor. Rarely has arms. Made in New England of maple; seat rails and stretchers sometimes of oak. Chair with original turkey work upholstery is very rare. *Ca. 1660–1700.* YY to Z

WILLIAM AND MARY

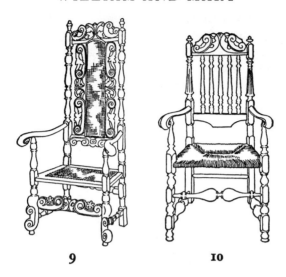

9   10

9. Restoration Chair

Also known as a Cane Chair, it has a tall back with caned panel and caned seat. Back uprights are turned and blocked, terminate in small turned finials and are flanked by foliage-carved scrolls, sometimes combined with a shell motif. Front legs are braced by ball-and-ring turned stretchers with front stretcher sometimes flat and foliage-carved. Open, downcurved molded arms are supported at front by extensions of front legs. Made in all sections of maple, walnut or other native hardwoods. With examples found today, upholstery sometimes replaces or covers cane work of back and seat. Not numerous. *Ca. 1675–1710.* YY to ZZZ

10. Banister-Back Chair

Banister is a corruption of *baluster,* the architectural term for the turned spindles supporting the handrail on the outer side of a stairway. This chair takes its name from the resemblance of the vertical splats that form the back to split banisters, since they are flat on the front and half-round at the back. The fashioning of these split banister splats involved two strips of wood, loosely glued with a paper between, which were then lathe-turned in ring-and-ball and vase shapings. After that glue and paper were removed and the split banisters were ready to be fitted to the chair back.

The general outline of this chair is similar to that of the Restoration or cane chair, with the split banisters, three to six in number, substituted for the cane back panel. Chair has slender uprights turned with vase, vase-and-ring, ball-and-ring or bobbin forms with back ones terminating in vase-shape, ball, or button finials. Front uprights have Flemish scroll or knob feet. The back uprights flank the split banister splats which are surmounted by an arched carved and pierced cresting or a curved solid one. At the bottom, the split banister splats are morticed into a straight cross rail with lower edge usually shaped in balancing concave curves. Has a rectangular flaring seat of rush or splint, 18 to 22 inches wide. The legs are braced by one or two box stretchers simply turned or with pronounced ring-and-ball turnings.

Made as side chair and armchair. The latter has shaped downcurved arms socketed onto the upper ends of the front uprights and terminating in knuckle carvings or shaped handgrips. Made in far greater numbers than the cane or Restoration chair in all sections, especially New England, of maple or sometimes of other native hardwoods. *Ca. 1700–1725.* Y to Z

Survival Example

Is usually a side chair. Back has straight cross rails top and bottom. Split banister splats are sometimes replaced by flat splats molded on the front. Generally painted a deep bottle green or finished with red filler. *Ca. 1725–1775.* XX to XXX

QUEEN ANNE

11   12

11. Corner or Roundabout Chair

Is so named because, with the diagonally placed seat, the back forms a right-angled corner. Has three vase-and-ring or knob turned uprights which support a low arm shaped in a continuous curve from end to end. At the front corner there is a seat-high upright or leg. The curved arm generally has a low, centered cresting shaped with a backward curve. All uprights terminate in small ball or in carved Spanish scroll feet. They are braced by a box stretcher with plain or ring-and-ball turned members. Between the rear seat rails and the arm are either two matching vase-shaped splats or horizontal slats with arched upper edges.

A chair with vase-shaped splats sometimes has a front cabriole leg terminating in a Dutch or drake foot. The uprights are then braced by a vase-turned X-shaped stretcher. The square seat is either rushed or upholstered; the fronts may have deeply valanced skirts. Made in all sections of walnut, maple or other close-grain native hardwoods with several different ones occasionally combined. *Ca. 1720–1750.* XX to Y

Corner chairs, all of the same basic construction but with slight variations in detail and ornamentation, continued to be made through the various furniture periods. Many were simple country-made pieces but handsome examples were also produced, especially in the Chippendale period.

12. Chippendale Corner Chair

Has either four cabriole legs terminating in claw-and-ball feet or a front one of this type and three square rear legs, chamfered on inner edges. Neither type has stretchers. The extensions of the rear supports are either simply or elaborately vase-turned and support the low curved arm which has a central flat cresting and terminates in either out-curved scrolls or knuckle carving. The matching splats of the back are plain or pierced in a balancing scrolled or lozenge pattern. The seat rails, into which fits a square upholstered slip seat, are bead-molded on the upper edges and at front frequently have deeply valanced skirts, either scrolled or with large semicircular pendents. Made in all sections of mahogany, walnut, plain or curly maple and sometimes cherry. *Ca. 1750–1775.* XXX to YY

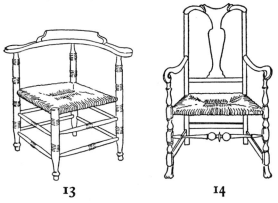

13   14

13. Nineteenth-Century Corner Chair

A simple country-made survival piece, the front leg and three rear uprights are plainly turned. The low curved arm is flat and frequently without central cresting. Back has plain horizontal slat or is sometimes completely open. Seat is square and rails are concealed by its rush or splint seating. Legs are generally braced by one or two box stretchers of plain turned members. Originally painted or finished with red filler. Made in all sections of maple, birch or assorted native hardwoods. Interesting and relatively plentiful. *Ca. 1775–1825.* X to XX

14. Queen Anne Vase-Splat Chair

Back is formed by a vase-shaped splat beneath a concave, yoke-shaped top rail and is flanked by vase-and-ball turned uprights that are continuations of plainly turned rear legs. When made with arms, the back uprights are sometimes square with front surface above the seat simply molded. With either a side or an arm chair, the front uprights have knob-and-ring or vase-and-ring turnings separated by square blocking and terminate in carved Spanish feet.

Rectangular rush seat is 18 to 20 inches wide. Legs are braced by a box stretcher with ring-and-ball turned front member and plain, slightly vase-shaped or square ones at sides and rear. As an armchair it has nearly flat scrolled arms that flare slightly and terminate in down-scrolled handgrips. Front ends of arms are socketed onto vase-and-ring turned extensions of front legs.

Made as both arm and side chair in all sections of maple and other native hardwoods. Frequently painted or finished originally with red filler. *Ca. 1710–1725.* Y to YY

Survival Example

Has turned front legs that are sometimes tapering and of kneeless cabriole type which terminate in small pad feet. Made of assorted native hardwoods as either arm or side chairs by country cabinetmakers in all sections as late as 1760. A simple chair of primitive character, it is interesting and relatively plentiful. *Ca. 1725–1760.* XX to XXX

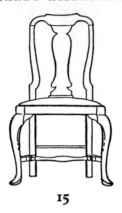

15

15. Spooned-Back Chair with Cabriole Legs

Has front cabriole legs terminating in Dutch feet. Back is slightly body conforming or "spooned" with vase-shaped back splat and arched top rail, supported by shaped and molded uprights. Has shield-shaped upholstered slip seat. Made in all sections of walnut, maple or other native hardwoods. *Ca. 1725–1740.* XXX to YY

16. Scrolled Splat Chair

Is more elaborate than the foregoing and has scrolled fiddle-shaped body-conforming back splat. Back uprights are slightly cyma-curved and are surmounted by yoke-shaped top rail with carved scallop shell at center. Front legs are cabriole, terminating in either Dutch or drake feet, and are shell-carved at knees. Made with or without a flat recessed box stretcher or an H-shaped stretcher of turned members.

Arms have serpentine curve, slightly flaring, and terminate in carved voluted rolls. Arm stumps are placed just behind front legs. Has shield-shaped upholstered slip seat. Made in all sections as either arm or side chair of walnut or sometimes of mahogany. *Ca. 1730–1750.* Y to YYY

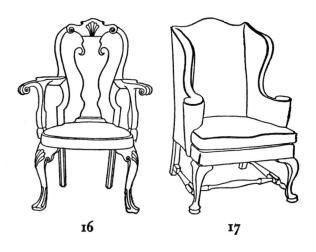

16   **17**

17. Wing Chair

Has upholstered body with stuffed seat, back, arms and wings. Its short front cabriole legs, sometimes with shell-carved knees, terminate in Dutch feet. Rear ones are square and canted backward. Legs are either unbraced or have an H-shaped or a box stretcher with recessed front of either vase-turned or flat shaped members. Top of upholstered back is either flat or slightly arched. Back is flanked by the wings which are an integral part of the out-scrolled arms. Made with legs of walnut and frame of assorted native hard and soft woods. *Ca. 1730–1750.* YY to Z

18. Upholstered Occasional Chair

Has stuffed seat and back. Front cabriole legs, sometimes with shell-carved knees, terminate in Dutch feet; back ones are square and slightly canted backward. Legs are braced by a box stretcher with recessed front

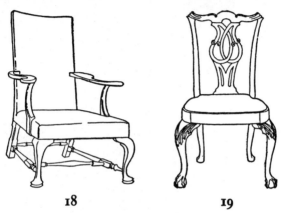

18   19

made of vase-turned members. The open out-scrolled arms terminate in rounded ends or voluted knuckle carving. Made in all sections with legs and arms of walnut and frame of assorted native woods. *Ca. 1730–1750.* Y to YYY

19. Early Georgian or Transitional Chair

Combines two periods in its lines and decorative detail, the passing Queen Anne and the coming Chippendale. Back has a scrolled fiddle-shaped splat that is either solid or symmetrically pierced, a serpentine top rail with central carved shell and voluted ends which is supported by slightly flaring uprights, molded on the front, that are continuations of the square canted back legs. Front legs are cabriole with shell-carved knees and terminate in either carved claw-and-ball or drake feet. The seat is rectangular and flaring or shield-shaped. It is fitted with an upholstered slip seat. Seat rails are of medium width. The front one has either a slightly valanced skirt or a pendent carved shell at its center. Arms, when present, are flaring and voluted, terminating in knuckle carvings. They are supported by shaped arm stumps attached to side seat rails a little behind the front legs. Made of walnut in all sections, especially Philadelphia and Newport, Rhode Island, or, in New England, of maple. *Ca. 1750–1760.* Y to Z

CHIPPENDALE

20. Chippendale Pierced Splat Chair

Has open flaring back surmounted by a boldly serpentined or cupid's-bow top rail with shell or shell-and-leafage scroll carving at center and terminating in carved volutes. Is supported by back uprights that are often fluted. The symmetrically pierced back splat is elaborately and intricately formed; is frequently leaf-carved and has a carved pendent tassel at center. Variations of this back splat have either Gothic details or a lozenge motif. Front legs are cabriole with shell-and-foliage or scroll-carved knees and terminate in boldly carved claw-and-ball feet. The canted rear legs are either square or rounded. The front seat rail is either plain or shell-carved with its lower edge straight or slightly valanced. The arms when present are outcurved and terminate in either voluted scrolls or carved knuckles. They are supported by arm stumps joined to side rails just behind the front legs. Has rectangular flaring upholstered slip seat or material may cover the seat rails. Made in all sections of mahogany or sometimes in New England of cherry. *Ca. 1760–1775.* YYY to ZZZ

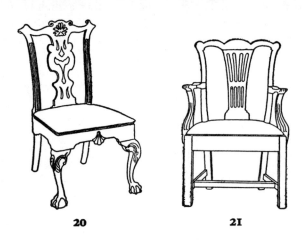

20 21

21. Chippendale Straight-Leg Chair

Has similar but generally less elaborate pierced back splat and top rail. Legs are square, chamfered on inner edge. The legs are braced by (1) a plain box stretcher, (2) box stretcher with recessed front member or (3) an H-shaped stretcher. The seat is rectangular and slightly flaring. If an armchair, the arms are outcurved, shaped, with rounded ends and are supported by recessed arm stumps. Either has an upholstered slip seat or upholstery covers the seat rails. Made in all sections of mahogany or cherry. *Ca. 1760–1775.* Y to Z

22

22. Ladder-Back Chair

Takes its name from similarity between its back with horizontal crossbars and a ladder. The open back is formed by slightly flaring molded uprights surmounted by a narrow serpentine or undulating pierced top rail. Beneath it, equally spaced, are two or, more frequently, three matching crossbars. The seat is rectangular, flaring and fitted with an upholstered slip seat. Seat rails when not covered by upholstery are of medium width and have straight edges, the upper ones bead-molded and lower ones plain. The legs are square with chamfered inner edges, the front two straight and the back ones canted. They are braced by a box stretcher, sometimes with front member recessed. Arms, when present, are molded, slightly outcurved and supported by concave, shaped and molded stumps attached to side seat rails. Made in all sections of mahogany or sometimes in New England of cherry. *Ca. 1760–1775.* YY to ZZ

23

23. Wing Chair

Is similar to that of the Queen Anne period (*see No. 17*) but wings are larger and more boldly shaped. There is usually a distinct line in upholstery where the wing bases rest on the arms. The latter are boldly out-scrolled, either horizontally or vertically. Chair is supported by (1) cabriole front legs with shell-carved knees and claw-and-ball feet and canted square or rounded back legs, usually not stretcher-braced, or (2) square front legs, either plain or molded and square canted rear legs, braced by a box stretcher, recessed at the front, made of square members.

Made in all sections with legs of mahogany and frame of assorted hard and soft woods. Especially fine examples with cabriole legs and claw-and-ball feet are generally of Philadelphia provenance. Not numerous and expensive. *Ca. 1760–1775.* YYY to ZZZ

HEPPLEWHITE

All chairs of the Hepplewhite period, except for the wing chair, are more delicate and graceful in design and appear to be smaller than those of preceding periods. Their openwork and low-relief carved backs are of five principal types: arched top with flaring uprights and central pierced splat, shield-shaped, oval, interlaced heart and shield, and "camel-back." Legs are slender, square and tapering. Those at front are straight, frequently fluted and sometimes inlaid. They may terminate in spade feet or have slight outward splay instead. Rear ones have less taper and a decided backward cant. Seats are rectangular with outward flare; fronts are either straight or serpentined. Upholstery is of two kinds — slip seat or covering seat rails. The latter is sometimes finished with festoons of brass-headed nails. These chairs were frequently made in matching sets and one or two were armchairs. With slight variations of design, the arms are always open, bowed or S-scrolled and either plain or molded. They are supported by incurvate arm stumps attached to side rails just behind the front legs.

24. Arched-Top Chair

The open back has an arched top rail supported by plain or molded flaring uprights and a central pierced splat like that of the simpler Chippendale chair. Front legs are square and tapering; rear ones are canted. Legs are braced by a box stretcher with front member either flush or recessed. Seat is rectangular and flaring with straight front. Upholstery is either slip seat or covering rails. Arms, if present, are of open bowed type. Made in all sections of mahogany. *Ca. 1785–1795.* XX to Y

 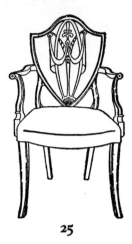

24   25

25. Shield-Back Chair

Open shield-shaped back with details carved in low relief is supported by short extensions of rear legs joined to sides of half-ellipse of shield. Top rail has arched curve and is sometimes carved with bowknotted foliage. Front of shield and supports are molded. At peak of shield there is a rosette segment, either carved or of satinwood inlay. Within the shield, back is completed by (1) an openwork oval splat with central forked leaf motif hung with drapery festoons and surmounted by a foliage cluster; (2) a triple-looped splat with drapery festoons and foliage sprays; (3) a balloon-shaped openwork splat with curved and clustered members carved in foliage details and pendent husks; (4) a carved splat

composed of the triple Prince of Wales feathers; or
(5) three to five converging shaped splats carved with
either leaf cluster and pendent husks or vase and sunburst motifs.

Arms, when present, are open, bowed and supported
by incurvate stumps placed just behind front legs. The
rectangular flaring seat has either a straight or a serpentine front. Upholstery either is a slip seat or covers
seat rails. Front legs are square and tapering, with or
without fluting, and may terminate in small spade feet.
Rear legs are square and canted. Stretcher, when present, is either H-shaped or a box with recessed front.
Most numerous of the finer Hepplewhite chairs. Made
of mahogany in all sections. *Ca. 1785–1800.* XXX to YY

26

26. Oval-Back Chair

Has oval open back with molded frame, carved in
low relief and supported by short shaped and molded
extensions of rear legs. Oval frames (1) three narrow,

shaped and sometimes carved vertical splats, (2) carved triple Prince of Wales feathers or (3) four branching feather plumes supported by a carved bowknot. The rectangular flaring seat usually has a serpentine front and the seat rails are covered by upholstery. Is supported by square tapering and fluted front legs, terminating in small spade feet, and square canted rear legs. Stretcher, if present, is a box with recessed front member. If with arms, these are open, bowed and supported by incurvate stumps attached to seat rails just behind front legs. Made in all sections of mahogany or, in Philadelphia, of beech and handsomely painted in Adam manner. Is rarer than other Hepplewhite chairs. *Ca. 1795–1800.* Y to YYY

27. Interlaced Heart-and-Shield-Back Chair

Has open molded back in form of an interlacing heart and shield, carved in low relief, which is supported by short shaped and molded extensions of rear legs. A central splat flares upward to contain a pierced, rayed fan with carved pendent husks below. This is flanked by upcurving narrower splats that support the central curve or cresting and form shield element of the design. All three splats spring from a carved or inlaid semi-rosette at base of back. Sometimes these splats are also hung with carved drapery festoons.

Seat is rectangular and flaring with serpentine front. Upholstery covers seat rails. Legs are square, tapering and terminate with either spade feet or slightly out-curved plain ends. They may be plain, fluted or inlaid with pendent bellflowers in satinwood. Stretcher, when present, is box-shaped with front recessed. If an arm-chair, open, bowed or S-scrolled arms are supported by incurvate molded stumps placed behind front legs. Is frequently the most elaborate example of Hepplewhite chairs.

Made in all sections of mahogany but probably of Baltimore provenance if front legs are inlaid. *Ca. 1790–1800.* Y to YYY

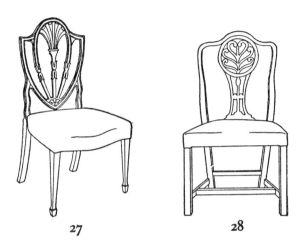

27

28

28. Camel-Back Chair

Top rail of the open back has a distinct but flattened arch similar to a camel's hump, hence the name. This rail, with slightly downcurved ends, and the back uprights are molded, enclosing a wide pierced central splat that is molded and carved with a Grecian honeysuckle or anthemion motif. The rectangular flaring seat has a straight front. Upholstery either is slip seat or covers the seat rails. Front legs are square and molded or slightly tapering and rear ones are canted backward. Legs are

braced by a box stretcher with recessed front. This chair
is sometimes considered as transitional from the Chippendale period. Is not generally as slender and delicate
as other Hepplewhite chairs. Made in all sections of
mahogany. *Ca. 1785-1795.* XXX to Y

29

29. Wing Chair

Shaping of back arms, wings and seat is the same as
with the Chippendale (*see No. 23*) but legs are square
and tapered. Rear ones have distinct backward cant.
Legs are sometimes braced by box stretcher with recessed
front member. Not widely made. Mahogany. *Ca. 1785-
1800.* YY to Z

30

30. Martha Washington Armchair

Is so named for chair of this design at Mount Vernon. Has upholstered back and seat. The high back is rectangular and slightly arched at the top. The seat is slightly flaring with rails covered by upholstery material and has a straight front. Open wooden arms are shaped, slightly bowed, and rest on quadrangular plain or molded stumps that curve downward in quarter-circles to the front legs. The square and tapering front legs are either plain or molded. The rear ones are square, plain and canted. They are braced by either an H-shaped or a box stretcher with recessed front member. Made in all sections with legs, arms and stretchers of mahogany and frame under upholstery of assorted woods. *Ca. 1785–1810.* YY to Z

SHERATON

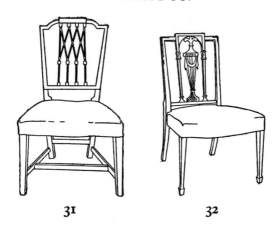

31   32

31. Sheraton Crested-Back Chair

Has open rectangular back. Top rail is slightly crested and has an oblong central panel, festoon or foliage-carved. Inside the molded frame of top rail and side uprights are either three or four narrow vertical splats, sometimes hung with festoons carved in low relief, or four or five bars forming a diamond-shaped or Gothic-arched lattice. Seat is rectangular and flaring. Upholstery is either a slip seat or covers rails. Front legs are square, tapering and fluted; rear ones, square and canted. Made in all sections of mahogany. *Ca. 1800–1810.* XX to Y

32. Sheraton Drawing-Book Chair

Is so called because design of back is taken from Sheraton's *The Cabinet-Maker and Upholsterer's Draw-ing-Book.* The open rectangular back has (1) interlaced rectangles, the inner one framing a carved tripod hung with drapery festoons and surmounted by Prince of Wales feathers; (2) interlaced rectangles with inner one containing balanced S-scrolls flanking a carved urn hung with drapery festoons; (3) diagonal bead-molded bars forming a diamond-shaped lattice or (4) four or five reeded colonnettes with capitals carved in palm-leaf motif. Has rectangular, flaring or shield-shaped seat with upholstery completely or partially covering seat rails. Front legs are turned, slightly tapering and fluted with feet simulated by ring turnings; rear ones are square or rounded and canted backward. Made in all sections of mahogany. *Ca. 1810–1820.* XX to YY

33

33. Colonnette-Back Armchair

Top rail has an oblong centered die hung with drapery festoons carved in low relief and is supported by uprights bead-molded on the front. The open rectangular back is arcaded with four slender, reeded, quadrangular colonnettes supporting palm-leaf carved spandrels. The arms curve slightly outward and are supported by quarter-round incurved molded arm stumps, attached to the seat rails a little behind the front legs. The flaring rectangular seat is covered by upholstery that completely or partially covers the seat rails. The front legs are square and tapering and terminate in spade feet. The rear ones are square and canted backward. Made of mahogany, especially in New York by Phyfe and his contemporaries. Was a popular design and made in considerable numbers. *Ca. 1795–1810.* XX to YY

PHYFE CHAIRS

These form a distinct group and show Duncan Phyfe's interpretation of the Sheraton and French Directoire styles. They were made in his own workshop and by many of his contemporaries in New York, Philadelphia and other cities. With minor variations in details or ornamentation and construction there are four types:

34. Turned-Leg Chair

Has slender turned and reeded front legs terminating in small turned knoblike feet. Rear legs are square and canted backward. Back is formed by reeded uprights with backward curve, a concave slightly backward curved top rail with oblong panel carved in spears of wheat, thunderbolts, arrows, bowknotted or drapery festoon. Below it is a latticework of diagonal bars or two tangent semicircles with carved rosettes at the joining. The seat is shield-shaped and either upholstered or

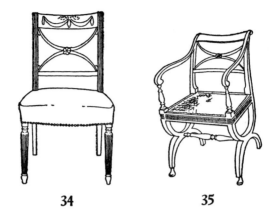

34   35

caned. The shaped seat rail, when exposed, is horizontally reeded to match front legs and back uprights.
Made of mahogany. *Ca. 1800–1820.* Y to YY

35. Curule Chair

Inspired by and takes name from Roman *sella curulis*
or curved chair. Legs are replaced by two tangent semicircular segments. Front ends of lower segment terminate in small carved or brass paw feet. These semicircular supports are braced by a single vase-turned
stretcher. Back consists of reeded, backward-curved uprights, a concave and backward-curved top rail with
oblong panel carved with (1) spears of wheat, (2) thunderbolts, (3) arrows or (4) leafed sprays all bowknotted
at center, two tangent semicircles with carved rosette
where they meet, and a lower, reeded, concave cross
rail. Has square caned seat and seat rails are reeded.
When made as armchair, the reeded arms are down-

curved and supported by vase-turned plain or reeded arm stumps. Made of mahogany. *Ca. 1810–1820.* YYY to ZZ

36

36. Saber-Leg Chair

Front legs are sharply incurved, giving them a profile like a saber, hence the name. They are water or acanthus-leaf carved, sometimes terminating in small carved or brass cast feet, or are carved to simulate fur and terminate in small animal paws ebonized. Rear legs are square and canted backward. Back uprights have a backward curve and are reeded. Top rail is concave, has slight backward curve and a bead-molded panel. Across center of the back is a horizontal splat with central oval medallion, flanked by leafage scrolls. Seat is bell-shaped, caned or upholstered, and shaped seat frame is reeded. When made as armchair the reeded arms are down-curved and supported by vase-turned plain or reeded arm stumps placed behind front legs. Made of mahogany. *Ca. 1810–1820.* YY to YYY

37. Lyre-Back Chair

Back splat is a classic lyre delicately leaf-carved with four brass rods simulating the strings. Has rectangular upholstered seat and reeded front seat rail. Rest of construction and decorative details are the same as the saber-leg chair except that front legs when leaf-carved are without paw feet. Seldom made as an armchair. It is considered the finest of the Phyfe designs. Made of mahogany. *Ca. 1810–1820.* YY to YYY

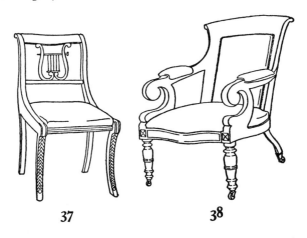

37   38

38. Sheraton Armchair

Has upholstered seat and back with exposed wooden top rail which is concave with rolled upper edge supported by plain uprights. The open arms terminate in horizontal scrolls and are supported by turned or curved arm stumps placed back of front legs which are turned and either plain or reeded. Rear legs are rounded and

canted backward. Made in all sections of mahogany.
Ca. 1810–1820. XX to YY

39

39. Painted Fancy Chair

Has turned, slightly tapering front legs with some
ring turnings and small ball or knob feet. Rear legs are
either plainly shaped or turned and canted backward.
Legs are braced by a box stretcher with front member
either decoratively turned or flat. Uprights of back have
slight backward curve and support a wide concave top
rail with rolled upper edge. Back contains either a
plain back splat or a cut-out horizontal bar. Has shield-
shaped rush seat. Is generally painted black with decorations and striping in various colors and gilt. Sometimes
has scrolled and slightly flaring arms supported by
turned arm stumps, placed behind front legs. Made in
all sections by fancy chairmakers of maple and other
close-grain native hardwoods. *Ca. 1800–1820.* X to XX

AMERICAN EMPIRE

40

40. Vase-Splat Chair

Is sometimes incorrectly called a *fiddle-back* although the large splat is always urn-shaped. The back top rail, always faced with crotch-grain veneer, is of two designs — a plain U-shaped or a wide concave cross member with rounded ends, a rolled cresting and scroll-cut lower edge. Either type is supported by plain rounded uprights that are continuations of the nearly square rear legs. These have a backward saber curve.

Back is open and the wide urn-shaped splat is crotch-grain veneered. Chair has an upholstered slip seat that is either rectangular or U-shaped with a bowed front. Front chair rail has conforming bow and is crotch-grain veneered. The front legs are flat and shaped in reverse ogee curves with front edges rounded. A variation of this chair has a horizontal splat with scrolled outline, either solid or pierced and faced with crotch-grain veneer instead of the urn-shape splat.

Made in all sections of mahogany, with liberal use of crotch-grain veneer. *Ca. 1820–1835.* XX to XXX

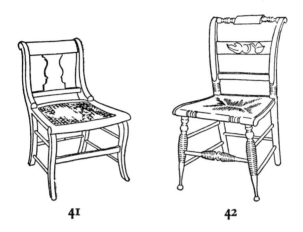

41   42

41. Vase-Splat Chair with Cane Seat

Design and construction are about the same as the preceding chair but this has cane seat and is made of straight grain or curly maple or a combination of the two. Top rail and splat are sometimes of bird's-eye maple. Sometimes vase-shaped back splat is replaced by a shaped horizontal splat of medium width that is pierced and foliage-carved.

Made in the early chair factories, particularly in New England, New York City and central New York State. Large quantities of these chairs were shipped to the South, the Middle West and the West Indies. William Marcy Tweed, later known as "Boss" Tweed, made this chair at his shop in New York City and sold it largely to the shipping trade before he forsook chairmaking for politics. The one illustrated is known to be Tweed-made. *Ca. 1825–1840.* X to XX

42. Hitchcock Chair

Is the painted fancy chair of American Empire period. Takes its name from Lambert Hitchcock in whose Connecticut factories large numbers of them were produced between 1822 and 1843. Some of the chairs made by Hitchcock bear a stencil label on back edge of seat. Before 1829 it read either "L.Hitchcock, Warranted" or "L.Hitchcock,Hitchcockville,Ct." After 1829 the label was "Hitchcock, Alford & Co."

This chair has slightly arched concave top rail that is either turned and shaped or flat with rounded ends. It is supported by rounded and slightly curved extensions of the plain turned back legs. Across middle of open back is a concave wide slat with or without a narrower one below it. The rush or cane seat is rectangular and slightly flaring. If of rush, there is a split turning about an inch wide at the front and thin flat strips at sides and back. These protect the twists of rush wrapped around the concealed seat rails. The front legs are turned, have some shallow ring turnings and taper slightly to terminate in small ball feet. The legs are braced at sides and back by plain turned stretchers and at front by a ring-turned stretcher or a flat one two inches wide placed boxlike.

To simulate rosewood, chair was originally painted brownish-black with irregular veinings. It was then stencil-decorated in colors and gilt with conventionalized designs and striped with yellow or gilt. When made as an armchair, it has scrolled downcurved arms supported by turned arm stumps. A late example can have a solid wooden seat, slightly conforming, about an inch and a half thick. A chair with original decoration and with Hitchcock label is the most desirable. Made chiefly of maple in a number of chair shops located in New England, New York and Pennsylvania and shipped in quantities to the South and Middle West. *Ca. 1820–1850.* X to XX

43. Boston Rocker

Has solid wooden seat upcurved at rear and boldly rolled at front with sides slightly cyma-curved. Its short turned legs, ring-turned at front and plain at rear, are mounted on short narrow rockers. The high, slightly conforming back is formed by plain turned uprights flanking seven to nine slender tapering spindles surmounted by a wide shaped top rail. This has a curved upper edge, rounded ends and arched lower edge. The arms are two inches wide, cyma-curved, have rolled ends and are supported by spindle-turned arm stumps. Painted and decorated like Hitchcock chair. Seat sometimes painted and grained to simulate either crotch-grain mahogany or bird's-eye maple. Made chiefly of maple with pine seat in same shops that produced Hitchcock chairs. *Ca. 1820–1850.* X to XX

44. Empire Armchair

Has stuffed and upholstered back framed by uprights with backward curve and concave top rail. Arms are open and formed by cyma curves extending from

back uprights to front of seat rails. Frequently have upholstered pads. The upholstered seat is rectangular with
bowed front. Front seat rail is generally bowed and
faced with crotch-grain veneer. The front legs are

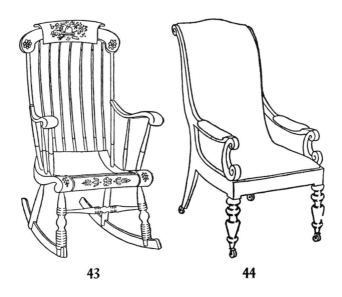

43   **44**

either turned or shaped in reverse ogee curve; rear ones
are square and curved backward. Sometimes chair has
long curved rockers. Made in all sections of mahogany.
Ca. 1820–1840. XX to XXX

Chair of similar design is made of straight-grain
maple with caned back and seat. Was originally painted
and striped, but not stencil-decorated. As inexpensive
substitute for the upholstered Empire armchair it was
popular and widely made. *Ca. 1830–1850.* X to XX

EARLY VICTORIAN

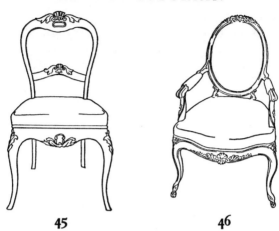

45   46

45. Victorian Side Chair

Design reflects the style of Louis XV. Has open cartouche-shaped back with top carved in leaf, flower and fruit motifs and an arched transverse scrolled splat. Seat is rectangular and flaring with slightly serpentined front and has carved and valanced skirt. Has slender cabriole front legs terminating in rudimentary feet. Rear ones are square with backward curve. Made in all sections of rosewood and later of black walnut. *Ca. 1850–1870.* X to XX

46. Victorian Armchair

Also copies the French style of Louis XV. Has cartouche-shaped or oval upholstered back surmounted by arched top, carved with leaf, flower and fruit motifs.

Top is supported by plain or deeply molded shaped uprights. Has either open or enclosed flaring scrolled arms supported by molded arm stumps. Arms are sometimes fitted with pads. Upholstered seat is rectangular and flaring with slightly serpentined front. Has cabriole front legs terminating in rudimentary feet that continue upward to form the scrolled arm stumps. Rear legs are square with backward curve. Made in all sections of rosewood and, later, black walnut. *Ca. 1850–1870.* XX to XXX

47

47. Belter Chair

Is named for John Henry Belter, New York City cabinetmaker, outstanding for his richly carved rosewood furniture. Has scroll-outlined concave back with central upholstered panel surmounted by cresting of carved foliage, flowers and fruits, done in high relief and flanked by scrolled and pierced framing with similar carving. The flaring upholstered seat has a serpentine front. Beneath it is an undulating carved and molded skirt. The short, molded cabriole front legs have carved knees and terminate in scroll feet. The rear legs are plain or molded, curve backward and sometimes terminate in small scrolled feet. If an armchair, the arms are either open or enclosed with upholstery. Outer ends and supports are flaring molded and frequently carved. Made of laminated rosewood. *Ca. 1844–1865.* XX to Y

Section **V**

Windsor Chairs. 1725–1850

THE American Windsor was made in nine different types, six of which were developed within the first seventy-five years. So marked were the differences of design and ornamentation that it is possible today to identify each kind clearly as to age and, sometimes, as to provenance.

This chair with solid plank seat, spindle-back and canted legs, was of English provincial origin. Made of elm, ash or yew, it was more the work of wheelwrights than of cabinetmakers and remained farmhouse or tavern furniture. It arrived in America about 1725. At the start, the handsome American versions were called Philadelphia chairs after the place where they were first made. Within a scant twenty-five years, they had spread northward to New England where a special type developed, now called Windsors. There were craftsmen in at least five colonies who made no other furniture and styled themselves "Windsor chair makers." Some had first learned the trade of making the small turned and decorative flax wheels used for spinning linen thread. The legs of these little spinning wheels are similar to those found on Windsor chairs and their wheel-spoke turnings have the same shaping as the arm supports of earlier Windsors. At the hands of such chair makers, Windsors became handsome enough to be used anywhere except in the drawing rooms of fine mansions.

They were made full-size for adults and smaller for children, including many high chairs. The earliest American Windsors were big and masculine, but about 1750 daintier ones with feminine appeal appeared.

The different types are: low-back, comb-back, bow-back, arched-back, fan-back, loop-back, rod-back, arrow-back and fire-house. This last, a decadent reversion to the early low-back, was a factory-made product of the mid-nineteenth century. There are also writing Windsors in five of these types and settles in three of them.

Comments on Windsors and Their Construction

The woods preferred by American Windsor chair makers are: pine, whitewood or basswood for seats; hickory or ash for spindles; maple, yellow birch or beech for turned legs, stretchers and arm supports; hickory, ash, oak or beech for turned legs, stretchers and arm supports; hickory, ash, oak or beech for hoops, bows and comb-pieces; and maple, ash or oak for one-piece curved arms. Pine and maple are the woods of the late fire-house Windsors.

Seats are from an inch and three quarters to two and a quarter inches thick. The upper side, except for some late examples, are carved or "saddled" to be body conforming. Sometimes this reduces the thickness of the center by half.

All parts are socketed together, including even the late fire-house type, except for the shaped arms of fan-back, rod-back and arrow-back chairs. Here the inner ends of the arms are doweled or screwed to the back uprights.

The legs are so socketed into the thick seat as to flare downward. The angle of this splay varies from 10 to 15 degrees from the perpendicular. The sideward splay is often noticeably more than that at front or back.

Legs with either cylinder or vase-and-ring shaping are of four kinds: (1) with blunt arrow at lower ends, found on Philadelphia and New York chairs; (2) with a long slender taper at lower ends, found on chairs of general New England provenance; (3) with taper of lower end incurved, Rhode Island origin; and (4) with a shorter and less slender taper which is peculiar to chairs of Connecticut make. Unshaped Windsor chair legs sometimes have slight ring turnings that simulate bamboo.

There are marked differences between American and English Windsors. The legs of English examples are never splayed and often not stretcher-braced. Some have front cabriole legs terminating in Dutch feet. Frequently there is a shaped and pierced back splat in place of the central spindles.

48. Low-Back Windsor Armchair

Has vase or cylinder-turned blunt-arrow splayed legs that are braced by an H-shaped stretcher of baluster or bobbin turned parts. The saddle seat has a straight front and half-round back. The low back has a heavy horseshoe-shaped continuous arm, slightly crested at center and terminating in plain or knuckle-carved ends. This is supported at the front by vase-turned uprights and the back is formed by from eleven to seventeen short plain spindles. Late example sometimes has vase-and-

ring turned instead of blunt-arrow legs. Made in or near
Philadelphia. *Ca. 1725–1760.* YY to YYY

48   49

49. Comb-Back Windsor Armchair

Has vase or cylinder and blunt-arrow or vase-and-ring
turned splayed legs that are braced by an H-shaped
stretcher of baluster or bobbin-turned parts. The
wide saddle seat is half-round with straight front. The
deeply curved one-piece arm is with or without a slight
cresting at the center and terminates in plain, outcurved or knuckle-carved ends. It is supported at front
by vase-turned uprights, sometimes canted forward. The
back is formed by seven or nine plain spindles that pass
through the arm and extend upward for about 18
inches. They are surmounted by a wide comb-piece with
ends plain or volute-carved. Back is sometimes braced
by two spindles that flare upward from seat tailpiece to comb. Made chiefly in or around Philadelphia
but sometimes in New York. *Ca. 1735–1775.* Y to YYY

50. Bow-Back Windsor Armchair

Has vase-and-ring turned splayed legs braced by an H-shaped stretcher of bobbin-turned parts. The wide saddle seat is oval in shape. The curved one-piece arm

50

terminates in plain or knuckle-carved ends and is supported at front by two slender vase-turned uprights. It is surmounted by a curved bow and the back is formed by seven rod spindles that pass through the arm and extend upward from 10 to 14 inches to the bow. Above this there is sometimes a comb-piece supported by the five central spindles. Made in all sections from New England to Pennsylvania. *Ca. 1750–1820.* XXX to YY

51. Fan-Back Windsor Chair

Has vase-and-ring turned splay legs that are braced by an H-shaped stretcher of bobbin-turned members.

These support a shield-shaped seat that is boldly saddled. The slightly sloping back is formed by from five
to nine long rod spindles which are flanked by slender
vase-turned uprights. These and the spindles are surmounted by a yoke-shaped, concave crest rail that has
either plain or volute carved ends. The back is sometimes braced by two spindles that flare upward from
tailpiece to cresting. Arms when present are flat, have
a flaring curve and terminate in rounded ends that
match those of comb-piece. They are supported by either
vase-turned or ram's-horn stumps. This is the first Windsor chair made in the smaller or lady size. Originally
made in Philadelphia and later in New Jersey, New
York and most of New England. *Ca. 1750–1800.* Y to
YY

51   52

52. Loop-Back Windsor Chair

Has bobbin or vase-turned splayed legs with bamboo ringings, braced by matching or bobbin-turned

H-shaped stretcher. These support a shield-shaped saddle seat. The sloping back consists of a U-shaped, slightly flaring loop and from seven to nine rod spindles. Made in all sections, especially New England, generally as a side chair. *Ca. 1750–1800.* XX to XXX

53

53. Arch-Back Windsor Armchair

Has vase-and-ring or bobbin-turned splayed legs braced by an H-shaped, bobbin-turned stretcher. These support a shield-shaped or oval saddle seat. The sloping back is formed by nine rod spindles, varying in length to conform to the one-piece arched hoop, ends of which are bent to form short flat arms with rounded ends. The arms are supported by slender vase-and-ring turned uprights, canted forward, and two short rod spindles. The back, sometimes braced by two rod spindles that flare upward from the seat tailpiece, can also be sur-

mounted by a comb-piece supported by extensions of the
five central spindles. This enhances its value. Construction is always lighter than that of earlier chairs. Made in
New England. *Ca. 1785–1810.* Y to YY

54

54. Rod-Back Windsor Chair

Has simply turned legs with bamboo ringings that
are splayed and braced by either an H-shaped or a box
stretcher with members turned to match legs. These support a shield-shaped or squarish saddle seat. The sloping back is formed by two simply turned slender uprights that support a matching top rail and contains from
five to seven rod spindles that sometimes have bamboo
ringings. When made as an armchair, has either short
turned and sometimes bamboo-ringed arms or flat and
shaped ones with rolled ends. These are supported by
plain or bamboo-ringed uprights and rod spindles. Many
of these chairs were originally painted black and ornamented with Sheraton details. Made in all sections. *Ca.
1800–1830.* XX to XXX

55. Arrow-Back Windsor Chair

Has simply turned splayed legs, plain or with bamboo ringings and braced by either an H-shaped or a box stretcher with matching members. The seat is shield-shaped or squarish with less pronounced saddling. The back frequently has a decided backward curve and is formed of two plain or bamboo-turned uprights con-

55

nected by a flat, shaped top rail. It contains from three to five flat arrow-shaped splats. Arms, when present, have a slight downward curve with rolled ends. They are supported by bamboo-ringed uprights. The top rail is sometimes surmounted by a comb-piece supported by five rod spindles with slight bend. This is the only Windsor originally made in quantity as a rocking chair. Many were painted black with Sheraton details. Made in all sections. *Ca. 1810–1835.* XX to XXX

56. Fire-House Windsor Chair

Is so called because of wide use in quarters of the volunteer fire companies of the day. Also extensively favored in hotels, meeting rooms and offices. The legs have less splay. The front ones are slightly ring-turned and tapering; rear legs are plain with decided backward flare. They are braced by a box stretcher with

56

front member ring-turned. Has a deep U-shaped seat that is either plain or slightly saddled. The heavy horseshoe-shaped continuous arm has a low cresting at the center and terminates in rounded ends. It is supported by seven to nine simply shaped spindles. Generally painted and grained like Boston rocker (*see No. 43*). A late revival of the low-back Windsor, it was made in all sections with seat and arm of pine and legs, stretchers and spindles of maple or birch. *Ca. 1840–1865.* X to XX

57. Windsor Writing Armchair

Was made in low-back, comb-back, bow-back, rod-back and arrow-back types. A broad writing tablet that is either rigid or pivoted is attached to the right arm.

57

If fixed, the tablet is generally supported by three turned spindles. A small drawer is sometimes attached to the underside of the tablet or the seat or both. *Ca. 1740–1810.* YY to YYY

58. Low-Back Windsor Settee

Is an enlargement of the low-back Windsor chair and is found in both large and love-seat sizes. Total length for the large size ranges from six to seven feet and for the love seat from three feet six inches to four feet six inches. The former has eight cylinder-turned blunt-arrow splayed legs that are braced by three H-shaped stretchers of baluster, bobbin or ball-and-ring turned members. The love seat has six legs and two H-shaped stretchers. The seat is saddle-shaped with pronounced

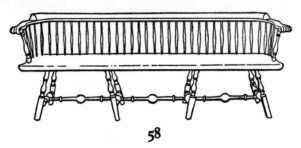

58

rounding of rear corners. The heavy U-shaped top rail of the low back has a low cresting and terminates in boldly done knuckle-carved ends. It is supported at the front by two vase-turned uprights and from twenty-two to thirty-eight plain or bobbin-turned spindles, according to size of settee. A late example sometimes has vase-and-ring turned instead of blunt-arrow legs. Made in or near Philadelphia. *Ca. 1730–1760.* YYY to Z

59. Bow-Back Windsor Settee

Is likewise an enlargement of the corresponding chair and is found in large and love-seat sizes. It varies in length from four to six feet. Has four, six and sometimes eight vase-and-ring turned splayed legs that are braced by one, two or three H-shaped stretchers made of bobbin-turned members. The wide saddle-shaped seat has a straight front with rear corners well rounded. The curved one-piece arm terminates in plain or knuckle-carved ends and is supported at the front by two slender vase-turned uprights. Arm is surmounted by an ample curved bow and the back is formed by from nine to

59

eleven rod spindles that pass through the arms and extend upward from 12 to 16 inches to the bow. Made in New England and parts of New York State. *Ca. 1760–1800.* YY to YYY

Comb-Back Windsor Settee

Is found only in the love-seat size, three to four feet long, with four or six vase-and-ring turned legs. Otherwise the lines and construction are like the foregoing except for the elongated comb-piece which is substituted for the curved bow. This comb-piece is supported by from nine to eleven plain rod spindles that pass through the arm. At each end there are also three shorter spindles which extend from seat to arm. Made in New England. *Ca. 1760–1790.* Y to YY

Rod-Back Windsor Settee

An enlargement of the rod-back Windsor chair, generally found in the large size with a total length of from five to six feet. Has six simply turned splayed legs with bamboo ringing that are braced by a double H-shaped stretcher of bobbin or bamboo-turned members. The shaping of the rectangular seat is less pronounced and the corners are only slightly rounded. The back usually has a decided backward curve and is formed by three or four chair-back units, each with six slender spindles flanked by slightly larger turned uprights, and a continuous slender turned top rail. The arms are either bamboo turned or are flat, downcurved shaped ones with rolled ends. They are supported by from four to six shorter spindles that are plain or bamboo turned. Made in all sections. *Ca. 1800–1820.* XXX to Y

SECTION VI

Tables

NEXT to chairs, tables were the most numerous of all household pieces during the two-hundred-year span when early American furniture was being made. Even the first meager furnishings of the early seventeenth-century home included a trestle table at which the family ate. Heavy and crude, it was probably the only table in a room where bare necessities existed. But as soon as the first rigors of existence lessened, cabinetmakers had orders to make the various types and sizes of tables common in England. Drawing on memory and adding individual touches of their own, they created tables that were English in design but had an American flavor.

This characteristic continued throughout the two centuries when furniture making was a handcraft and in the course of which American cabinetmakers produced over fifty varieties of tables. Their names, save for the Pembroke, indicate either the purpose for which they were made or some special feature of construction. All, except possibly the sawbuck and butterfly, were similar to those made in England at about the same time.

Special Comments on Tables and Their Construction

The height is uniformly 27 to 29 inches unless otherwise specified in the description of a particular table.

Mortice and tenon joints are consistently used for joining legs to frame, swinging legs to pivoting brackets and stretchers to legs. They are generally pegged with wooden pins about a quarter inch in diameter with ends visible.

Dovetail joints are used for joinings of front, side-pieces and back of drawers.

Stretchers are of three kinds — box, X-shaped, and H-shaped. A box stretcher is either square or oblong with members on all four sides. An X-shaped stretcher has diagonal members, lap-jointed at center crossing. An H-shaped stretcher has members at the ends which are joined by a centered transverse one. All stretchers are placed just above the feet or, when legs are without feet, two to six inches from the floor.

Table tops consistently overhang their bases. With small tables this is from half an inch to two inches and with larger ones from four to six inches. With drop-leaf tables the overhang at the sides is just sufficient to allow the leaves to hang vertically; at the ends, it is from two to six inches, depending on size. When a table is without leaves, the overhang at the sides is usually half of that at the ends.

A rule or knuckle joint is formed by a matching straight-concave and a straight-convex molded finish on the sides of a table top and its hinged drop leaves. When leaves are dropped, they provide molded edges and when raised, top and leaves fit closely. Rule joints are found on all leaved tables except very early examples, double-top card tables, and late farm-made pieces.

A swinging bracket is a horizontal which supports a table leaf. It is attached to the table bed by a pivot-and-pin joint to enable it to swing to a right angle. Most brackets are the same width as the table bed and have shaped ends.

The hinged legs that support table leaves are of two types — gate-leg and swinging bracket leg. The gate-leg is so named for its resemblance to a fence gate. It is constructed with upper and lower cross members. The upper one is connected to the upper end of the leg by a mortice and tenon joint and its other end is pivot-joined to the table bed. The lower cross member is morticed at one end to the leg, just above the foot, and pivot-joined at the other to the side of the box stretcher. A swinging bracket leg has only the upper cross member.

A table bed is the horizontal framework beneath the top to which legs or pedestals are attached. When there are drawers, they fit within the bed.

The top or the fixed leaf of a table with drop leaves is attached to its bed by unseen screws, located on the inner sides of it. Here tapering cuts, done with a half-round chisel, extend to within three quarters to an inch of the upper edge of the bed. The screws are put in these semicircular cuts. From six to eight so set are used to fasten a top of average size.

With all card and gaming tables the fold-over leaves are attached by a pair of toggle hinges made especially for this purpose. These hinges are of cast brass and are set in shallow recesses cut in the sides of the fixed and movable leaves at the back edges. Each hinge consists of two rectangular leaves about half an inch wide and two to three inches long which are joined by a small toggle piece tenoned into the rear ends of the leaves and held fast by pins on which they pivot. Each leaf has two or three screw holes reamed so that the heads of the seated screws are flush. For gaming tables with two movable leaves, special three-leaved toggle hinges are used.

The bed of a pedestal table is screwed to an unseen flat crosspiece from six to 10 inches wide that is mortice-jointed to the upper end of the pedestal shaft.

The cabriole legs of a tripod table are joined to the base of its turned shaft by large vertical dovetails. These are cut into the base so that the legs slide upward into place. This joining is reinforced by a wrought-iron plate with three extensions, three to four inches long, which are screwed to the undersides of the legs.

The skirt of a table is the finished horizontal member connecting the upper ends of the legs or, with a pedestal table, concealing the bed. Tables without leaves have four skirt pieces; drop-leaf tables have one at each end; and half-round tables a conforming semicircular skirt with upper ends of the front legs sometimes forming slight outsquared breaks which project about a quarter of an inch. Pedestal tables are skirted on all sides.

PURITAN SPAN

60. Trestle Table

Has one-board plank top up to 12 feet long by 24 to 30 inches wide supported by two or three heavy T-shaped oak trestles with chamfered edges. Each rests on a blocklike foot, sharply beveled from ends to upright, known as a shoe foot. Trestles are connected by a single wide, flat stretcher passing through mortices cut in them a third to half of the way from floor and held in place by pairs of exposed wooden pins. Its original use was

probably that of a church communion table. Excessively
rare. Most examples are now in museum collections.
Ca. 1650–1660. Q to QQ

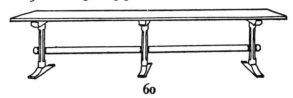

60

New England Survival Type

Has two-board top with cleated ends and lighter,
plainer trestles. Flat stretcher is mortice-joined to uprights. A farm-made piece, measuring four to six feet in
length, it is usually all of pine or with pine top and maple
understructure. *Made as late as 1825.* XXX to Y

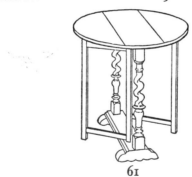

61

61. Tuckaway Trestle Table

When not in use and with leaves lowered, this table can
be stored readily as it occupies little floor space, hence
its name. It has round, oval, or oblong top with narrow

central fixed leaf and two drop leaves. Trestle consists
of two spirally or vase-and-ring turned uprights braced
by a flat stretcher and supported by shoe feet. Fixed leaf
is attached directly to trestle uprights. When raised,
leaves are supported by swinging gates with either square
or vase-and-ring turned uprights and matching stretcher
pieces. Made in New England, generally with pine top
and understructure of various hardwoods, but sometimes
all of maple or walnut. Rare. *Ca. 1675–1730.* XXX to YY

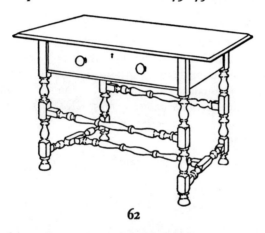

62

62. Five-Stretcher Cromwellian Table

Has small, oblong top with molded edges or cleated
ends fixed to shallow bed which contains a full-width
drawer fitted with elongated turned wooden knobs or
pendent iron rings. Supported by spiral, vase-and-ring,
or ring-and-ball turned legs with square sections that
terminate in small pear-shaped or knob feet. Legs are
braced by five stretchers turned to match. At front and

back these are halfway from floor and at ends, just above the feet. Lower ones are joined at center by a fifth stretcher. Made mostly in New England of maple or walnut with top sometimes of pine. Rare. *Ca. 1650–1700.* YY to Z

63

63. Jacobean Table

Has pine top, one and one half to two inches thick, that is up to eight feet long by about 34 inches wide. The side and end skirts are plain or valanced. One side skirt sometimes contains two drawers of medium depth, the fronts of which are each fitted with an elongated turned wooden knob. Table is supported by four baluster-turned legs about four inches in diameter that terminate in ball feet. The legs are braced by a box stretcher, with parts of nearly the same width, placed above the feet. Legs, stretchers and skirts are of oak, top is of pine. Probably made only in Massachusetts and Connecticut. Rare. *Ca. 1670–1690.* Z to Q

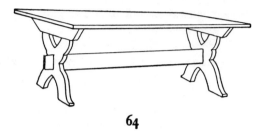

64

64. Sawbuck Table

Is so named for the similarity of its X-shaped trestles to a sawbuck frame. Has thick, planklike two- or three-board top up to six feet long and 32 to 34 inches wide. It is supported by two X-shaped trestles, lap-jointed at their crossings, that have scrolled edges and are braced by a wide stretcher morticed through the crossings with shaped projecting ends. All of oak and probably first made by early Swedish settlers in Delaware. *Ca. 1670–1680.* Very rare. YY to Z

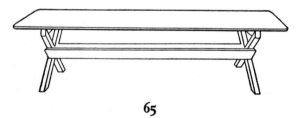

65

65. Eighteenth-Century Sawbuck Table

Has two-board pine top with cleated ends which is five to eight feet long and 30 to 36 inches wide. The X-shaped trestles are somewhat lighter and have chamfered edges. The stretcher is either a single horizontal, four to six

inches wide, morticed to the trestles, or two pieces
attached to them either just above or a little below the
crossings. Made in all sections, particularly New England
and Pennsylvania, with pine top and understructure of
maple or other native hardwoods. *Ca. 1700–1800.* XX
to Y

Nineteenth-Century Survival Sawbuck Table

Has same construction as earlier sawbuck tables but
trestles are lighter and their edges are not chamfered.
Top is generally from three to five feet long and 26 to 32
inches wide. Was farm-made in all sections with either
pine top and hardwood understructure or all of pine
Ca. 1800–1840. X to XX

Table-Chair

See Section IV (No. 7).

WILLIAM AND MARY

66. Gate-Leg Table

Named for gatelike form of the swinging legs which
support the drop leaves. Has oval or oblong top formed
of a narrow fixed leaf flanked by hinged drop leaves.
With leaves raised is from three to six feet long. Bed
contains a full-width, medium-deep drawer at one end
with plain front fitted with turned elongated wooden
knob. Table has six stationary and two swinging legs
all vase-and-ring or baluster-and-ring turned, terminating in pear-shaped, knob, or occasionally carved Spanish
feet. The stationary legs are braced just above the feet
by a box stretcher with parts turned to match the legs.

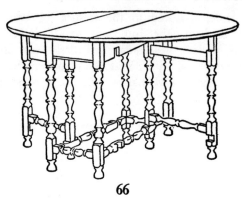

66

Made in all sections of walnut, straight-grained or curly maple, and occasionally cherry or other native hardwoods. Some very large tables have two gates on each side and some small ones have tops under three feet long with leaves raised. *Ca. 1690–1730.* YY to ZZ

67. Tuckaway Gate-Leg Table

Is so named because it can be tucked against a wall when its top is raised. Has a circular one-piece top, 22 to 28 inches in diameter, attached by two pivots to the single cross rail that forms the table bed. Two stationary legs are joined to the ends of this rail and stretcher-braced just above the feet. At the center there is an upright extending from the stretcher to the cross rail with its ends loosely socketed. The two swinging legs are attached to this, gatelike. When top is tilted upright the fixed and swinging legs nest together. When it is lowered, the swinging legs and their stretchers are at right angles to the fixed ones and the single stretcher.

All legs are vase-and-ring or baluster turned and

67

terminate in small knob or pear-shaped feet. The central upright and the stretchers have matching turnings. Made of maple or cherry, probably only in New England. Rare. *Ca. 1690–1710.* Y to YYY

Tavern Tables

Tavern Table takes its name from its wide use in eighteenth- and early nineteenth-century inns. Many variations were made but the seven which are most representative are:

68. Jacobean Tavern Table

Its construction and design are like the slightly earlier Jacobean table (*see No. 63*). Has large two- or three-board top, with or without cleated ends, up to five feet long and about 30 inches wide. It overhangs the bed from six to eight inches. Side and end skirts are plain. One side skirt contains one or two drawers, six to eight inches deep. Drawer fronts are fitted with elongated turned wooden knobs. The lower edges of skirts are either plain or valanced in balancing scrolls. Table is supported by four vase or vase-and-ring turned legs, about

68

two inches in diameter, which terminate in knob or ball feet. Legs are braced just above the feet by a plain box stretcher. Made in all sections, especially Pennsylvania, of walnut, maple or other native hardwoods. Top may be pine or other softwood. *Ca. 1700–1750.* Y to YYY

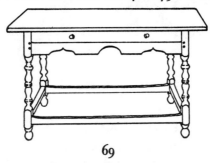

69

69. Small Early Tavern Table

Has oblong top from 30 to 40 inches long and 20 to 24 inches wide. Skirt on one side usually contains a drawer with turned wooden knob. Lower edge of side and end skirts are usually plain. Is supported by four vase or vase-and-ring turned legs terminating in knob or ball feet. Legs are braced either by an H-shaped stretcher, turned to match the legs, or by a plain box stretcher.

Made in all sections of walnut, maple or other **native** hardwood. *Ca. 1700–1750.* XXX to YY

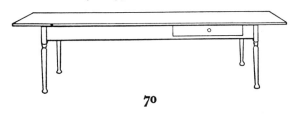

70

70. Large Queen Anne Tavern Table

Has rectangular top from five to eight feet long. Skirt at one side contains from one to three drawers fitted with wooden knobs. Is supported by four plain tapering turned legs terminating in small button feet. Legs not stretcher-braced. Made chiefly in New England with top of pine or other softwood and skirts and legs of maple. *Ca. 1725–1775.* XXX to Y

71

71. Small Queen Anne Tavern Table

Has one- or two-board round, oval, square or rectangular top. Skirts are deeply valanced, with or without drawer. Is supported by turned tapering legs, straight or splayed, that terminate in small pad feet. Made in all sections, especially New England, of curly or plain-grained maple, walnut or cherry. Top is sometimes of pine. *Ca. 1725–1760.* XX to Y

72

72. Windsor Tavern Table

Has small circular or rectangular top supported by splayed vase-and-ring turned legs like those of a Windsor chair but about 26 to 30 inches long. Eight to 10 inches from the floor, the legs are braced by a plain box stretcher consisting of plain turned members. Made in New England and Philadelphia of walnut, maple or cherry. Probably work of Windsor chair makers. Unusual and not numerous. *Ca. 1790–1820.* X to XXX

73. Large Nineteenth-Century Survival Tavern Table

Two-board top with cleated ends is from five to six feet long and 30 to 34 inches wide. Has plain skirt without drawers. Is supported by four two-inch square straight legs without feet. They are braced by a box stretcher made of pieces two inches wide and half the thickness of the legs. With some examples, the legs are

slightly tapering and without stretcher. A farm piece
made as far west as Ohio and Kentucky with pine top
and understructure of maple or other native hardwood.
Ca. 1800–1830. XX to XXX

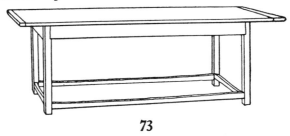

73

Small Nineteenth-Century Tavern Table

Has top about 30 inches long and 18 inches wide with
molded edges. Skirt is plain with or without a drawer.
Is supported by square slender tapering legs, usually
splayed and *not* stretcher-braced. Made in all sections of
maple, cherry, birch or other native hardwood. Sometimes finished with red filler. *Ca. 1800–1830.* XX to
XXX

74. Butterfly Table

The winglike shaping of its swinging leaf brackets
accounts for name. Has a round, oval or rectangular top
with square or rounded edge. Top is 26 to 32 inches
wide and from 34 to 42 inches long with leaves raised.
The latter are supported by pivoted, solid, wing-shaped
brackets which are socketed at top into side pieces of
the bed and at bottom into the box stretcher. Otherwise
construction of understructure is like that of a joined
stool (*see No. 6*). The four flaring legs are baluster or

vase-and-ring turned and terminate in knob feet. Legs are braced just above feet by a plain box stretcher. The narrow bed contains a long narrow drawer with canted sides which conform to the flare of the legs. It is fitted with an elongated turned wooden knob. Height varies

74

from 22 to 28 inches. Made only in Connecticut, southern Massachusetts and possibly Rhode Island of plain or curly maple, walnut or cherry. Some examples have pine top and a few are all of pine. May still have original red filler finish. Feet are apt to be partially or completely worn away. Rare and in much demand. *Ca. 1700–1730.* YYY to Z

Double Butterfly Table

Construction is the same as that of smaller table but it has two butterfly brackets on each side. These support long rectangular leaves that are less than 18 inches wide. Top with leaves raised is nearly five feet wide and six to seven long. Less than twelve such tables are known. *Ca. 1700–1730.* ZZ to ZZZ

QUEEN ANNE

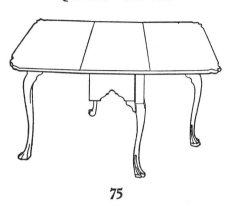

75

75. Queen Anne Drop-Leaf Table

Has round, oval or rectangular top with rounded edge that measures from 26 to 66 inches in diameter or length with leaves raised. The small-sized table generally has a round top; with the larger size, the top is usually oval or rectangular and is practical for use as a dining table. Has plain or valanced skirts at ends, one of which sometimes contains a shallow full-width drawer with front slightly overlapping and thumb-molded. It is fitted with a brass bat's-wing plate with bail handle.

Table is supported by four cabriole legs with uncarved knees that terminate in either Dutch or drake feet. Two of these legs, diagonally opposite, swing out and support the raised leaves. Made in all sections of walnut, plain or curly maple, cherry, birch or, toward the close of the period, of mahogany. *Ca. 1720–1750.* Y to YYY

76

76. Tray-Top Table

Is so named for its rectangular top with raised and molded edge which looks like a tray. Top is approximately 32 inches long by 20 inches wide and has no overhang. Skirt, plain or molded, is from four to six inches deep and has straight or scroll-valanced lower edge. It sometimes contains a full-width drawer fitted with willow brasses. Table is supported by four slender cabriole legs, with plain or shell-carved knees, terminating in Dutch feet. Made from Boston to Philadelphia of walnut, plain or curly maple or mahogany. A sophisticated piece, chiefly used as a tea table. Scarce and high-priced. *Ca. 1740–1750.* YYY to Z

77. Queen Anne Tea Table

Has round, oval, square or rectangular top, with rounded or molded edge, approximately 30 inches in

77

length or diameter. When top is rectangular, it sometimes has shaped corners. Skirts are plain with lower
edges bead-molded or deeper and valanced. One of them
may contain one to three shallow drawers. These have
overlapping fronts fitted with brass knobs or brass bail
handles. Table has either cabriole legs with Dutch feet
or turned tapering ones of cabriole type, but lacking
curved knees, which terminate in button or pad feet.
Made in all sections of walnut, cherry, and maple, either
plain or curly. *Ca. 1720–1750.* XXX to YY

78. Sideboard Table

Has rectangular marble or slate top from 44 to 58
inches long by 20 to 28 inches wide, usually with rounded
front corners. Sometimes front is slightly serpentined
with ends cyma-curved. Skirt is plain or slightly valanced.
Table is supported by four cabriole legs with Dutch feet.
Used in dining room for serving dishes heated by bra-
ziers or spirit lamps, hence the stone top. Sometimes

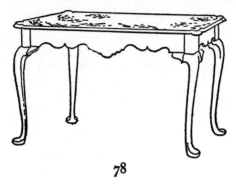

78

found with wooden top which is probably an old replacement. Made infrequently New England to Philadelphia with understructure of walnut. *Ca. 1740–1750.* YYY to Z

79. Gaming Table

Playing cards for money became socially acceptable in some of the American colonies about 1740. The favorite game was loo, for which cabinetmakers made a special "loo table," now known as a gaming table. It has a square top from 36 to 38 inches across that is formed of two matching leaves. The upper one is hinged at the back and folds over on the lower fixed leaf, forming a double top when closed. When open, upper leaf is supported by a swinging rear leg. Corners of top are outsquared or outrounded to provide places for candlesticks. The open top has four oval incised saucers with slightly raised rims, called guinea pockets after the English gold coin. They are so placed as to be at a player's left. The skirt is outblocked to conform to shaping of top, is either straight or valanced, and sometimes contains a centered shallow drawer with overlapping front that is

79

fitted with a single willow brass handle or a brass knob. Table is supported by four cabriole legs with Dutch feet. The right-hand rear leg swings out to support the open top. Made only in the larger urban centers of walnut or mahogany. Not numerous. *Ca. 1740–1750.* YY to Z

CHIPPENDALE

80. Chippendale Drop-Leaf Table

Has oval or rectangular top, with rounded or molded edge, 32 to 36 inches wide by four to seven feet long with leaves raised. The fixed central leaf is about half as wide as the drop leaves. End skirts are valanced and sometimes one of them contains a shallow drawer with over-lapping front, fitted with a single brass bail handle. Table has four, six or eight cabriole legs, with knees generally shell, foliage or scroll-carved, terminating in bold claw-

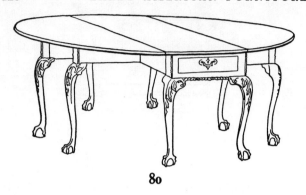

80

and-ball feet. When table has only four legs, two at diagonally opposite corners swing out to support the leaves. Where table has six or eight, those at the corners are stationary and the extra ones are swinging legs. These nest inside the stationary legs when leaves are down. Made in all sections of mahogany, walnut, cherry, plain or curly maple. Were the dining tables of the period. *Ca. 1750–1775.* YY to Z

81. Pembroke Table

Named for the Earl of Pembroke for whom Thomas Chippendale designed and made such a table with broad bed and narrow drop leaves. As made in America, this table has an oblong fixed leaf, about 26 to 30 inches long and 16 to 18 inches wide with drop leaves half that width. When raised, these leaves are supported by pivoted, shaped brackets. Rectangular leaves are either plain or serpentined with outrounded corners. End skirts are straight with molded lower edges and one contains a full-width drawer with the opening framed by a cock-

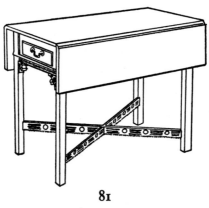

81

bead molding. Drawer front is fitted with a brass willow plate with bail handle.

Table is supported by four square legs chamfered on inner edge and either plain or molded. Sometimes they terminate in small block feet and have fretwork brackets where they join skirts. Legs are braced by an X-shaped stretcher, sometimes arched. Stretcher parts are plain, carved, or pierced with either scrolls or Chinese fretwork. Made in all sections, especially Newport, Rhode Island, or Philadelphia, of mahogany, cherry or sometimes curly maple. *Ca. 1750–1790.* Y to Z

Chippendale Tray-Top Table

Is a more elaborate version of the same table made in the Queen Anne period (*see No. 76*). Has same rectangular top with raised and molded edge resembling a tray which is 32 to 34 inches long by 20 to 22 inches wide. Sometimes the raised and molded rim is replaced by a scroll-carved gallery. The corners of the top can be slightly outsquared and the skirt is shaped to conform to this. Valancing of the skirt is deeper and more pronounced. Table is supported by four cabriole legs with foliage or scroll-carved knees that terminate in boldly carved claw-and-ball feet. Made only of mahogany from Boston to Philadelphia. Scarce. Finest known example was made in Newport, Rhode Island. *Ca. 1750–1770.* Z to QQQ

Tilt-Top Tables

Divide into five kinds according to shape and size of top, but all have same understructure. It consists of a tripod pedestal formed of three ample arching cabriole legs that terminate in either claw-and-ball or snake's-head feet and have a spread of a little less than the size of the top. This tripod supports a shaft about half as tall as the total height of the table. It tapers slightly, is either plain or fluted, and has a vase-shaped lower element, either carved or spirally fluted.

Where carving is present, it consists of foliage on the knees of cabriole legs which is sometimes repeated on knopped element of the shaft. This and the carving of the claw-and-ball feet are always handsomely done and the fluting of the shaft is deeply cut. Sometimes the entire shaft is ball-and-ring turned in simple but bold detail.

Two parallel cleats are screwed to the underside of the table top and into them fit two pivots that project about half an inch from the sides of the pedestal block. This allows the top to be either tilted to a vertical position or lowered for use. When lowered, it is secured by a cast-brass latch.

Some tables have a double block construction, known as a "bird cage," which allows the top to rotate as well as tilt. It is constructed of two blocks connected by four turned corner posts about three inches long. The lower block has a central hole so that the bird cage fits loosely over the upper end of the pedestal shaft. A short wooden key or wedge, located above the upper side of the lower block, fits into a mortice in the shaft and holds the bird cage in place.

Circular tops vary from 24 to 36 inches in diameter; square ones are from 28 to 36 inches wide.

82

82. Piecrust Table

Takes name from scalloped rim of its circular top. This top is always one-piece and extra thick to allow for carving of raised rim. Design of piecrust edge is usually three units of balancing curves that are repeated from eight to ten times in the circumference. This table usually has the bird-cage detail. Always an elaborate and sophisticated piece. Made in all sections, most frequently of mahogany or, in Connecticut, of cherry. One very fine example is of curly maple with pronounced dark stripes. Especially fine pieces were made in Philadelphia. *Ca. 1750–1770.* ZZ to QQQ

83

83. Dish-Top Table

Has one-piece top with bead-molded rim about half an inch high which is like the beaded rim of a large pewter dish. Otherwise is like the piecrust table, including bird cage, though carving is not always as elaborate on understructure. Made in all sections of mahogany, cherry, maple or walnut. A walnut table top is necessarily made of three pieces instead of one because of the narrowness of walnut lumber. *Ca. 1750–1770.* YY to ZZ

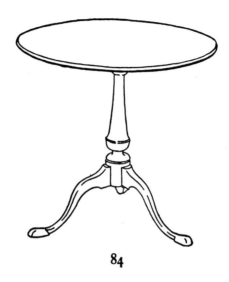

84

84. Plain Circular-Top Table

Has flat top with rounded edge, frequently of three pieces. Occasionally top has an inlaid chessboard with alternate squares of light and dark wood. The pedestal is usually vase or ball-and-ring turned with plain block instead of bird-cage detail. The cabriole legs often have uncarved knees and terminate in either claw-and-ball or snake's-head feet. Tables of this type were made at least twenty-five years longer than the piecrust or dish-top designs. Made in all sections of mahogany, walnut, cherry, plain and fancy-grained maple. *Ca. 1750–1800.* **XXX to YY**

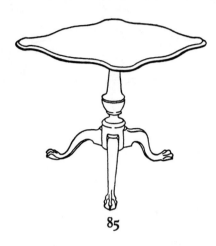

85

85. Square-Top Table

Has molded and slightly serpentined edges and tilts diagonally. Shaft is either tapering and fluted or turned in vase or ring-and-ball motifs. Has single block instead of bird-cage construction. The cabriole legs, with un-carved knees, terminate in either claw-and-ball or snake's-head feet. Made mostly in New England of mahogany, cherry or maple. Less numerous than plain circular-top table. *Ca. 1750–1790.* Y to YYY

86. Tilt-Top Candlestand

Has round, oval, square, oblong or elongated-oval top with diameter or greater dimension 16 to 24 inches. Shaft of pedestal is turned and fluted or, more fre-quently, vase or ring-and-ball turned. Cabriole legs have

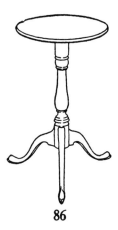

86

uncarved knees and terminate in either claw-and-ball or snake's-head feet. Frequently is a little lower than other tilt-top tables, being from 22 to 26 inches high. Made in all sections of mahogany, walnut, maple, cherry or birch. *Ca. 1750–1790.* XX to Y

87. Sideboard Table

Structure is like that of Queen Anne sideboard table (*see No. 78*). Has oblong marble top, five to six feet long, with square corners and, sometimes, shaped front. The base has either a valanced skirt and cabriole legs or a plain skirt and square legs. Foliage carving decorates the valanced skirt and the knees of the cabriole legs which terminate in boldly executed claw-and-ball feet. The straight lower edge of the plain skirt is molded or gadrooned-carved; the outer sides of the square legs are molded or fluted, and their inner edges are chamfered.

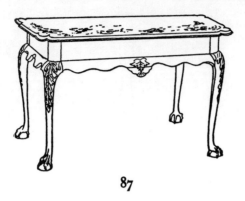

87

Also, where these legs join the skirt there are pierced fretwork brackets. Made of mahogany, chiefly in New England, New York and Philadelphia. Not numerous. Are high-priced rarities. *Ca. 1760–1770.* YYY to QQQ

88. Chippendale Gaming Table

Has same construction as Queen Anne gaming table (*see No. 79*) but with more carving and more elaborate details. Square top, 32 to 40 inches wide, is found in five designs. They are: (1) serpentine with bold outsquared corners, (2) serpentine with rounded corners, (3) serpentine with square corners, (4) straight with slightly outsquared corners, and (5) straight with square corners. The front and side edges of both the fixed and the fold-over leaf are either rounded or carved in low relief.

Sometimes there are two hinged leaves, one above the other, thus providing two different tops — the upper one inlaid with a combination chess and backgammon board and the lower one provided with the incised guinea pockets.

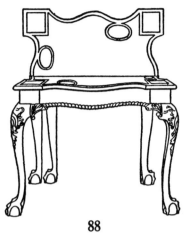

88

The skirt at front and sides is either plain or shaped to conform to the outline of the top with lower edge either bead-molded or gadrooned. Sometimes the skirt contains a shallow drawer, located at the front or at one end, which has an overlapping front and is fitted with willow brasses. The legs are either cabriole with foliage, scroll or shell-carved knees and boldly carved claw-and-ball feet, or square and chamfered with outer sides plain, molded or fluted. With some examples these square legs end in small box or Marlborough feet. Also, triangular fretwork brackets may be present where legs and skirt join.

A cabriole-legged table may have a fifth leg attached to a swinging bracket which supports the upper leaf and occasionally conceals a small secret drawer inserted in the table bed. Made chiefly of mahogany, sometimes of walnut, principally in Philadelphia, New York and Newport, Rhode Island. The more elaborate examples are distinct rarities. *Ca. 1760–1770.* YYY to QQQ

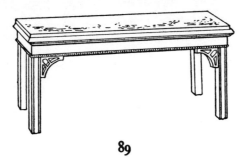

89

89. Pier Table

Takes name from the architectural term for a comparatively narrow wall space between two openings. Designed to stand against such a wall, the back is always unfinished. Top consists of a single fixed leaf of wood or, more frequently, of marble, up to five feet long and less than half as wide. May be straight-sided with right-angle corners or serpentined with outrounded corners.

With the former, the rectangular top rests on a frieze-like skirt having an ample convex molding along its upper edge and a narrower molding, generally carved with a fish-scale motif, on its straight lower edge. It is supported by four square legs with outer surfaces molded and inner edges chamfered. The joinings of legs and skirt are braced by pierced triangular brackets. This design is characteristic of the "Chinese conceit" as introduced by Chippendale.

The serpentined top is found with a table of European eighteenth-century rococo designing. The skirt is shaped to conform to the top and has a scroll-carved lower edge with central pendent finial. It is supported by four cabriole legs, generally with foliage, scroll or shell-carved knees, and boldly done claw-and-ball feet.

Made of mahogany, mostly in Philadelphia, but some examples in the Chinese conceit are of Massachusetts or Rhode Island provenance. About six ornate rococo pier tables are known. Both types are rare but do not command corresponding high prices. *Ca. 1760–1770.* YYY to Q

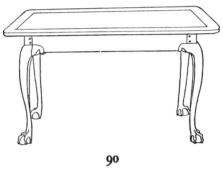

90

90. Library Table

Has rectangular top from 25 to 36 inches long and 16 to 24 inches wide with rounded or molded edges. Top sometimes has large inset leather panel. The skirt is plain with straight lower edge, sometimes bead-molded, and on one side may contain a wide shallow drawer with overlapping front, fitted with brass willow plates and bail handles. Table is supported by four cabriole legs with plain or shell-carved knees ending in bold claw-and-ball feet. Made in all sections of mahogany or walnut. *Ca. 1760–1770.* Y to YYY

HEPPLEWHITE

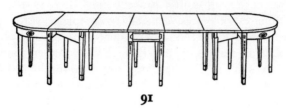

91

91. Part Dining Table

Made in two, three, and four parts, it consists of (1) a pair of end tables, each with an oblong drop leaf, or two drop-leaf tables; (2) a central drop-leaf table with matching half-round end tables; or (3) two drop-leaf tables with matching end tables. The top varies in width from 48 to 54 inches. Total length with all leaves ranges from six to eight feet for a two-part table; eight to 14 feet for a three-part table; and 12 to 16 feet for a four-part table. Skirts are plain with straight lower edges, sometimes ornamented by inlaid checkered fillet or stringing done in light-colored wood. Has square tapered legs with one or two swinging ones to support the drop leaves. Made in all sections of mahogany and, in parts of New England, of cherry or curly maple. Through the years parts of such tables often became separated, so one with all original parts is rare today. *Ca. 1785–1800.* YYY to ZZZ

92. Pembroke Table

Structurally the same as that of the Chippendale period (*see No. 81*) but *without* X-stretcher. Has oval or rectangular top with central fixed leaf from 26 to 30 inches long and 16 to 18 inches wide. The oblong or curved drop leaves are from eight to 12 inches wide. When top is rectangular, the outer corners of the leaves are sometimes rounded or segmented; when oval, the outer edges of all leaves are cut in a convex curve.

92

The end skirts are either straight or bowed to conform to an oval top. One skirt frequently contains a full-width shallow drawer with front cock-beaded on the edges and fitted with a single brass oval plate with bail handle. Top and drawer front have single or double inlay stringing of light-colored wood. The four slender tapering legs are frequently inlaid at upper ends with vase, oval or other motif and pendent husk or bellflower below. Inlay crossbanding near lower ends to simulate feet may also be present. Made in all sections of mahogany with satinwood inlay or, in Connecticut, of cherry. *Ca. 1785–1800.* Y to Z

93. Hepplewhite Card Table

Frequently made as a pair and when not in use served as pier tables. Fundamental construction like that of Chippendale gaming table (*see No. 88*) but none are found with top inlaid for chess or backgammon and incised guinea pockets are also lacking. Two-leaf fold-over top when open is either circular, measuring 36 to 42 inches in diameter, or a shaped square, 32 to 40 inches wide. Shaping of square top is of five kinds: (1) corners boldly rounded, (2) corners deeply canted, (3) front serpentined, (4) front bowed, and (5) cartouche out-

93

line. With circular top, the upper side of the fold-over leaf is plain or decorated with outline stringing in light-colored wood, banded with satinwood or fancy-grain maple veneer, or has a half sunburst done in veneer of alternating dark and light colors. The semicircular edges of both leaves are plain, have double lines of stringing, or are faced with veneer to match banding of top. With oblong leaves, the fold-over is without stringing, band-ing, or inlaid pattern, but edges of both leaves are either plain or decorated with stringing.

The skirt conforms to shaping of the top, is often faced

with fancy-grain veneer and its lower straight edge defined by an inlaid checkered fillet. It may be plain, have oval or oblong stringing panels, a central plaquette of satinwood or curly maple, or a carved one done in low relief. Infrequently the skirt contains a shallow drawer in the center or at one end. This has a front with cock-beaded or overlapping molded edges and is fitted with either an oval brass plate with bail handle or a small brass knob. The table is supported by four square tapering legs, the right rear one swinging on a pivoted bracket to support the fold-over leaf when top is open. Legs are either plain or decorated with a variation of inlaid medallions at upper ends; stringing below sometimes frames inlaid pendent bellflowers, and crossbanding near lower ends simulates feet.

Made in all sections of mahogany with satinwood, curly or bird's-eye maple veneer and stringing of box or holly. Those made in Baltimore with characteristic decorative details or designed by McIntire of Salem, Massachusetts, with carved central panels of baskets of flowers and fruits done in low relief are high-priced rarities. Others are among the more numerous of the smaller tables. *Ca. 1785–1800.* Y to Q

94. Survival Hepplewhite Card Table

Has identical construction and lines as No. 93, but details are simple. The leaves of fold-over top are oblong with straight edges and either square corners or outer ones slightly rounded with small incut quarter rounds. Skirt is plain with straight lower edge either plain or bead-molded. It sometimes contains a shallow drawer at one end. The four square tapering legs are less delicate and are plain with edges sometimes bead-molded. Made of cherry, maple or birch in rural New England, New York State, New Jersey and parts of Pennsylvania. *Ca. 1800–1820.* XX to Y

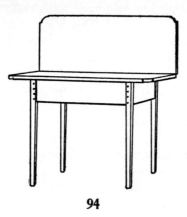

94

Pier Table

Lines are like the card table of this period but with single fixed top and stationary legs. Top is either half-oval or a shaped oblong from 38 to 54 inches wide. It is either plain or decorated with stringing, banding or inlaid design. Skirt conforms to shape of top, has straight lower edge, sometimes with checkered inlaid fillet and decorated with stringing. Occasionally has a centered plaquette of light-colored fancy-grain veneer. Table is supported by four tapering legs, slender and square, that are from 30 to 34 inches tall and generally have inlaid medallions at upper ends with stringing below that frames inlaid pendent bellflowers. Crossbanding simulates feet. Made of mahogany with satinwood veneer and inlay, chiefly in Baltimore. Not numerous but do not command high prices. *Ca. 1785–1800.* Y to YYY

95

95. Sewing Table

Has square or octagonal top, 18 to 20 inches wide, with square or canted corners. The skirt is plain or faced with crotch-grain veneer, has straight lower edge with or without an inlaid fillet, and at the front generally contains single full-width shallow drawer. Its front has cock-beaded edges and is fitted with either oval brass plates with bail handles or small rosette knobs. Interior of drawer is sometimes compartmented to hold sewing supplies. Beneath this is a deep pendent sewing bag of plaited silk stretched over a concealed wooden frame that pulls forward, drawerlike. Sometimes table is constructed without a drawer, has a fixed bag and top is hinged at back to give access to sewing materials. The four square tapering legs are very delicate and may be plain or decorated with stringing. Made in all sections of mahogany and satinwood, curly maple, cherry or, infrequently, all of satinwood. *Ca. 1785–1800.* Y to YYY

96

96. Dressing Table

Has oblong top, 34 to 40 inches wide, sometimes with a hinged central section that gives access to an interior fitted with easel-mounted and hinged dressing glass and small compartments for pomade jars and other toilet accessories. Skirt is of medium depth with straight lower edge. Contains either a full-width drawer, fitted with folding mirror and compartments, or three narrower drawers. Beneath are, occasionally, one or two narrow pendent drawers flanking a central open section. Drawer fronts have cock-beaded edges and are fitted with oval plate and bail handle brasses. Table is supported by four square tapering legs from 30 to 32 inches tall. Made of mahogany with satinwood veneer and inlay stringing of boxwood or holly, chiefly in New York, Philadelphia and Baltimore. Not numerous but do not command high prices. *Ca. 1785–1800.* XXX to YY

97

97. Lamp Stand

Is so named for its principal use, a stand for the whale-oil lamps then coming into general use. Its four legs made it safer than the three-legged candlestand. Has square or nearly square top, from 16 to 20 inches wide, which may be plain or decorated with stringing, banding or inlaid design. The skirt, usually about three inches deep, contains a shallow drawer at front, full-width or narrower. Drawer front is either plain or has cock-beaded edges and is fitted with a small brass knob. Occasionally skirt is deeper and contains two drawers of same sort. Made in all sections of mahogany, with or without satin-wood veneer or inlay, cherry, plain or fancy-grain maple or other native hardwoods and, infrequently, all of satin-wood. *Ca. 1785–1800.* XXX to YY

Survival Example

Made as late as 1825, it is frequently of pine or assorted hard and soft woods, originally finished with red filler. *Ca. 1800–1825.* X to XX

98

98. Tripod Candlestand

Has round, oval, square, oblong or octagon top, from
14 to 18 inches wide, with rounded or molded edge. Is
either fixed or tilts like candlestand of Chippendale
period (*see No. 86*) and may be plain or decorated with
stringing, banding or a central inlaid medallion. Skirt
is lacking but sometimes a pendent candle drawer, fitted
with a small brass knob, is attached by cleats to the
underside of a fixed top. Tripod base consists of a vase-
shaped or ball-and-ring turned shaft, infrequently, with
bird-cage detail, and three legs that are either cabriole-
curved or have only a convex curve. Legs are plain, with
snake's-head or spade feet. Made in all sections of mahogany, with or without satinwood veneer, cherry, curly
or plain maple or birch. *Ca. 1790–1800.* XX to YY

SHERATON

Two types of tables were made during this period — those supported by four or more slender turned and reeded legs, and those supported by pedestals. The former is earlier; the latter shows the Directoire influence and dates from about the middle of the period.

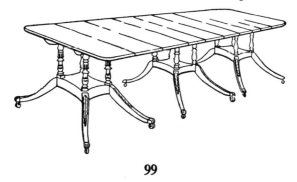

99

99. Part Dining Table

Early example is like that of Hepplewhite period (*see No. 91*) but has rectangular top with rounded outer corners and turned and reeded legs. Pedestals of the later table parts are supported by four curved and splayed legs terminating in brass paw feet, castered. The pedestal treatment is of four kinds — (1) a turned vase-shaped shaft with carved foliage, (2) a turned and fluted shaft, (3) crossed lyres with leaf carvings and slender brass rods simulating strings and (4) four matching, turned, acanthus-leaf carved colonnettes. Both the crossed lyres and the colonnettes are mounted on a shaped plinth that is supported by the four concave and splayed legs.

With turned pedestal the legs are joined directly to its base. Some three-part pedestal examples have an unusually wide top, as much as 56 inches.

The part table with turned and reeded legs was made in all sections of mahogany, with skirt faced with crotch-grain veneer, or, in New England and New York State, of cherry or curly maple. The pedestal-base type is of mahogany only and a fine example is often of Phyfe origin. *Ca. 1800–1820.* YY to ZZ

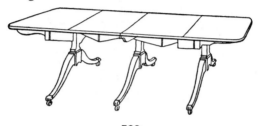

100

100. Expanding Dining Table

Is a "mechanical" substitute for the part dining table. Its bed is constructed of pivot-hinged sections and expands to its full length when ends are pulled out. On it rests a rectangular top, with square or rounded corners, which is composed of three or four leaves. These are either hinged so as to fold and form the top of the closed table or one is fixed and the others are removable. The base consists of two end pedestals, each with three or four curved legs terminating in brass paw feet and a central flat one with only two legs.

These pedestals fit closely together when table is closed, and when open the central pedestal supports the center of the expanded top. Top is usually 48 to 52 inches wide by about five feet six inches long when closed and 10 to 12 feet long when expanded. Made of mahogany, chiefly in New York City. Is an American adaptation of the mechanical tables designed by Thomas Sheraton. Not numerous. *Ca. 1815–1820.* YYY to Z

101

101. Sheraton Pembroke Table

Design and construction are about the same as earlier Pembroke tables (*see No. 81 and No. 92*). Fixed leaf of top is from 26 to 30 inches long and frequently from four to six inches wider than earlier examples or 20 to 24 inches wide. The drop leaves are from 10 to 14 inches wide and their outer sides are either straight with in-cut clover-leaf corners or slightly serpentined. They are supported by shaped swinging brackets. The end skirts have straight cock-beaded lower edges and are sometimes faced with crotch-grain mahogany or satin-wood veneer. One contains a shallow full-width drawer with front cock-bead-edged and fitted with a brass rosette knob. Table is supported by four turned and reeded slender legs that are sometimes fitted with either brass cup casters or small brass ball feet with cups above. Made of mahogany in all sections, especially Boston to Philadelphia. *Ca. 1800–1815.* YY to Z

Survival Example

Has drop leaves with either square or rounded corners. The end skirts are plain and drawer is generally lacking. Is supported by four legs, either square with a slight taper or turned and unreeded. Made in all sections as far west as Ohio and Kentucky of maple, especially of curly maple in central New York State, cherry, walnut, birch or assorted hardwoods, sometimes with softwood top and originally finished with red filler. *Ca. 1815–1830.* X to Y

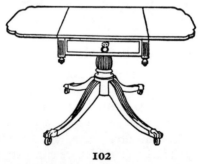

102

102. Pedestal Drop-Leaf Table

Has a nearly square top with rounded corners and edge, from 44 to 48 inches wide by 46 to 52 inches long with leaves raised. The central fixed leaf is from 20 to 24 inches wide and drop leaves from 11 to 15 inches wide.

The leaves are supported by swinging brackets. The end skirts, faced with crotch-grain veneer, have cock-bead-molded edges and sometimes small turned pendent finials. One skirt generally contains a full-width drawer of medium depth. Its front has cock-beaded edges and is fitted with a brass rosette knob. Column of pedestal may be (1) turned foliage-carved urn, (2) spirally reeded globe, or (3) four acanthus-leaf carved colonnettes resting on an oblong-shaped plinth. Beneath are four splayed legs. These are either concave or cyma-curved with reeding or are in the form of animal legs, carved with acanthus leafage or to simulate fur. They terminate in either carved or brass paw feet and are castered. Made in all sections of mahogany. Originally used as tea, small dining or center table. *Ca. 1805–1820.* Y to Z

103

103. Sheraton Card Table

Construction is the same as Hepplewhite card table (*see No. 93*). The open top is square and its sides are either serpentined with outrounded corners or straight with in-cut clover-leaf corners. The skirt is shaped to

conform to top, has straight molded lower edge and is
generally faced with crotch-grain veneer. It sometimes
has a centered panel of satinwood veneer or a low-relief
carved detail of drapery festoons or a basket of fruit and
flowers. The front corners of the skirt are half or three-
quarter round pilasters that may be plain, satinwood
veneered, or carved in low relief or bamboo detail.
Table is supported by slender turned and reeded legs
that terminate in either restrained ring-and-ball turned
feet or small brass ball feet with cups above. Infrequently
a table has four fixed legs and a fifth that swings out to
support the open top. Made in all sections of mahogany
with crotch-grain, satinwood or, occasionally, curly or
bird's-eye maple veneer. Particularly fine examples are
of New York, Philadelphia or Salem, Massachusetts,
provenance. *Ca. 1800–1820.* Y to Z

104

104. Survival Example

Has simpler details. Top when closed is either oblong
with plain corners or half-round. Skirt is plain and does
not have veneer or carved panel. Is supported by four

turned and slightly tapering but unreeded legs. Made in rural sections of New England, New York, Pennsylvania and as far west as the Ohio River Valley of cherry, plain or fancy-grain maple or birch. *Ca. 1820–1835.* XX to XXX

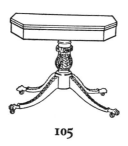

105

105. Pedestal Card Table

Has same two-piece fold-over top as other card tables. Top measures 34 to 38 inches wide and has either a bowed front with square corners or a straight front with in-cut clover-leaf corners. Edges are sometimes banded with crotch-grain veneer. When open, top is square, rotates 90 degrees with both leaves supported by table bed. The skirt, somewhat narrower than that of other card tables, is shaped to conform to top and generally has facing of crotch-grain veneer with small turned pendent finials at front corners. The pedestal has either a slightly tapering and partly fluted column or a turned urn, carved or fluted. Is supported by four splayed, concave legs that are either reeded or leaf-carved and terminate in brass paw or box feet, castered. Made of mahogany with crotch-grain veneer, mostly in the larger cities. *Ca. 1805–1820.* YY to Z

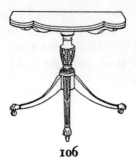

106

106. Phyfe Mechanical Card Table

Duncan Phyfe designed a unique "mechanical" tripod card table. The lower leaf of the top is attached directly to the shaft of the base and there is no skirt. The mechanical feature is a steel rod concealed in the hollow turned and foliage-carved, urn-shaped column, which moves the rear legs and leaf brackets when top is opened. He made these tables in pairs of mahogany, and, infrequently, of satinwood. They were also used as pier tables. Rare. *Ca. 1805–1815.* ZZ to Q

107. Lyre Card Table

Has rotating top from 34 to 38 inches wide which is oblong when closed. Front is straight or bowed with square or deeply canted corners. The skirt conforms to shape of top and has straight cock-beaded lower edge. It is generally faced with crotch-grain or satinwood veneer and decorated with brass rosettes at center and ends. The pedestal is formed of two lyres that are either leaf-carved or veneered with satinwood and have slender brass rods to simulate strings. The lyres are either

107

crossed or parallel and rest on an oblong plinth with
brass rosettes. Supported by four splayed concave legs,
reeded or leaf-carved, that terminate in brass paw feet,
castered. Made mostly in New York and Philadelphia of
mahogany with crotch-grain or satinwood veneer. Not
numerous. *Ca. 1805–1820.* YY to Z

108

108. Pier Table

Lines and construction are like card table (*see No.
103*) but with single rectangular fixed top, 42 to 48

inches wide, with rounded front corners. It has a plain or shaped crotch-grain, veneered skirt with straight cock-beaded lower edge. Supported by four turned and tapering reeded legs. Made in all sections of mahogany with crotch-grain veneer. Not numerous. *Ca. 1800–1820.* XXX to Y

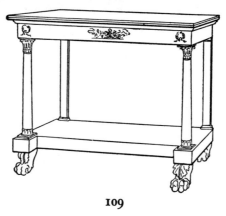

109

109. Directoire Console Table

Has oblong top, frequently of white marble, with molded edge, and is from 38 to 44 inches wide. Skirt is plain or ogee-molded and sometimes ornamented with pierced bronze doré mounts at center and ends. Is supported at front by tapering columns, usually Doric, about four inches in diameter with carved or bronze doré capitals and bases, and at the back by matching pilasters. The latter generally flank a large mirror panel. Columns and pilasters rest on a shaped oblong plinth that is either supported by carved paw feet or rests directly on the floor. With a late example the columns can be replaced by heavy cyma-curved scrolls and the paw feet by convex scrolls.

Made of mahogany with liberal use of crotch-grain veneer or, less frequently, of rosewood in such cities as New York, Philadelphia and Baltimore. Sometimes were made by cabinetmakers who had migrated from France. Not numerous. *Ca. 1810–1825.* XX to Y

110

110. Serving Table

Has oblong top with square corners, 36 to 48 inches wide. A plain skirt with straight molded lower edge contains one or two tiers of wide drawers faced with crotch-grain veneer. They have bead-molded edges and are fitted with either brass lion's-head plates with pendent rings or brass rosette knobs and inset brass keyhole surrounds. Table is supported by four turned and reeded legs that terminate in small brass paw or ball feet. There is sometimes an oblong shelf with shaped front six to eight inches from floor. Height of table is from 36 to 38 inches. Often called a buffet and sometimes served as a small sideboard. Made of mahogany with crotch-grain veneer in the larger cities. *Ca. 1800–1820.* Y to YYY

111. Sofa Table

Has rectangular top, 34 to 40 inches long and 16 to 20 inches wide, with small drop leaves at ends supported by shaped swinging brackets. The skirt is plain with bead-molded lower edge and contains two wide shallow

111

drawers. These have bead-molded edges and are fitted with either stamped-brass oblong plates and bail handles or brass rosette knobs. At the ends, table bed is supported by lyres, square tapering columns or pairs of foliage-carved colonnettes that rest on concave legs, plain, reeded or leaf-carved, which terminate in carved or brass paw feet, castered. These end supports are braced by a vase-shaped turned stretcher or a flat one with cyma-curved outline.

A later example has an oblong top about 24 inches long by 18 inches wide without leaves. The skirt is ogee-molded and contains a single shallow drawer without brasses. The lyre supports are taller, plainer and rest on scrolled feet, braced by a flat, shaped stretcher. Made of

mahogany with crotch-grain veneer, sometimes with rosewood banding. Made mostly in larger cities. A sophisticated piece. Not numerous. *Ca. 1810–1830.* XX to YYY

Dressing Table

Has oblong top from 32 to 36 inches wide with
rounded corners and sometimes a serpentined front.
Frequently the rear third of the top is raised four to five
inches to form a recessed cabinet containing two or three
smaller drawers. The skirt conforms to the shaping of
the top and contains either a full-width drawer or a
narrower one, centered. The drawers are faced with
either crotch-grain, satinwood or fancy-grain maple
veneer and are fitted with brass rosette knobs and inset brass keyhole surrounds. At the front corners the
skirt sometimes has semicircular pilasters, foliage-carved
in low relief, that are extensions of the front legs. Table
is supported by four turned and reeded slender legs.
Made in all sections of mahogany with crotch-grain,
satinwood or fancy-grain maple veneer. Some of the
finest examples are of Salem, Massachusetts, provenance.
Ca. 1800–1820. XXX to YYY

112. Martha Washington Sewing Table

So named because Mrs. Washington is reputed to
have owned a table of this distinctive design with its
deep semicircular end pockets that flank the legs to
right and left. Top, shaped to conform to these rounded
ends, is from 24 to 26 inches wide and hinged to give
access to the pockets and also to a fitted central tray.
Beneath tray is a deep drawer with front usually fitted
with a single classic-shaped brass handle. Below a nar-

row friezelike skirt, front, back and pocket sides are so
finely reeded as to look like tambour work or are covered with plaited silk. Is supported by four turned

112

and reeded legs but an early example may have square
and tapering ones. Made chiefly in New York, Philadelphia and Baltimore of mahogany, sometimes with satinwood veneering, or of curly maple or cherry. Always
a sophisticated piece of furniture. High-priced today.
Ca. 1795-1810. YYY to ZZ

113. Martha Washington Pedestal-Base Sewing Table

Under the Directoire influence a pedestal replaced
the legs. It has a small urn-shaped turned shaft, reeded
and foliage-carved, supported by four concave, reeded
legs that terminate in carved or brass paw feet, castered.
With this type, the central drawer is generally replaced
by a cupboard with sliding tambour front. A shallow
drawer above it sometimes is fitted with a baize-covered
writing flap.

Made of mahogany, sometimes with satinwood bands, in the larger cities, especially in New York by Duncan Phyfe. About six of the pedestal sewing tables bearing his label are known. All are high-priced rarities. *Ca. 1805–1815.* Z to ZZZ

113   114

114. Sewing Table with Work Bag

Has square or slightly oblong top, from 18 to 24 inches wide, sometimes with end drop leaves eight to 10 inches wide. Plain skirt contains two full-width drawers, upper one may be fitted with a writing flap and compartments for pens, ink bottle and sand shaker. Drawer fronts are faced with crotch-grain veneer, fitted with brass rosette knobs or pendent rings and inset brass keyhole surrounds. Beneath lower drawer is a deep pull-out bag of plaited silk stretched over a wooden frame.

Turned tapering and reeded legs with turned feet or brass cup casters. Made in all sections. Finest examples from eastern Massachusetts of mahogany with crotch-grain veneering. *Ca. 1800–1820.* Y to YYY

115

115. Sheraton Lamp Stand

Has square or slightly oblong top, 16 to 22 inches wide, with deeply canted or semicircular outrounded corners. The plain front skirt is deep enough to contain one to three full-width shallow drawers. They are faced with crotch-grain or satinwood veneer and fitted with pairs of small brass rosette knobs and either diamond-shaped inlaid keyhole escutcheons or inset brass keyhole surrounds. Table is supported by four slender tapering legs, turned and reeded. Sometimes their upper ends, where they overlap the skirt, form semicircular pilasters carved in low relief or ring-turned. The legs terminate in small turned feet or are fitted with brass cup casters. Made in all sections of mahogany with crotch-grain, satinwood or fancy-grain maple veneer. *Ca. 1800–1820.* XXX to YY

Survival Example

Has square top. Plain skirt contains two or three full-width shallow drawers with plain fronts, fitted with small brass rosette, pressed glass or turned wooden knobs. The plain turned legs are sometimes decorated with ring turning below skirt and above small turned ball feet. Made by country cabinetmakers in all sections of cherry, maple, walnut, birch or an assortment of native hardwoods. Some were originally mahogany stained or finished with red filler. *Ca. 1820–1835.* X to XX

116

116. Pedestal Candlestand

Has square or slightly rectangular top, 18 to 24 inches wide. The plain skirt contains a single full-width drawer with a brass rosette knob, sometimes fitted with a writing flap like No. 114. The top rests on a leaf-carved, urn-shaped or lyre pedestal. This is supported by three concave splayed legs, plain, reeded or water-leaf carved, which terminate in brass paw feet, castered.

Made in the larger towns of all sections of mahogany with crotch-grain, satinwood or fancy maple veneer, or of cherry or fancy-grain maple. *Ca. 1800–1820.* XXX to YYY

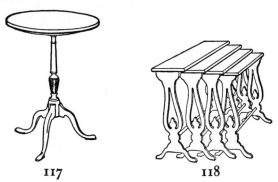

117   118

117. Sheraton-American Empire Candlestand

Has round, square or oblong top, sometimes with shaped or canted corners. Table with square top may have a narrow skirt containing a shallow drawer with plain front fitted with a small brass knob. Pedestal has a vase-shaped column, sometimes pineapple-carved or ball-and-ring turned. Is supported by three or four legs, either cyma-curved and terminating in small spade feet or concave and reeded with paw feet. Made in all sections of mahogany, cherry or maple. *Ca. 1800–1830.* XX to Y

118. Nest of Tables

Consists of three or four tables, nested. Largest has oblong top about 20 inches wide with rounded edges and square or slightly rounded corners. Is supported by four slender turned legs mounted on narrow block feet with convex ends or by lyre-shaped supports. Both are braced near floor by a single flat stretcher. The other tables are identical but graduated in size so that they fit one inside the other. Made chiefly in the larger cities of mahogany or maple, lacquered in the Chinese manner. Sometimes imported from China. Complete original sets not numerous. *Ca. 1800–1830.* XX to XXX

AMERICAN EMPIRE

Part Dining Table

Construction is like that of other part dining tables (*see No. 91 and No. 99*) but it generally consists of only two parts. Assembled and with leaves raised, has a rectangular top with rounded corners, measuring from 46 to 54 inches wide and six to eight feet long. Each table has a single extra-wide drop-leaf supported by a fifth swinging leg or by two swinging brackets with shaped ends. The plain skirt is usually faced with crotch-grain veneer. Table is supported by either four legs or a pedestal. Legs are turned and may be plain, spirally reeded or acanthus-leaf carved and fitted with brass cup casters.

With the pedestal type there is either a circular or a rectangular tapering column that rests on a shaped plinth supported by carved paw, concave scrolled or flattened ball feet, castered. Column, plinth and scrolled feet are crotch-grain veneered. Made in all sections of mahogany with liberal use of veneer, cherry, plain or fancy-grain maple, or walnut. Those with pedestals were made only of mahogany. *Ca. 1820–1840.* XX to Y

119

119. Drop-Leaf Table

Has slightly oblong top, 36 to 42 inches wide, with outer corners of drop leaves well rounded. Leaves are supported by pivoted or sliding brackets. Skirt is plain or has wide ogee molding. Often contains a wide shallow drawer at one end. Is supported by legs slightly turned and tapering that are acanthus-leaf carved or with later examples are square with turned sections top and bottom. Legs terminate in brass cup casters. Made in all sections of mahogany with skirt faced with crotchgrain veneer. *Ca. 1820–1840.* XX to Y

120. Pedestal Base Drop-Leaf Table

Is like the foregoing but has a pedestal instead of legs. Column of the pedestal is either circular and sometimes acanthus-leaf carved or rectangular. If the former, it rests on a circular plinth that is supported by four cyma-curved legs that are acanthus-leaf carved and terminate

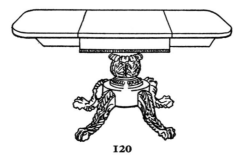

120

in carved paw feet. If the latter, the plinth is oblong and shaped and supported by concave scroll or flattened ball feet. Made in all sections with liberal use of crotch-grain veneer. *Ca. 1820–1840.* XX to YY

121. American Empire Card Table

Has same two-leaf fold-over top as other card tables (*see No. 93 and No. 103*). Top is from 36 to 40 inches wide and has rounded or canted corners. Skirt is crotch-grain veneered with bead-molded or banded lower edge. Sometimes contains a shallow full-width drawer at one end. This has a veneered front and an incised finger grip at back of lower edge. Table is supported either by four turned legs or by a pedestal. The legs may be plain, spirally reeded or acanthus-leaf carved and are fitted with brass cup casters. With a pedestal base the fold-over top rotates and when open is supported by the table bed.

The pedestal column may be (1) either circular or rectangular, tapering and faced with crotch-grain veneer, (2) vase-shaped and foliage-carved or fluted or (3) an oversize lyre, faced with crotch-grain veneer. The vase-shaped column is supported by four cyma-curved legs, carved or reeded, that terminate in brass paw feet, castered. The other two forms rest on shaped plinths sup-

121

ported by carved paw, concave scroll or flattened ball feet, castered. Made in all sections of mahogany with crotch-grain veneer and sometimes rosewood banding. *Ca. 1820–1840.* XX to Y

122. American Empire Sewing Table

Has a rectangular top, 22 to 26 inches wide and 16 to 18 inches deep, that is slightly overhanging. The plain skirt contains two full-width drawers, the upper one sometimes fitted with a writing flap and compartments for pens, ink bottle and sand shaker. Skirt and drawer fronts are faced with crotch-grain veneer. The latter are fitted with brass rosette, pressed glass or mushroom-turned wooden knobs and inset brass keyhole surrounds. The upper part is supported by (1) a pedestal consisting of four turned and carved colonnettes resting on a shaped plinth supported by four carved animal legs terminating in paw feet, castered; (2) a circular or square crotch-veneered column centered on a shaped plinth supported by either carved paw or convex scroll

122 **123**

feet, castered, or (3) four legs that are acanthus-leaf carved, spirally or plainly turned and fitted with brass cup casters. When the table has legs, it may be equipped with a pendent pull-out work bag that is shallower and has less flaring sides than pieces of earlier periods.

Made in all sections of mahogany with crotch-grain veneer, cherry, plain or fancy-grain maple. When of mahogany, it is sometimes decorated with stencil gilding. *Ca. 1820–1840.* XXX to YY

123. Serving Table

Construction and design like that of earlier serving tables (*see No. 110*). Has oblong top, 36 to 48 inches long, with rounded front corners, that is sometimes of white or light-colored veined marble. Skirt is plain with lower edge generally veneer-banded. It usually contains two or three drawers of medium depth, placed side by

side. These are faced with crotch-grain veneer and
fitted with brass rosette, pressed glass or mushroom-
turned wooden knobs and inset brass keyhole surrounds. Is supported by four turned legs, acanthus-
leaf carved or spirally reeded, that terminate in small
turned feet. Made in all sections of mahogany with
crotch-grain veneer and sometimes rosewood banding.
Ca. 1820–1840. XX to Y

124

124. Dressing Table

Size and construction are the same as Sheraton dressing table. An oblong mirror with ogee-molded frame
sometimes surmounts the top and is supported by cyma-
curved uprights. Mirror frame, supports and drawers
are faced with crotch-grain veneer and the latter are

fitted with brass rosette, pressed-glass or mushroom-turned wooden knobs. Is supported by four turned legs. These are plain, spirally turned, foliage-carved or have long square sections. Made in all sections of mahogany, with crotch-grain veneer, cherry, maple or birch. Tables of maple or birch were often stained to simulate mahogany or finished with red filler. *Ca. 1820–1840.* XX to XXX

125

125. Lamp Stand

Has square or slightly oblong top with plain or rounded edges, and is 18 to 24 inches wide. Sometimes has drop leaves at the sides. The plain skirt contains from one to three shallow full-width drawers that are crotch-grain veneered and fitted with brass rosette, pressed-glass or mushroom-turned wooden knobs. The four turned legs are plain, spirally reeded, foliage-carved or have long square sections. Made in all sections of mahogany with crotch-grain veneer, cherry, plain or fancy-grain maple, birch or walnut. Some country-made examples originally were stained to simulate mahogany or finished with red filler. *Ca. 1820–1840.* X to XXX

EARLY VICTORIAN

126

126. Victorian Center Table

Has cartouche-shaped or circular top of marble or wood with molded edge and is from 28 to 36 inches across. The skirt, shaped to conform to the top, is plain or molded with lower edge either straight or scrolled and carved. There are four incurved, shaped and carved cabriole legs that terminate in plain or small scrolled feet, castered. The legs are braced by a cyma-curved, X-shaped stretcher which sometimes has an urn-shaped carved central finial. Made of rosewood, mahogany or black walnut. *Ca. 1840–1865.* XX to XXX

127. Victorian Tilt-Top Table

Is finished in black lacquer. Has either a large circular top, 36 to 42 inches in diameter, or a shaped oval one, 24 to 28 inches long, that is generally of papier-mâché. Top has painted decoration in naturalistic colors of flowers, tropical birds, a landscape vignette or central panel copied from a contemporary genre painting. It may

127

also be inlaid with irregular pieces of mother-of-pearl. Is supported by a vase or vase-and-ring shaped pedestal that rests on a circular base of wood or papier-mâché, painted to match the top. There are either four low scrolled legs, terminating in scrolled feet, or three small cast-iron painted feet on which the base rests. Made in some of the larger cities or may have been imported from England. *Ca. 1860–1870.* XX to Y

Chests and Chests of Drawers

THE first containers for household linens and articles of wearing apparel were rude chests, made by the recently arrived American colonists as part of the sparse furnishings of their makeshift homes. But as conditions improved, trained cabinetmakers began coming over from England to try their luck in the newly settled America. By 1660 or possibly a little before, such craftsmen as Thomas Dennis of Ipswich, Massachusetts, were making paneled and carved oak chests that were both handsome and useful. They were fashioned according to remembered English designs but with distinctly American touches in the carved decoration and in the use of a wide, one-board pine top.

Then others, like Nicholas Disbrowe of Hartford, Connecticut, added a wide drawer or two below the capacious well. From this beginning, it was just another step to insert two more drawers in what had been the well space and convert the lid into a fixed top. So the chest of drawers evolved and became a useful piece of furniture. Its acceptance was swift and widespread. During the nearly two centuries that followed, American cabinetmakers produced the chest of drawers with many variations. That with four graduated drawers and a broad top was the most popular. For variety, its straight front was bowed or serpentined. Its supports changed from feet to brackets, to legs and back to feet. It was also made tall enough in some instances to contain seven wide drawers.

At the same time, its ancestor with drawer beneath was not discarded as obsolete. Known as a blanket chest, it too continued to be made, uncarved and frequently painted, until furniture making shifted from craftsmen's shops to factories and machinery.

Special Comments on Chests and Chests of Drawers and Their Construction

Dovetails join top, sides and bottom of a chest of drawers except where a top is overhanging. Then it is attached to the sides by glued blocks placed on the inside. These dovetails are generally not visible on the outside of the piece but can sometimes be seen at the corners of the interior.

The front, back and sides of most chests are joined by dovetails, but the bottom is attached with nails or screws and its edges are flush with front, back and sides.

Fronts and backs of drawers are also joined to their sidepieces by dovetails.

Dovetails are found on early blanket chests; with later examples, rebated joints are used instead.

Lids of seventeenth- and early eighteenth-century chests have wrought-iron strap hinges; later eighteenth-century ones have wrought-iron snipe hinges; and either snipe or butt hinges of wrought iron are found on early nineteenth-century lids. These lids are generally one-piece boards cleated at ends on the underside to prevent warping.

Drawer parts, except for the fronts, are of pine, spruce, basswood or other native softwood. The sides and back are each of one piece, as is the bottom, generally. Side and front edges of bottom are usually beveled on the underside and fit into grooves in sides and front.

Drawer openings are separated by narrow bearer strips which are sometimes dovetailed to the sides of the carcase. If front is serpentined or bowed, the strips are shaped to conform.

Drawers are supported by runners on which the sides slide. These runners are horizontal strips, glued or nailed to the inside of the carcase behind the bearer strips.

Drawers are usually of graduated depth with top drawer four to five inches deep and the bottom one eight to 10 inches deep, or a graduation of an inch to an inch and a half per drawer.

Chests of drawers are supported by brackets, feet, or short legs. These are generally from seven to nine inches high. The only exception is the very early type where the corner stiles are extended downward and serve as short legs.

Tops, except where there is a cornice molding at front and sides, generally overhang the carcase about two inches on the sides and an inch to an inch and a half at the front.

Stile and rail construction is found on all seventeenth- and early eighteenth-century chests and with the earliest chests of drawers.

Backboards of chests of drawers are always of some softwood and not necessarily all of the same wood. These boards vary in width from four to 10 inches and are from three quarters to an inch thick. They can be either vertical or horizontal, are generally lap-jointed and more often held in place by handmade or cut nails than by screws. The surfaces of these boards are roughly planed and may retain saw marks.

Drawer locks are set in mortices cut into the back of the drawer front and the keyhole is always at the center. Wrought-iron plate locks were used for all but the very finest pieces. These were equipped with brass plate locks.

PURITAN SPAN

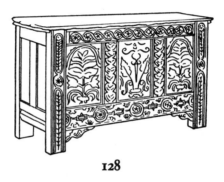

128

128. Ipswich Chest

Is of stile and rail construction with slightly sunk panels, three in front and two at each end. Front panels are intaglio-carved. Design may vary from arcades enclosing leafage and lozenge-shaped medallions to either panels with identical formal foliage palmettes, or a central panel of stylized leafage flanked by one on either side enclosing a tulip motif. Fronts of both rails and stiles are plain or carved with characteristic Jacobean lunettes or running rose motif bands. End panels are un-

carved as are their stiles and rails. Stiles at corners are
extended to form short straight legs. The plain one-
piece pine top has molded or beveled edges at front and
sides and cleats on underside at ends. An occasional
chest has a top of oak with four plain sunk panels.
Dimensions are about 48 inches long and 30 inches
high. Rare. Made of oak with pine top, chiefly at
Ipswich, Massachusetts, by Thomas Dennis. *Ca. 1660–
1680.* Z to ZZZ

129

129. Connecticut Sunflower Chest

Takes name from arrangement of three sunflowers
on front central panel. Is of stile and rail construction,
with three carved panels on the front and a plain one at
each end. The central front panel is carved in a formalized arrangement of three sunflowers or asters in full
bloom supported on single stalk and combined with

tulips in profile. The flanking panels are carved with tulips and leafage scrolls.

The carving may originally have been painted, red and yellow for flowers, green for leafage, and with yellow for molding that frames the panels. Rails are slightly molded; stiles are plain but ornamented with applied split balusters. The end panels have centered applied bosses. Extensions of corner stiles serve as short legs. The one-piece pine top has molded or beveled edges. The dimensions are 48 inches long by about 25 inches high. Some examples are about 45 inches high with two full-width drawers beneath the well section. Drawer fronts have octagon-shaped molded panels, applied bosses in pairs, and are fitted with elongated turned wooden knobs. Made of oak with pine top. Sunflower chests, with or without drawers, are attributed to Nicholas Disbrowe of Hartford, Connecticut. *Ca. 1660–1680.* ZZ to Q

130. Hadley Chest

Is of stile and rail construction and has one or two full-width drawers fitted with small turned knobs. Front of well has three sunk panels; ends have two or four plain ones. Entire front — panels, drawer fronts, stiles and rails — is carved with incised allover design of tulips, scrolling stems and voluted foliation. Outer panels of the front match in design and that of the central panel frequently includes the two initials of the original owner. The entire front is stained or paint-darkened to resemble ebony. Extensions of corner stiles, carved to floor level, serve as short legs. With some examples these extended corner stiles have been replaced by short ring or vase-and-ball

130

turned feet. Chest measures about 46 inches long and
from 36 to 45 inches high.

About one hundred examples are known; some have
been cut down so drawers are missing. Originally used
as hope chests are today. All believed the work of Cap-
tain John Allis of Hadley, Massachusetts, grandnephew
of Disbrowe. Made of oak with one-piece pine top. *Ca.
1675–1700.* YYY to ZZZ

131. Paneled and Molded Chest

Is of stile and rail construction with three sunk panels
in front. Instead of carving, decoration is achieved by
moldings and applied diamond and oblong blocks arranged in a geometric pattern. Some of these and the split
baluster turnings applied to the stiles are ebonized, as are
the inlaid initials of the original owner, placed on upper
rail, flanking the keyhole. Beneath the well is a single
full-width drawer with front divided into three oblong

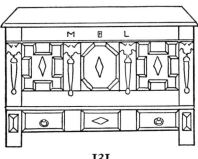

131

panels by moldings with applied blocks. The short legs are extensions of corner stiles. It is about 48 inches long and 30 inches high. Made of oak with one-piece pine top. Made in Massachusetts or Connecticut. *Ca. 1660–1680.* YYY to Z

132

132. Guilford Painted Chest

Takes name from Guilford, Connecticut, where a good proportion of such chests were made. Has stile and rail construction. Front has a wide panel with a single full-width drawer beneath and there is a large panel at each end of chest. Front and ends are decorated with an all-over polychrome design of flowers, foliage and running bands of scrolls and leaves. Design on end panels includes large bird in silhouette. Drawer is fitted with elongated turned wooden knobs. Chest stands on extension of corner stiles. Examples retaining original painted decoration are the most desirable. Made in southern Connecticut of oak with one-piece pine top. *Ca. 1690–1720.* YY to YYY

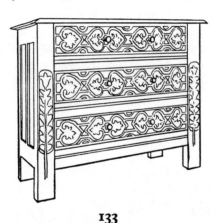

133

133. Chip Carved Chest of Drawers

Has stile and rail construction. Carcase contains two or three full-width drawers that are fitted with turned wooden knobs. Drawer fronts, stiles and rails are carved intaglio with a design of formalized tulips, foliage and scrolls with running bands. The background is sometimes ebonized. Extensions of corner stiles serve as legs. Edges of overhanging top, 36 to 42 inches wide, are molded on front and sides. Is earliest form of American-made chest of drawers. Made of oak with pine top in New England, chiefly Massachusetts and Connecticut. Not numerous. *Ca. 1675–1700.* Y to Z

WILLIAM AND MARY

134

134. Paneled Chest of Drawers

Has oblong overhanging top about 40 inches wide with molded edge. Carcase contains four full-width drawers. Fronts have oblong sunk panels framed by applied moldings set in geometric patterns and are fitted with either brass teardrop handles or turned wooden knobs. Has a slightly projecting molded base and is supported by four boldly turned ball or turnip feet.

Molded base and turned feet were originally ebonized. Made in New England with stiles and rails of oak and balance of pine. *Ca. 1680–1700.* YY to Z

135

135. Plain Chest of Drawers

Has oblong overhanging top from 38 to 44 inches wide with deeply molded edge. Carcase contains four to six tiers of drawers, the top one consisting of two half-width drawers; the others are full-width. Drawer openings are framed by single or double arched moldings. With some examples, the drawer fronts have stringing of light-colored wood, done in balancing S-scroll outlines. All are fitted with brass teardrop handles. Has a molded base and is supported by turned ball or turnip feet, ebonized. Height varies from 40 to 56 inches. Made of walnut or maple from Massachusetts to Pennsylvania. *Ca. 1690–1720.* XXX to YYY

136

136. Early Blanket Chest

Is similar in construction to later chests of drawers of period. Has oblong lid, 38 to 44 inches wide, with molded edge. Is fitted with wrought-iron snipe hinges. Real or simulated drawer fronts are plain and separated by single or double arched moldings. Two upper tiers mask the well and beneath may be one or three full-width drawers. Drawer fronts are fitted with brass teardrop handles or bat's-wing plates with bail handles. Has a molded base and is supported by four turned bun or peg feet. Made all of maple or pine from Massachusetts to Pennsylvania. *Ca. 1700–1720.* XX to Y

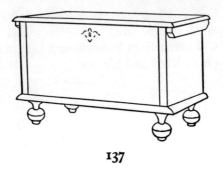

137

137. Plain Chest

Sturdily constructed and undecorated, with dovetailed corners. Lid, front, back and sides are of one-piece boards. Lid overhangs the width of its cleats at ends. Has molded base and is supported by boldly turned ball feet. From 30 to 42 inches long and 16 to 20 inches high. Made of pine, tulipwood, or other native softwoods in all sections, especially Pennsylvania. *Ca. 1700–1720.* XX to Y

QUEEN ANNE

138. Chest-on-Frame

Is in two sections. The upper one is a case piece containing five or six tiers of graduated drawers, and the lower section a low supporting frame. Top of upper section measures 34 to 38 inches wide, is oblong with square corners and has a deeply molded flush cornice. The top tier of drawers may consist of two or three narrow ones or one of full width. Drawer fronts have thumb-mold overlapping edges. The brasses are either bat's-wing or willow plates with bail handles and match-

138

ing keyhole escutcheons. The upper section fits within the raised molding of the frame which has either a plain narrow skirt or a wider, deeply valanced one. It is supported by four short cabriole legs that terminate in Dutch or drake feet. The frame is from 16 to 24 inches high. Total height varies from four to six feet. Made in all sections of walnut, cherry, plain and fancy-grain maple. With the latter, curly-grain wood was sometimes used for cornice, drawer fronts and frame with straight-grain maple for the rest. *Ca. 1720–1750.* Y to YYY

139

139. Low Chest of Drawers

Has oblong top, 34 to 38 inches wide, with deeply molded cornice applied to sides and front like chest-on-frame (*see foregoing*). Carcase contains three or four full-width graduated drawers. The fronts have thumb-mold overlapping edges and are fitted with brass bat's-wing or willow plates with bail handles and matching keyhole escutcheons or with rosette-and-bail handles and oval escutcheons. Has molded base, very narrow skirt, and is supported by four plain bracket feet. Height is from 34 to 36 inches. Made in all sections of walnut, plain or curly maple, cherry or infrequently of mahogany. Sometimes was made of assorted native hard and soft woods, originally finished with red filler. *Ca. 1720–1750.* XXX to YY

This chest of drawers is frequently classed incorrectly

as Chippendale, especially examples made late in Queen Anne period. It is similar to the Chippendale straight-front, but always has a projecting cornice molding set flush with top instead of an overhanging applied top. Also the feet are plain brackets instead of the scrolled or molded bracket characteristic of Chippendale. Further, the top can be of pine or other softwood and dovetails are to be seen at each end of it inside the cornice. Survival examples were made in New England as late as 1800. With these the full-width drawers range from four to six.

CHIPPENDALE

140

140. Straight-Front Chest of Drawers

Has oblong, slightly overhanging top, 34 to 42 inches wide, with molded edge. Carcase contains four gradu-ated full-width drawers, or may have two or three narrower ones at top. Drawer fronts have thumb-molded overlapping edges and are fitted with brass willow plates with bail handles and matching keyhole escutcheons or small rosette-and-bail handles and oval keyhole escutcheons. Front corners of carcase are sometimes chamfered and fluted or have inset quarter-round reeded pilasters. The molded base without skirt is supported by scrolled bracket or molded bracket feet. Height varies from 34 to 42 inches. Made in all sections of mahogany, walnut, cherry, plain or curly maple. *Ca. 1750–1775.* Y to YYY

141

141. Serpentine-Front Chest of Drawers

Has oblong slightly overhanging top from 36 to 44 inches wide with serpentined front and molded edge. The carcase contains four graduated full-width drawers. Fronts conform to serpentine outline of top and are bead-molded. This is repeated on edges of openings.

Fronts are fitted with plain or pierced brass willow plates with bail handles and matching or oval escutcheons. Front corners may be chamfered and fluted or have quarter-round reeded pilasters. Base is molded and serpentined at front and may have a small shell or fan-carved central pendant. Is supported on high scrolled or boldly molded bracket feet or on short cabriole brackets terminating in claw-and-ball feet. Height varies from 30 to 36 inches. Made in all sections of mahogany, walnut, cherry, plain or curly maple. *Ca. 1750– 1775.* YY to Z

142

142. Philadelphia Serpentine Chest of Drawers

Structure is the same as foregoing piece but it is larger, being 46 to 50 inches wide, 20 to 22 inches deep and 32 to 38 inches tall, with more elaborate details. The oblong top has a boldly serpentined front and its molded edge is deeply cut. Fronts of the four graduated drawers are faced with crotch-grain veneer and may have plain or pierced brass willow plates with bail handles and matching keyhole escutcheons. The front corners of carcase are deeply chamfered and are either carved in an incised fretwork design or boldly fluted. It is supported by canted molded bracket feet or by short cabriole brackets terminating in boldly carved claw-and-ball feet. Made only of mahogany by such cabinetmakers as Gostelowe and his contemporaries. Relatively few examples known. *Ca. 1760–1770*. Z to ZZZ

143

143. Reverse Serpentine-Front Chest of Drawers

Has oblong, overhanging top, 36 to 42 inches wide, with reverse serpentine front and molded edges. The carcase contains four graduated drawers with fronts that repeat shaping of top and are bead-molded as are openings. Drawers are fitted with brass willow plates with bail handles and matching keyhole escutcheons or rosette-and-bail handles and oval escutcheons. The molded base also has a reverse serpentine outline. Is supported by boldly molded and scrolled bracket feet or short cabriole brackets terminating in claw-and-ball feet. Made of mahogany or walnut. From New Jersey to Maryland. *Ca. 1760–1780.* YYY to Z

144

144. Bow-Front Chest of Drawers

Has oblong top about 40 inches wide; front is shaped in continuous convex curve, molded or inlaid with stringing or checker banding. Carcase contains four graduated drawers with fronts conforming to curve of top. Drawer fronts are bead-molded and fitted with brass rosette-and-bail handles or circular plates with ring bails. Both have oval keyhole escutcheons. The molded base has bowed front and is supported by short cabriole brackets with wings, ending in claw-and-ball feet. Made in all sections of mahogany or, in New England, of cherry. *Ca. 1770–1780.* Y to YYY

145

145. Tall Chest of Drawers

Sometimes made as companion to low straight-front of same period (*see No. 140*). Has oblong top, 44 to 46 inches wide, with molded cornice. The carcase contains five, six or seven tiers of graduated drawers. Some examples have three narrow drawers at top with half-width ones in tier below. Drawer fronts have thumb-molded, overlapping edges and are fitted with brass willow plates and bail handles and matching keyhole escutcheons or inset brass keyhole surrounds. Front corners of carcase may have inset quarter-round reeded pilasters. Molded base is supported by scrolled or molded bracket feet. Height varies from five feet to five feet 10 inches. Made from New York south of walnut and in New England of cherry, birch or maple. Survival examples with plain bracket feet were made in rural sections of New England and elsewhere at least twenty years longer than in large centers. *Ca. 1750–1780.* Y to YYY

146

146. Chest-on-Frame

Made early in period only. Is similar to that of the
Queen Anne (*see No. 138*) except for the frame. Here
skirt is wider, more boldly valanced, and frame is supported by short cabriole legs terminating in claw-and-
ball or drake feet. Drawers have rosette-and-bail handles.
Piece measures from 40 to 44 inches wide by five to five
and a half feet tall. Not numerous. Made in all sections,
generally of walnut. *Ca. 1750–1760.* Y to YYY

147

147. Blanket Chest

Has oblong lid 38 to 44 inches wide with applied
molded edge. Hinges are wrought-iron snipes. Front
may be plain or have two tiers of simulated drawers
above a full-width drawer which has molded or beaded
edges. Drawer fronts, simulated and real, have thumb-
molded overlapping edges and are fitted with bail
handles. Has slightly molded base supported by scrolled
bracket feet. Height is from 32 to 36 inches. Always a

simple piece, it is made mostly of pine but examples of walnut or of maple with curly-grain drawer fronts also are found. *Ca. 1750–1775.* XX to Y

HEPPLEWHITE

148

148. Straight-Front Chest of Drawers

Has overhanging oblong top from 38 to 40 inches wide with edge either plain or inlaid with stringing or checkered banding. Corners are always square. The carcase contains four full-width graduated drawers. Fronts are cock-beaded and have inlaid stringing forming oblong or oval panels. Brasses are oval plates with bail handles and small oval or oblong keyhole escutcheons. Diamond-shaped inlays are sometimes substituted for the latter. Is supported by outcurved French feet, connected by deeply valanced skirt with balancing cyma curves that flank either a small, semicircular arch or a semicircular pendant. Made in all sections of mahogany, cherry, birch, or maple with drawer fronts of crotch-grain mahogany, satinwood, or fancy-grain maple veneer. *Ca. 1785–1800.* Y to YYY

149

149. Country-Made Survival

Is of an assortment of native hardwoods without inlay or veneer. Originally it was stained to simulate mahogany or finished with red filler. *Ca. 1800–1820.* XXX to Y

150. Chest of Drawers with Deep Top Drawer

Construction and lines are the same as the foregoing (*see No. 148*) except that top drawer is from 10 to 14 inches deep. Its front often has a large central oval panel of crotch-grain veneer, flanked by two lozenge-shaped panels of satinwood or fancy-grain maple. Made of mahogany in all sections. A considerable number of

150

such chests of drawers that bear the label of Michael Allison, New York City cabinetmaker, are known. *Ca. 1790–1800.* YY to Z

151. Bow-Front Chest of Drawers

Has oblong top, 38 to 44 inches wide, with bowed front. Edge is plain and inlaid with stringing or check-ered banding or faced with crotch-grain veneer. Carcase contains four graduated drawers with fronts conform-ing to curve of top and edges cock-bead molded. Fronts may be (1) plain, (2) faced with satinwood or fancy-grain maple veneer, or (3) crotch-grain veneered and banded. Further ornamentation is sometimes achieved by a central oval and flanking oblong panels of veneer with banding of contrasting color. With some examples the central panel is a light-colored oval on a darker back-ground and all panels are framed with checkered inlaid fillets or stringing. Brasses are oval plates with bail handles and oval or oblong keyhole escutcheons.

151

A few examples have light or dark diamond-shaped inlays in place of keyhole escutcheons. Is supported by French feet connected by a conforming valanced skirt. May have a small oblong central pendant veneered to match drawer fronts. A checkered inlaid fillet defines its upper edge. Height varies from 36 to 42 inches. Made in all sections of mahogany, cherry or birch with crotch-grain, satinwood, or fancy-grain maple veneer. *Ca. 1785–1800.* YY to Z

152. Serpentine-Front Chest of Drawers

Has overhanging top serpentined at front, measures 38 to 44 inches wide, and sides are either straight with edge plain or inlaid with stringing or narrow checkered banding, or slightly scrolled with front corners out-rounded and edge molded. Carcase contains four full-width drawers with conforming fronts and cock-beaded edges. These fronts may be (1) of same wood as rest

152

of piece and plain, (2) inlaid with stringing that outlines large veneer panels or (3) faced with satinwood or fancy-grain maple veneer in decorative designs like those of bow-front type (*see No. 151*).

Brasses are oval plates with bail handles and small oval or oblong keyhole escutcheons. Diamond-shaped inlays may take place of latter. Front corners of the carcase are either plain or chamfered and fluted. Is supported by either French feet with serpentine valanced skirt or scrolled bracket feet with narrow unvalanced skirt. Height varies from 34 to 38 inches. Made in all sections of mahogany, cherry or maple, often with liberal use of satinwood or fancy-grain maple veneer. *Ca. 1785–1800.* YY to Z

153

153. Blanket Chest

Has oblong lid, 36 to 44 inches long, with molded cleats on underside where ends overhang case. Front is plain or may have two tiers of simulated drawer fronts above one or two full-width drawers. All drawer fronts have thumb-molded, overlapping edges and are fitted with oval brass plates with bail handles or small turned wooden knobs. The single keyhole at the top has an oval or oblong escutcheon. Instead of feet, end boards of carcase are cut in balancing cyma curves, forming arches eight to 10 inches high. Made in all sections of plain or curly maple, cherry, walnut, or, most frequently, of pine sometimes painted or grained. *Ca. 1785-1800.* XXX to YY

154

154. Survival Example

Construction is the same as foregoing, but details **are** often crudely executed. Has oblong top with applied molded edge front and sides instead of cleats on underside of ends. Hinges are either snipe or butt. There is only one drawer beneath well. Real and simulated drawer fronts have thumb-molded edges and are fitted with oval or oblong brass plates with bail handles or mushroom-turned wooden knobs. Originally finished with red filler, painted bluish-green or crudely grained. Farm-made in all sections of pine or other softwoods. *Ca. 1800–1830.* X to XX

SHERATON

155

155. Straight-Front Chest of Drawers

Has overhanging oblong top, 40 to 48 inches wide, generally with outset three-quarter round front corners. Edge is plain, rounded or banded, with inlaid fillet or veneered. Carcase contains four full-width drawers. The fronts have cock-bead edges and are (1) of same wood as rest of piece, (2) faced with satinwood or fancy-grain maple and banded with crotch-grain veneer or (3) faced with crotch-grain veneer framed by inlaid fillets. Brasses are oval or oblong plates with bail handles or rosette knobs and oval or oblong keyhole escutcheons or inset surrounds.

The front corners of the carcase may have (1) three-quarter round, straight or spirally reeded pilasters with or without carved capitals or (2) plain or reeded flat stiles. Is supported by four legs that are ring-turned or noticeably taller ones, baluster-turned and either plain or reeded. Front legs are sometimes connected by a narrow, slightly valanced skirt. Ends of carcase are either solid or stile and rail constructed with large sunk panels. Height varies from 36 to 44 inches. Made in all sections of mahogany, with crotch-grain, satinwood or fancy-grain maple veneer, cherry, plain or curly maple. Examples of New England provenance have especially fine details. *Ca. 1800–1820.* Y to YYY

Survival Example

Is of same construction but without veneering. Has plain turned pilasters and no skirt. Drawer fronts are fitted with brass, pressed glass or mushroom-turned wooden knobs and inset brass keyhole surrounds. Made as far west as Indiana and Tennessee by country cabinet-makers, of assorted native hardwoods with pine top. Generally finished with red filler. *Ca. 1820–1840.* XX to XXX

156. Bow-Front Chest of Drawers

Is like foregoing (*see No. 155*) in construction, decorative details and size, but entire front is bowed in a continuous outward curve. Skirt (when present) is narrow and seldom valanced. Top is sometimes surmounted by a small case at rear, with same bow front, which contains two half-width shallow drawers. Some examples have a backboard with voluted ends. Made in all sections of

156

mahogany or cherry, sometimes with satinwood or curly maple veneered drawer fronts, plain or curly maple or birch. *Ca. 1800–1820.* YY to YYY

157. Chest of Drawers with Attached Mirror

Has straight-front oblong top, 40 to 44 inches wide, with plain or veneer-banded edges and outset three-quarter round front corners. Top is surmounted at rear by a small case, four to six inches high, that contains three drawers and has a pivoted mirror with boldly voluted supports. Front corners of carcase have three-quarter round pilasters that extend downward into high reeded and ring-turned tapering legs. Back legs are also reeded and ring-turned. Carcase contains three tiers of

157

graduated drawers with half-width drawers in the top
one. Fronts are (1) plain, (2) faced with satinwood or
fancy-grain maple or (3) banded with crotch-grain
veneer. Brasses are rosette knobs and inset keyhole surrounds. Height to top of mirror frame is five and a half
to six feet. Made of mahogany with crotch-grain veneer
in chief urban centers. Especially fine examples are of
Salem provenance. *Ca. 1810–1820.* YY to YYY

AMERICAN EMPIRE

158

158. Bow-Front Chest of Drawers

Oblong, overhanging top is 38 to 44 inches wide and has three-quarter outrounded front corners and rounded edge. May be surmounted at back by case containing two shallow drawers of equal width. Behind it is a backboard with voluted ends. Front corners of carcase have three-quarter round pilasters, spirally reeded and ring-turned, that extend downward into turned legs of medium length. Carcase contains four graduated drawers. Top drawer is often the deepest. Fronts are fitted with brass rosettes, pressed glass or mushroom-turned wooden knobs, oval or oblong keyhole escutcheons or inset surrounds. Ends of carcase are either plain or of stile and rail construction with single large sunk panels. Made in all sections of mahogany with crotch-grain veneer drawer fronts, cherry, maple or birch. Those of cherry frequently have drawer fronts faced with curly or bird's-eye maple veneer. *Ca. 1800–1840.* XXX to Y

159

159. Survival Example

Is of same construction but simpler. Drawer fronts are either of same wood as rest of piece or are faced with crotch-grain mahogany veneer. They are fitted with either pressed glass or mushroom-turned wooden knobs and small oblong keyhole escutcheons or inset keyhole surrounds. The three-quarter round pilasters at the front corners (when present) are unreeded but have some ring turnings. Is supported by four simply turned legs. Made by country cabinetmakers in all sections of the East and in some of the older parts of the Middle West of various native hardwoods stained to simulate mahogany or finished in red filler. *Ca. 1840–1850.* XX to XXX

160

160. Chest of Drawers with Overhanging Drawer

Has slightly overhanging oblong top, 38 to 44 inches wide, with edge veneer-faced or rounded. At rear, top is often surmounted by a case, four to six inches high, with matching top that contains two or three drawers Behind it is a shaped or oblong backboard, sometimes with voluted corners. The carcase has a frieze that projects about two inches and contains a full-width drawer, sometimes eight to 10 inches deep. The frieze is supported at the corners by tapering columns, three to four inches in diameter, that are crotch-grain veneered or by acanthus-leaf carved pilasters. These columns or pilasters rest on square plinths and flank three full-width graduated drawers. All drawer fronts are plain and faced with crotch-grain veneer. They are fitted with brass rosettes, pressed glass or mushroom-turned wooden knobs. The wide drawers have oblong brass keyhole escutcheons or inset surrounds.

The sides of the carcase are either solid or stile and rail constructed with large oblong sunk panels. Supported by either tall paw feet with acanthus-leaf carved knees at front and turned legs at rear or by four tall turned legs, three to four inches in diameter, with ring turnings and sometimes reeded. Height to top of backboard varies from 48 to 54 inches. Made in all sections of mahogany, with crotch-grain veneer, cherry or maple with vase-and-ring turned columns or carved pilasters of curly maple. *Ca. 1820–1840.* XXX to Y

161. Survival Example

Is of same construction and size as the foregoing, but details are simpler. The backboard has a straight upper edge with applied molding and square corners. Fronts of the small drawers and of the wide frieze drawer are frequently ogee-molded and the frieze is supported by either plain pilasters or heavy cyma-curved scrolls about three inches wide with flat crotch-grain veneered fronts. All drawer fronts are faced with crotch-grain veneer and fitted with either pressed glass or mushroom-turned wooden knobs. Front feet are convex scrolls about three inches wide with flat, crotch-grain veneered fronts; rear

161

ones are square and plain. Made by country cabinet-makers in the East and in older parts of the Middle West of mahogany, or mahogany-stained cherry, maple or birch with crotch-grain veneer. *Ca. 1840–1860.* X to XX.

EARLY VICTORIAN

162. Early Victorian Chest of Drawers

Has rectangular, slightly overhanging top of either wood or white marble, 40 to 52 inches wide with rounded corners and edges. At rear is a case with serpentine front, rounded edges and corners, that contains two half-width shallow drawers and has an oblong vertical mirror with undulating frame and rounded corners. The mirror sup-

162

ports are pierced and consist of large S and smaller C scrolls. The straight-front carcase has rounded corners and contains four graduated drawers, generally framed with the characteristic crinkled French molding. All drawers are fitted with either mushroom-turned wooden knobs or leaf-and-fruit carved wooden handles and inset brass keyhole surrounds. A low shaped base which is castered has a slightly valanced skirt with applied scrolled carving on lower edge. Height to top of mirror varies from six to seven feet. Made in all sections of veneered rosewood or black walnut. *Ca. 1850–1870.* XX to XXX

163

163. Pine Painted Chest of Drawers

Has rectangular, slightly overhanging top, 35 to 39 inches wide, with rounded corners and a rounded or concave molded edge. Top may (1) be plain, (2) have a low gallery board or (3) be surmounted by a tilting mirror with frame conforming to the scrolled brackets which support it and are mounted on low recessed boxes. The carcase is from 36 to 39 inches high, has a straight front with rounded corners and generally contains four full-width drawers. These are either six and a half inches deep or may be graduated, varying from five inches for the top drawer to seven inches for the bottom one. Drawer fronts are plain and fitted with mushroom-turned wooden knobs and inset cast-iron keyhole surrounds. Ends of carcase are either solid or have large, slightly sunk rectangular panels. Back generally has four narrow vertical backboards, groove-joined. Base of piece is from three to five inches high, projects about a half inch, has conforming rounded corners and scroll-valanced skirt. Original fittings or iron socket casters or wooden rollers are frequently missing.

Made in all sections of pine, interior parts sometimes

are of other softwoods. Drawers often have machine-cut dovetails. Original finish was either graining, done in light and dark tones of brown with scrolling and sometimes a landscape vignette at center of top drawer, or solid color paint, usually a dark brown to simulate black walnut. This chest of drawers was a product of early furniture factories and was frequently part of a bedroom suite that included a double bed, washstand, two to four cane-seated chairs and a towel rack. It is the least expensive chest of drawers to be found in antique shops and is considered too late by some dealers. Plentiful to numerous. *Ca. 1860–1880.* X to XX

Section VIII

Desks and Secretaries

THE desk was first made as a separate piece of furniture by American cabinetmakers between 1680 and 1690. Before that a writing or Bible box, placed on a joined stool or small table, did duty. Consequently the first desks all reflected this usage. They were two-part pieces consisting of a larger and more elaborate writing box with either sloping lid or slanting front, placed on a topless frame.

About 1700 the one-piece bureau desk made its appearance. With three or four wide drawers beneath the slanting front, it was so serviceable that regardless of numerous other designs, it remained in demand as long as furniture making was a handcraft.

With the addition of an enclosed cupboard, placed on its top, the desk became a secretary and an imposing piece. Variations in desk and secretary design began about 1790. The chief change was the front of the writing section with six different types substituted for the hinged slant-front. They were (1) fall-front, (2) fold-over writing flap, (3) pull-out writing shelf, (4) quarter-round cylinder front, (5) tambour roll-top and (6) drop-front. Many desks and secretaries were made during the following half-century with one or another of these features but cabinetmakers still went right on making as many if not more slant-front bureau desks along with them until the Early Victorian period.

Special Notes on Desks and Secretaries and Their Construction

A sloping lid reflects the box origin of the desk. It is hinged at the top, has batten strips on the sides to prevent warping and a slightly raised molded edge at the bottom. This lid serves as writing surface and when raised to gain access to writing materials in the well beneath is braced by a pivoted wooden bar.

A slant-front is hinged at the bottom. It consists of transverse flush end pieces from two to four inches wide which are joined to the central one- or two-piece section by glued tongue-and-groove joints. A slightly overhanging thumb-molding usually finishes the top and side edges. The centered lock at the top is mortice-countersunk on the inside. When open, lid is supported by pull brackets that flank a wide drawer beneath.

A fall-front is drawerlike in construction, hinged at the bottom and supported by brass quadrant brackets. It pulls out to about half its depth. The back third has the usual pigeonholes and small drawers and the writing surface generally has a large fabric or leather-covered panel with veneer banding.

A writing flap, whether flat or sloping, is hinged on its outer side and most frequently supported by pull brackets, though occasionally by the drawer beneath. Its writing surface also has a large fabric or leather-covered panel, veneer-banded.

The pull-out writing shelf is a full-width slide that fits into an opening in the carcase of the lower part of a secretary above the top drawer. Its front is usually fitted with small knobs and its writing surface has a large fabric or leather-covered panel, veneer-banded.

A cylinder-front is quarter-round and pivots on concealed brackets. When open it disappears behind the compartment of pigeonholes and small drawers of the interior. Below these is a pull-out writing shelf. In some desks and secretaries, the cylinder-front is mechanically connected to the shelf so that the latter slides out when the cylinder is raised.

A tambour roll-top consists of a horizontal panel that slides or rolls back in curved grooves in the sides of the desk compartment. The tambour slide is made of strips of wood, about an eighth of an inch wide, with fronts rounded. These are mounted on a heavy canvas backing and when assembled the slide has a reeded appearance. The outer edge of the panel is finished with a heavier cross rail that is fitted with small brass knobs and may have a centered lock.

Except in rare instances, the writing surface of a desk, whatever its type, is from 30 to 34 inches from the floor.

Most desks and secretaries with slanting-front or fold-over writing flap have pull brackets which support front or flap when opened. They flank the drawer beneath and are generally about one inch thick by three to four inches high. They are always fitted with small brass knobs.

Dovetail joints are used on top, sides and bottom of a desk and those of both parts of a secretary. They are visible at the top of a desk, except with a veneered piece. Indications of them can also be seen in the interior.

Large drawers in all types of desks and secretaries

have same construction details as those of chests of drawers. (*See Section VII, page 175*).

Small drawers of writing compartment, as well as secret drawers, have sides, backs and bottoms of thin soft wood, generally about a quarter-inch thick. Pine and spruce are the most favored woods. Fronts and backs are dovetailed to the sides or fastened by small wooden pegs or brad-size nails. Bottoms are flush and pegged or nailed to sides and backs. These drawers were always left "in the raw" and *never* stained or varnished. They can be tested for genuineness by putting them in upside down. If they slide as readily in that position as when right side up, they are as the old craftsmen made them originally — square, true and fitted so carefully that they do not bind or stick when reversed. When such a drawer has to be replaced or repaired, the man who does it is generally satisfied if it works properly in normal position.

Secret compartments are found more often in a desk or secretary than in any other piece of furniture. They are generally located (1) behind the arched tops of pigeonholes, (2) masked by the pilasters or narrow reeded panels that flank the door of the central locker, (3) concealed by a removable cabinet in the locker, (4) at rear of pigeonholes and small drawers and (5) beneath the writing compartment in place of the wide top drawer of the carcase. This hiding place occurs only with William and Mary and Queen Anne desks. Here the drawer front is false or lacking and the space behind it is a well reached by a sliding panel set in the writing surface just in front of the compartment of drawers and pigeonholes.

Secret drawers behind arched pigeonhole tops are only half to three quarters of an inch deep and fitted so tightly that pressure has to be exerted to move them. The tall narrow drawers behind the pilasters or reeded panels on either side of the locker are called document boxes since they were designed for important papers. They are from eight to 10 inches tall, an inch and a half to two inches wide, five to six inches deep and open at the top. They are "locked" by small wooden slides, pegs or springlike narrow wooden strips concealed just inside the locker.

A removable cabinet in the locker is generally secured by two small slides at top or bottom with finger-tip depressions near the ends which slide inward and release it. This cabinet is not of full depth and behind it are located two or three secret drawers, one above the other, fitted with either pendent brass rings or short leather thongs.

Secret drawers at rear of pigeonholes and small drawers are shaped like document boxes and access to them is through the back of the piece. The top horizontal board is removable and held in place by two springlike wooden strips. If pressed slightly and pushed down about a quarter of an inch, it can be taken out to reveal four secret containers four to five inches wide, an inch and a half deep and from eight to 10 inches tall.

Secretaries are always in two parts — the upper one a cupboard or bookcase and the lower one a desk. The upper section is consistently about half as deep as and an inch and a half to three inches narrower than the lower section and fits into a molded finish on its top.

Secretary doors are usually hung with plain butt hinges with only the rounded pin joints visible. Ornamental hinges, such as the H-shape, are mounted on the fronts of doors and uprights. The right-hand door is fitted with a lock and the key serves as a handle. The left-hand door is secured by small catches or sliding bolts. Mortices are frequently used for these and for the lock.

The upper section of a secretary is surmounted by (1) a flat molded cornice, (2) a broken arch pediment or (3) a shaped pediment. There are two types of broken pediments, the bonnet top that is enclosed and the plain which is in silhouette.

The bonnet top is formed by a pair of balancing molded cyma curves with ends frequently terminating in carved rosettes, three to five inches in diameter. In the break between these curved elements is a molded plinth, generally surmounted by a turned or carved finial, with or without matching plinths and finials at the corners. The sides have flat cornices that continue the molding of the front curved pieces. The boards of the back are shaped to conform to the front and the top is enclosed by thin boards also shaped to conform. Behind the central finial, on either side of the break, other boards are placed vertically and complete the closing, thus giving the top a bonnet shape with a deep central crease.

The plain broken arch has the same outline but is in silhouette with space behind *not* enclosed.

A shaped pediment is always in silhouette and may be removable. It is formed by a central plinth, with or without a finial, which is flanked by wide vertical pieces with upper edges either cyma-curved or concave and terminating at corners in matching plinths, with or without finials.

PURITAN SPAN

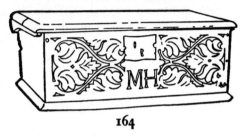

164

164. Bible or Writing Box

Has an oblong, slightly overhanging pine lid, 24 to 28 inches wide and 14 to 16 inches deep. The edges are rounded or molded with molded cleats on underside of ends. Sides are of oak with large dovetail joints at corners. Lid is attached either by two wrought-iron snipe hinges or by wooden pegs projecting through the end cleats. Top is generally flat but may slope slightly toward front which is from eight to 10 inches high and intaglio-carved in either a design of interlacing lunettes with leaf motif or an allover decoration of tulips, leaves and tendrils. Sometimes the two initials of the original owner are included in the carved decoration, either flanking the keyhole or below the front plate of the lock.

A box without lock usually has centered holes in lid and front for a cord or chain. The box bottom is of pine and has either flush or projecting and molded edges. Was originally painted partially or all over. Made chiefly in Massachusetts and Connecticut of oak and pine. Most of these writing boxes are now in museum collections. Some survival examples, made as late as 1725, are of walnut and uncarved. *Ca. 1650–1700.* XXX to Y

WILLIAM AND MARY

165

165. Slant-Front Desk-on-Frame

Made in two sections, upper one is essentially a slant-front writing box with narrow oblong top, 28 to 32 inches wide. Front slants at about a 60-degree angle, is hinged at bottom, has simple overlapping edges and a centered brass scrolled keyhole escutcheon. Open, writing flap rests on pull brackets. Interior may contain (1) eight to ten small drawers, (2) three to five small drawers with pigeonholes above or (3) central locker flanked by pairs of small drawers with arched pigeonholes above. Drawers are fitted with either brass pendent rings or bat's-wing plates. Locker door has a shaped keyhole escutcheon or brass knob. The full-width drawer beneath writing flap has overlapping thumb-molded edges and is fitted with brass teardrop handles and matching keyhole escutcheon.

Upper edge of lower section or frame is molded at front and sides. The skirt beneath is sometimes deep enough to contain a full-width drawer with molded overlapping edges and fitted with brasses matching those above. Lower edge of skirt is valanced in balancing scrolls.

Desk is supported on four vase-and-ring or trumpet-turned legs, terminating in large ball feet. Legs are braced by either an X-shape flat stretcher with balancing cyma-curved outline, or a flat cyma-curved box stretcher. Total height is from 32 to 36 inches. Made of walnut and generally of New England or Philadelphia provenance. Relatively few examples known. *1700–1710*. Z to ZZZ

166. Slant-Front Bureau Desk

Has narrow oblong top, 34 to 38 inches wide. Front slants at about a 45-degree angle and is fitted with a brass scrolled keyhole escutcheon. Interior is compartmented with symmetrically arranged small drawers and pigeonholes and may include a central locker with plain or paneled door. Locker usually has small graduated drawers, sometimes contained in a removable case with secret compartment at back, and is nearly always flanked by split-turned pilasters or reeded panels which mask the fronts of document boxes.

166

Drawers and locker door are fitted with brass knobs. Pigeonholes may be plain or have arched tops. Rear of writing surface usually has slightly sunk sliding panel that gives access to a well beneath. Carcase contains three full-width graduated drawers. Fronts are framed by single or double arched moldings or have simple overlapping edges, and brasses are either teardrop handles or bat's-wing plates and matching keyhole escutcheons. Slant-front and drawer fronts may be decorated with inlaid stringing forming oblong panels and geometric shapes. Sides of carcase are either plain or stile and rail constructed with large oblong panels. Has a molded base, sometimes deeply cut, and is supported by four boldly turned ball feet, ebonized.

Made in New England and probably as far south as Pennsylvania of walnut or other native hardwoods, sometimes combined with pine. When of walnut, the slant-front and drawer fronts are sometimes faced and banded with burl veneer. When of maple, the fronts may be of curly maple. *Ca. 1700–1720.* YY to Z

QUEEN ANNE

167

167. Slant-Front Desk on Turned Frame

Has narrow top from 22 to 28 inches wide. Front slants at a little less than a 60-degree angle and is fitted with a bat's-wing keyhole escutcheon. Writing interior is compartmented with drawers and pigeonholes. Drawer fronts are plain with small brass knobs; pigeonholes are plain or arched and dividers are frequently scrolled. Full-width drawer below has molded overlapping edges and is fitted with bat's-wing brasses or elongated wooden knobs.

Upper edges of supporting frame are cove-molded. Its skirt is of medium depth and has straight-molded lower edge. It sometimes contains a full-width drawer with front matching that of wide drawer above. Both are fitted with either brasses or elongated knobs to match those above. Frame has four vase-and-ring turned legs terminating in small ball or knob feet. Legs are braced above feet by a plain box stretcher. Total height varies from 36 to 40 inches. Made in all sections of walnut, maple and sometimes partly of pine. Occasionally is of smaller size for child. Not numerous. *Ca. 1720–1740.* YY to YYY

168

168. Sloping Lid Desk on Turned Frame

Has narrow oblong top, 25 to 32 inches wide, to which is hinged a deep lid that slopes at about a 30-degree angle. It gives access to a well of medium depth that is compartmented at rear with drawers or pigeon-holes or both. Drawers are fitted with small brass knobs or pendent brass rings. Supporting frame is like that of foregoing desk. Made in all sections of walnut, maple and sometimes partly of pine. *Ca. 1720–1750.* YY to YYY

169

169. Countinghouse Desk

Is a survival piece of like lines and construction, made for about seventy-five years longer. It is generally taller and wider than the earlier desk. Well interior has a simple arrangement of pigeonholes with small drawers sometimes included. If the skirt is deeper it may contain two full-width drawers, fitted with rosette-and-bail handles and oval keyhole escutcheons. Has square or turned legs, sometimes slightly tapering, with or without a plain box stretcher. Made in all sections of walnut, maple or other native hardwoods, sometimes with pine lid, and originally finished with red filler. *Ca. 1750–1820.* XXX to Y

170. Slant-Front Desk on Cabriole Leg Frame

Lines of upper section are still those of an enlarged writing box. Has a narrow oblong top 32 to 38 inches wide. Front slants at nearly a 60-degree angle, is slightly overlapping and fitted with a brass bat's-wing keyhole escutcheon. Interior is compartmented with six to eight pigeonholes above three to five small shallow drawers

170

that are fitted with brass knobs. May have locker instead of two central pigeonholes and drawer. Beneath writing compartment is a single full-width drawer with overlapping edges and fitted with bat's-wing brasses.

Upper section is slightly narrower and shallower than supporting frame. Top of latter is cove-molded and the valanced triple-arched skirt contains a full-width drawer with overlapping edges. Front is sometimes paneled to simulate three narrower drawers with fan carving at center and is fitted with brasses matching those above. Base is supported by four cabriole legs, terminating in Dutch or drake feet, or it may have kneeless cabriole turned legs terminating in small button feet. Total height varies from 38 to 46 inches. Made in all sections of walnut, maple, plain or curly, cherry and occasionally of pine with maple legs. *Ca. 1720–1740.* YY to YYY

171

171. Slant-Front Bureau Desk on Low Frame

Has narrow oblong top, 38 to 46 inches wide. Front
slants at about a 45-degree angle, has thumb-molded
edges and brass bat's-wing escutcheon. Interior is compartmented with six to eight pigeonholes with scrolled
dividers above a single or double tier of small drawers.
Sometimes has a central locker with plain or sunburst-
carved door, flanked by pilaster-fronted document boxes.
Carcase contains four full-width drawers with overlapping thumb-molded edges, and fitted with bat's-wing
brasses. Rests on very low frame with top edge molded
and well-valanced skirt. Is supported by short cabriole
legs terminating in either Dutch or drake feet. Total
height varies from 42 to 48 inches. Made in all sections
of walnut, plain or curly maple or cherry. Not numerous. *Ca. 1720–1740.* YY to Z

172

172. Slant-Front Bureau Desk

Has narrow oblong top, 36 to 42 inches wide. Front slants at about a 45-degree angle, has overlapping thumb-molded edges and is fitted with a brass bat's-wing or willow keyhole escutcheon. Interior is compartmented with arrangement of arched pigeonholes with a single or double tier of small drawers beneath. Central locker has a plain, paneled or sunburst-carved door, frequently flanked by plain or pilaster-fronted document boxes. Drawers are fitted with brass knobs and pigeonhole dividers have either straight or scrolled edges.

The carcase contains four full-width graduated drawers with overlapping thumb-molded edges and fitted with either bat's-wing or willow brasses. Base has slightly molded upper edge, narrow skirt, plain or with scrolled central finial, and four bracket feet. Height from 40 to 43 inches. Made in all sections of walnut, plain or curly maple, cherry or birch. *Ca. 1720–1750.* YY to Z

173

173. Survival Slant-Front Bureau Desk

Has simple decorative details and brasses characteristic of the succeeding periods, but basic design and construction remain unchanged. Pigeonholes are unarched, their dividers unscrolled, and when there is a central locker the flanking document boxes are sometimes omitted. Seldom has secret compartments. Skirt is always plain and without central pendent finial. Is supported by plain bracket feet.

Such a desk is an example of country cabinetwork. Made from Maine to Georgia and as far west as the Ohio River Valley of walnut, maple, cherry, birch and other native hardwoods sometimes combined with pine and finished with red filler. Southern desks were frequently made entirely of southern hard pine and finished natural. Because of their usefulness these desks are popular with collectors. *Ca. 1750–1830.* XXX to YYY

174

174. Flat-Top Secretary

Upper section is from 38 to 46 inches wide and from 46 to 50 inches high. Has a boldly done cove molding cornice that overhangs two to three inches. Below is a pair of doors with large, slightly sunk, rectangular wooden panels. They are hung with butt or H-shape hinges and fitted with scrolled brass keyhole escutcheons. Centered beneath each door are candlestick slides, four to six inches wide, with slightly overlapping molded fronts and brass knobs. Interior of section has a varied arrangement of shelves, pigeonholes, including tall vertical ones with scrolled dividers for account books, and small drawers.

Lower or bureau desk section has same features previously described (*see No. 172 and No. 173*). It is supported by plain or molded bracket feet or may rest on a very low frame with cabriole brackets terminating in Dutch feet. Total height of secretary varies from five feet 10 inches to seven feet. Made in all sections of walnut, plain or curly maple, cherry, occasionally mahogany or pine combined with other softwoods and finished with red filler. Not numerous. *Ca. 1740–1750.* YYY to **Z**

175

175. Bonnet-Top Secretary

Is surmounted by a bonnet top which overhangs the body from two to three inches at front and sides and may contain secret compartments in enclosure back of central finial. Balance of secretary is similar to foregoing flat-top type just described. Usually is supported by molded bracket feet; very rarely has the low frame with cabriole brackets. Total height varies from six feet three inches to seven feet six inches. Made in all sections of walnut with drawer fronts, door panels, slant-front and pediment-front sometimes faced with burl veneer, of plain or curly maple, cherry or mahogany. Not numerous. *Ca. 1740–1750.* Z to ZZ

CHIPPENDALE

176. Slant-Front Desk with Square Legs

Has narrow oblong top, 34 to 38 inches wide. Front slants at about a 45-degree angle, has slightly overlapping edges and is fitted with a willow brass keyhole escutcheon. Compartmented interior has from six to eight plain or arched pigeonholes with scrolled dividers. Beneath are small drawers fitted with brass knobs. Skirt is deep, contains a full-width drawer of medium depth, and its lower edge is valanced. Drawer has overlapping thumb-molded edges and is fitted with willow brasses. Desk is supported by four long legs with bead-molded edges and braced by an H-shape stretcher placed about four inches from the floor. Height varies from 38 to 42

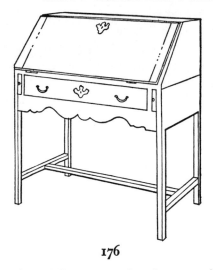

176

inches. Made in all sections of walnut, maple, cherry and sometimes of assorted hard and soft woods, finished with red filler. Possible variation of the countinghouse desk. Not numerous. *Ca. 1750–1760.* Y to YY

177. Straight-Front Bureau Desk

Lines and construction are the same as with similar desk of Queen Anne period (*see No. 172*). Slant-front is sometimes decorated with a large incised fan or sunburst carving. Elaboration of interior is pronounced. Small drawers beneath the pigeonholes are frequently in two tiers with the upper one recessed about an inch, forming a "stepped" arrangement. These drawer fronts are flat, serpentined or cut in a concave curve. Pigeonhole tops are arched and sometimes decorated with centered carved shells. The central locker door is either

177

plain or has a raised panel with a carved shell at the top and is fitted with a scrolled keyhole escutcheon. Small drawers are fitted with brass knobs.

Below slanting front the carcase contains four graduated drawers. Their fronts either are overlapping and thumb-molded or have cock-bead edges and are fitted with brass willow plates or rosette-and-bail handles and matching keyhole escutcheons. Front corners of the carcase may be plain, chamfered and fluted or have inset quarter-round reeded pilasters. The sides are plain and sometimes fitted with large willow brass chest handles with pendent bails. Desk has a slightly projecting molded base, sometimes gadrooned, and is supported by plain or molded bracket feet or by short cabriole brackets terminating in claw-and-ball feet. Height varies from 42 to 44 inches. Made in all sections of mahogany, walnut, plain or curly maple or cherry. *Ca. 1750–1775.* YY to Z

178

178. Serpentine-Front Bureau Desk

Always more elaborate than desk just described. Refinements include serpentine shaping of bureau front and treatment of writing interior. Here small drawers above and flanking the pigeonholes are apt to be boldly shell-carved, incised and in relief. Also the front line of drawers and pigeonholes on either side of a flat central section is frequently recessed in balancing curves. Beneath it is the stepped arrangement of the tiers of drawers which are fitted with brass knobs. The central section has two or three small drawers, set vertically, in place of the usual locker and is flanked by reeded, molded or pilaster-fronted document boxes.

The top bureau drawer has a straight upper edge and a boldly serpentined lower edge. This is accomplished by two projecting arcs on either side of the center which conform to the serpentine curve of the lower drawers. Drawers are graduated, fitted with plain or pierced willow brasses and matching keyhole escutcheons and have cock-bead edges. The conforming molded base either is plain or has a central shell-carved pendent finial. Is usually supported by short cabriole brackets terminating in claw-and-ball feet, but sometimes molded bracket feet are used. Made in all sections of mahogany, walnut, plain and curly maple. Some of finest examples are of Massachusetts provenance. *Ca. 1760–1775.* Z to Q

179

179. Flat-Top Secretary

Upper section is a bookcase cupboard from 38 to 48 inches wide, surmounted by a boldly executed, slightly overhanging cornice that is sometimes denticulated.

Front has a pair of doors with either wooden or glazed panels. If the latter, muntins form a rectangular trellis and the top row of panes are sometimes arched. Doors are hung with butt hinges and fitted with scrolled brass keyhole escutcheons or brass pendent loop handles. Cupboard front corners match those of lower or bureau desk section and are plain or have inset quarter-round reeded pilasters. Base of cupboard usually has candlestick slides with molded overlapping fronts and fitted with brass knobs. Interior of cupboard has three or four shelves with molded front edges and occasionally there are tall account-book pigeonholes and small drawers at the bottom like those of the desk interior below.

The lower section has the same construction and arrangement of writing compartment details as the straight-front desk already described (*see No. 177*). Total height of secretary varies from six feet six inches to seven feet four inches. Made in all sections of mahogany, walnut, plain or curly maple or cherry. *Ca. 1750–1775.* YYY to Q

180. Bonnet-Top Secretary

Cupboard section is from 38 to 46 inches wide and capped by a characteristic bonnet top which may contain secret compartments and have either turned wooden or brass ball-and-steeple finials. Cupboard doors have either plain or cartouche-shape wooden panels, are butt-hinged and fitted with scrolled brass keyhole escutcheons. Corners of upper section are either plain or have inset quarter-round pilasters to match lower section. Candlestick slides may be present.

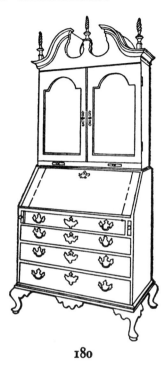

180

Lower section is like straight-front bureau desk (*see No. 177*) with four graduated drawers fitted with brass willow plates. May have short cabriole brackets, or plain or molded bracket feet. Total height varies from seven to eight feet. Made in all parts of the country of mahogany, walnut, plain and curly maple or cherry. Especially fine examples are known to have been made by Aaron Chapin of Connecticut. *Ga. 1750–1775.* Z to Q

HEPPLEWHITE

181

181. Slant-Front Bureau Desk

Has narrow oblong top 38 to 44 inches wide. Front slopes at about a 45-degree angle, has slightly overlapping molded edge and is fitted with an oval brass keyhole escutcheon or an inset brass keyhole surround. With a more elaborate example, the slanting front has a central inlaid medallion, lozenge or oval, or a spread eagle surrounded by inlaid checkered banding or stringing which is repeated on the locker door, bureau drawer fronts and across the top of the skirt.

Writing compartment contains six to eight plain or arched pigeonholes and the same number of small drawers arranged on either side of the plain or pilaster-fronted document boxes which flank the locker. Four graduated full-width drawers in the carcase have cockbead edges. Their fronts are sometimes faced with crotch-grain mahogany, satinwood or curly maple veneer. They are fitted with oval brasses with bail handles

and matching escutcheons or inset keyhole surrounds.
Desk is supported by four outcurving French feet and
has valanced connecting skirt. Height varies from 43
to 45 inches. Made in all sections of mahogany, cherry,
maple and occasionally birch in northern New England.
Ca. 1785–1800. YY to Z

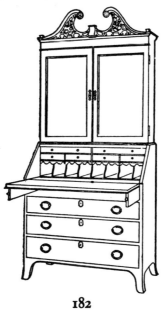

182

182. Slant-Front Secretary

Upper or cupboard section is from 38 to 44 inches
wide with either a flat molded and sometimes denticulated cornice that is slightly overhanging or a broken
pediment top. This has molded cyma curves terminating
in inlaid rosettes and the plinth of the central urn-

shape finial sometimes has a floral or spread-eagle inlaid medallion. The frieze above the pair of oblong
doors is faced with a band of contrasting inlay or has
inlaid stringing in a curved interlocking design.

Cupboard doors may (1) have slightly sunk wooden
panels, with or without either central inlaid medallions
or larger veneer ovals or (2) be glazed with geometric-
shape panes set in muntins that form a latticework pattern. Brass fittings are small oval escutcheons or inset
keyhole surrounds. Cupboard contains three or four adjustable shelves with molded front edges. Lower section
is like bureau desk just described.

Total height of secretary varies from seven feet to
eight feet six inches. Made in all sections of mahogany,
cherry, maple or occasionally walnut. Door panels,
drawer fronts and locker door are sometimes faced with
crotch-grain mahogany, satinwood or fancy-grain maple
veneer. *Ca. 1785–1800.* YYY to ZZ

183. Fall-Front Bureau Desk

Closely resembles deep-drawer type chest of drawers
also made in the Hepplewhite period (*see No. 150*).
Has oblong, slightly overhanging top, from 46 to 48
inches wide, edged with inlaid stringing. Carcase contains four full-width drawers. Top one is from 10 to 14
inches deep and pulls out about halfway. Front, hinged
at bottom and supported by brass quadrant brackets,
falls forward to form writing surface. This device gives
the piece its name. Interior is compartmented with from
six to eight plain or arched pigeonholes, as many small
drawers and usually a locker with flanking document
boxes. Small drawers are fitted with brass knobs and

183

are plain or faced with crotch-grain veneer inlaid with stringing. Locker door has inset brass keyhole surround and may have an inlaid central medallion. Fronts of document boxes are plain or veneered and have stringing.

The fall-front is faced with crotch-grain mahogany and sometimes has a central oval panel flanked by lozenge plaquettes of satinwood. The full-width drawers below are graduated with fronts likewise faced with crotch-grain veneer, with cock-bead edges, and frequently have stringing panels. They are fitted with oval brass plates with bail handles and (1) matching keyhole escutcheons, (2) diamond-shape satinwood inlays or (3) inset brass keyhole surrounds.

Desk is supported by four outcurved French feet connected by a valanced skirt, frequently with a fillet of inlay across the top and stringing-edged below. Made in all sections of mahogany with satinwood inlay and stringing of holly or boxwood. *Ca. 1790–1800.* YY to YYY

184

184. Fall-Front Secretary

The upper bookcase section is from 42 to 48 inches wide with either a flat molded cornice, sometimes arcaded, or a shaped pediment top. With the latter the central finial is a carved and gilded wooden or brass eagle and there are usually brass ball-and-spire finials at the corners. These finials are mounted on plinths that are plain with inlaid medallions or faced with satinwood veneer. There is a narrow frieze of crotch-grain veneer above the pair of oblong doors which are generally glazed with geometrically shaped panes set in latticed or Gothic-arched muntins.

Some examples have doors with wooden panels, often

inlaid with small oval medallions in the center. Doors have inset brass keyhole surrounds or diamond-shape satinwood inlays. Lower section is like desk just described. Total height varies from seven to eight feet. Made in all sections of mahogany with satinwood inlay and box or holly stringing. *Ca. 1790–1810.* YYY to ZZ

185. Break-Front Secretary

Takes its name from the central section of both upper and lower parts which breaks or projects two to four inches further than the narrower sections that flank it.

The upper part is from five feet two inches to five feet 10 inches wide and is surmounted by a slightly overhanging shaped pediment that lifts off. It has a conforming central break and balancing cyma curves. The central finial is frequently an eagle with outspread wings made of carved and gilded wood or brass. Corner finials are turned wooden urns or brass spired balls. The pediment is faced with crotch-grain veneer and generally paneled with stringing. Under this frieze are three cupboards, a wide central one with double doors flanked by narrower ones with single doors, all glazed with geometric-shaped panes set in latticed muntins. The pattern is often elaborate, such as two tiers of interlacing arcs formed by narrow muntins that are stringing-edged. Keyhole fittings may be oval brass escutcheons, diamond-shape satinwood inlays or inset brass surrounds.

The projecting central section of the lower part contains either three wide drawers with the top one a fall-front or simply a fall-front with an open knee-hole

185

beneath. The flanking recessed sections each have a shallow full-width drawer above a tall cupboard. Drawer fronts and doors are faced with crotch-grain veneer with cock-bead edges and have oval self-panels outlined with checkered fillets or stringing. They are fitted with oval brass plates with bail handles and matching keyhole escutcheons, diamond-shape satinwood inlays or brass keyhole surrounds. Stiles of outer corners and those of the central projection are outlined with stringing and inlaid with pendent bellflowers or husks. Secretary is supported by eight square tapering legs inlaid to match the stiles above them. Total height varies from seven feet eight inches to eight feet six inches.

Made of mahogany with satinwood inlay and string-ing of box or holly. Most of the known examples are of Salem, Massachusetts, provenance. Some break-front secretaries have Sheraton details, such as doors with Gothic-arched panes set in reeded pilaster-like muntins, drawer fronts without paneling or stringing, brasses, lion's-head with pendent rings, and turned and reeded legs. *Ca. 1790–1810.* QQ to QQQ

186. Secretary with Fold-Over Writing Flap

Upper bookcase section is from 38 to 42 inches wide and is surmounted by a shaped pediment with plinths at center and corners sometimes faced with satinwood, curly or bird's-eye maple veneer. Central finial is a carved and gilded or brass eagle with spired ball finials at corners. The narrow frieze may mask a shallow full-width drawer and is faced with crotch-grain veneer with stringing. Below are a pair of oblong or nearly square glazed doors with geometric panes set in lat-ticed or Gothic arched muntins. The interior has two or three adjustable shelves with molded front edges. Some-times there is an arrangement of pigeonholes and small drawers at the bottom.

On the top of the lower section in front of the cup-board is a fold-over writing flap, eight to 10 inches deep. It slopes slightly and overhangs the sides of the carcase about an inch. Its inner surface is covered with baize and banded with crotch-grain veneer. Beneath are full-width graduated drawers with cock-bead edges. Their fronts are faced with crotch-grain mahogany, satinwood or fancy-grain maple veneer and are fre-

186

quently banded or framed with herringbone or check-ered fillets. They are fitted with oval brass plates with bail handles, matching or diamond-shape inlay keyhole escutcheons or inset brass keyhole surrounds. Supported by four outcurved French feet connected by a valanced skirt with a herringbone or checkered fillet at the top or by four square and tapering legs without valance.

A late example sometimes has slender turned and reeded legs with or without valanced skirt, and draw-ers fitted with brass rosette, pressed glass or mushroom-turned wooden knobs. Total height varies from five feet 10 inches to seven feet. Made in all sections, par-ticularly New England, of mahogany or cherry with satinwood or bird's-eye maple veneer, or curly maple with mahogany veneer. *Ca. 1785–1810.* YY to Z

187

187. Tambour Secretary

Takes its name from sliding shutters of tambour work that replace the usual doors of upper section. Has an oblong top with square or slightly molded edges from 36 to 40 inches wide. The low cabinet beneath has a pair of reeded tambour vertical slides, made all of the same wood or of alternating satinwood stripes, infrequently decorated with inlaid festoons and pendent bellflowers or husks. The narrow uprights at the inner ends of these slides are fitted with small brass knobs. Front corners of the cabinet have slender pilasters or narrow panels of satinwood veneer that simulate them. There is also a matching pilaster at center between the tambour slides.

Interior of cabinet is compartmented with pigeonholes and small drawers. Their arrangement is usually two tiers of shallow drawers above arched pigeonholes.

The drawers are faced with the same veneer as the full-width drawers in lower section and fitted with brass, ivory or turned wooden knobs.

On top of the lower section in front of the tambour shutters is a slightly overhanging, fold-over writing flap that is flat or has a very slight slope. Its inner surface is covered with fabric or leather and is veneer-banded. Below it are from one to four full-width drawers with cock-bead edges and faced with crotch-grain veneer, banded and paneled with stringing or with large oval inlay panels of satinwood or bird's-eye maple. They are fitted with oval brass plates with bail handles, matching or diamond-shape inlay keyhole escutcheons or inset brass keyhole surrounds. Supported by four square tapering legs with stringing and sometimes pendent bellflower or husks of satinwood inlay or by outcurved French feet connected by a valanced skirt.

A late example sometimes has four turned and reeded legs and drawers are fitted with brass rosette knobs. Total height varies from 41 to 51 inches. Made of mahogany with crotch-grain, satinwood, or bird's-eye maple veneer and stringing of box or holly, in New England, mostly in or near Boston. The finest example known, with the label of John Seymour & Son, Boston, was sold in 1930 for $30,000. *Ca. 1790–1805.* YYY to QQQ

188. Cupboard Secretary

Is like tambour secretary just described in construction and basic design except that cabinet section has doors instead of sliding tambour shutters. Has an oblong top 38 to 42 inches wide with square edges. The

188

pair of wide short doors beneath are either faced with crotch-grain veneer or finely reeded to look like tambour work and are fitted with oval brass keyhole escutcheons or inset brass keyhole surrounds.

Was the work of country cabinetmakers whose customers did not wish to pay for tambour work. Made in all sections of New England of mahogany with crotch-grain veneer, maple with much of the piece bird's-eye veneered, cherry or birch. *Ca. 1790–1810.* Y to YYY

189. Tambour Roll-Top Desk

Has slightly overhanging top, 36 to 42 inches wide, with edge plain or inlaid with stringing or a checkered fillet. Under this slides a horizontal tambour shutter, terminating in a crossbar fitted with small brass knobs, which gives access to an interior compartment at the back with small drawers either flanking or placed below four to six pigeonholes. A writing shelf pulls for-

189

ward and is paneled in green baize and veneer-banded. Small drawers, faced with veneer to match larger ones in skirt, are fitted with brass knobs, as is the writing shelf. Tambour shutter when closed has a quarter-oval downward curve.

The skirt beneath has a straight molded lower edge and contains either two half-width drawers or a wide central drawer flanked by two narrower ones. They are faced with crotch-grain or satinwood veneer, have cock-bead edges and their brasses are rosettes with bail handles or oval plates with bail handles and inset keyhole surrounds. Desk is supported by four square tapering legs decorated with stringing or satinwood panels and crossbanding to simulate feet. Height varies from 36 to 42 inches. Made of mahogany with satinwood veneer and box or holly stringing, chiefly in Philadelphia and Baltimore. Not numerous. Unusual rather than rare. *Ca. 1790–1800.* YYY to Z

190

190. Cylinder-Front Desk

Has oblong slightly overhanging top, 38 to 42 inches wide, with plain or inlaid edge. Beneath it is a narrow frieze faced with crotch-grain veneer and sometimes paneled with stringing. The front is a quarter-round solid shutter that pivots on unseen brackets. When raised, it disappears behind the small drawers and pigeonholes of the interior. Has a pull-out writing shelf covered with fabric or leather and veneer-banded.

Beneath it, carcase contains one to three full-width graduated drawers or a single tier of shallow half-width ones. They are faced with crotch-grain veneer, have cock-bead edges and are fitted with oval brass plates with bail handles and matching escutcheons or inset keyhole surrounds. Is supported by outcurved French feet connected by a valanced skirt or by four square tapering legs.

Made of mahogany with satinwood or bird's-eye maple veneer and box or holly stringing in the larger cities, such as Boston, New York, Philadelphia and Baltimore. Those of Baltimore provenance usually have oval glass insets depicting figures in classic flowing robes done in gold leaf with black background. A later example has slender turned and reeded legs and brasses are oblong plates with bail handles or rosette knobs and keyhole surrounds. Not numerous. *Ca. 1795–1810.* YY to Z

191. Cylinder-Front Secretary

Upper or bookcase section is from 38 to 42 inches wide with shaped pediment that has central and corner plinths on which urn-shaped wooden finials are mounted. Beneath a narrow frieze of crotch-grain veneer are oblong doors with glass panes forming three narrow Gothic-arched panels set in molded muntins. Inner door stiles are fitted with inset keyhole surrounds. Bookcase interior has adjustable shelves with molded front edges. Below doors may be a tier of two or three shallow drawers with veneer facing, cock-bead edges and brasses that are either oval plates with bail handles or rosette knobs and inset keyhole surrounds.

The lower or desk section has a solid veneer-faced quarter-round shutter and pull-out writing shelf like the foregoing desk. Beneath are three full-width drawers with cock-bead edges, crotch-grain veneer facing and stringing, and fitted with oval brass plates with bail handles and matching escutcheons or inset keyhole surrounds. Is supported by four outcurved French feet connected by a valanced skirt with an inlay fillet across the top.

191

Made in the larger cities of mahogany with crotch-grain or satinwood veneer and stringing of holly or box. A late example may have turned and reeded legs and only crotch-grain mahogany veneering. Not numerous. *Ca. 1795–1815.* YY to Z

SHERATON

192. Secretary with Fold-Over Writing Flap

Resembles like secretary of Hepplewhite period (*see No. 186*) but the upper section is either tall enough to accommodate four adjustable shelves or noticeably shorter, with only two shelves above a shallow arrangement of small drawers and pigeonholes. Cupboard section is from 38 to 42 inches wide and has either a shaped

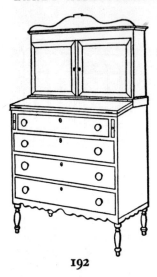

192

pediment with turned wood or brass finials or a flat, slightly overhanging cove-molded cornice. Beneath it is a frieze faced with crotch-grain veneer. The bookcase doors have either wooden panels or glazed ones with panes that form narrow muntin-framed panels with Gothic arches. If pigeonholes and small drawers are present, the glazing stops just above them and they are concealed by oblong cross panels veneered with satinwood or bird's-eye maple. Brasses on doors are inset keyhole surrounds.

The outside of the fold-over writing flap is faced with crotch-grain veneer and has the usual fabric panel with veneer banding inside. The lower section contains three full-width drawers faced with crotch-grain mahogany, satinwood or fancy-grain maple veneer and edges cock-beaded. Brasses are oblong plates with bail

handles or rosette knobs and either oblong keyhole escutcheons or keyhole surrounds.

Corners of carcase may have three-quarter round outset reeded pilasters that terminate in vase-and-ring turned
plain or reeded legs 10 to 12 inches long (*see No. 155*).
Total height varies from six feet four inches to seven
feet 10 inches. Made in all sections, particularly New
England, of mahogany or cherry with crotch-grain mahogany, satinwood or bird's-eye maple veneer, or of
curly maple or birch with mahogany veneer. *Ca. 1800–
1820.* YY to Z

193. Fall-Front Secretary

Upper part varies in width from 44 to 56 inches and
has either a flat molded cornice or a lift-off shaped pediment with turned wooden urn-shaped or spired ball
brass finials at center and corners. Below is a frieze
faced with crotch-grain veneer above a pair of oblong
doors. These either have crotch-grain veneered panels
with stringing or are glazed with geometric-shaped
panes set in latticework of interlocking curved muntins.
Doors are fitted with inset brass keyhole surrounds. Interior contains three or four adjustable shelves with
molded or rounded edges.

Lower section is like the fall-front desk in construction (*see No. 183*). Beneath the writing section, the
carcase contains either three full-width drawers or a
cupboard enclosed by a pair of rectangular solid doors.
Drawers are faced with crotch-grain veneer, have cock-
bead edges and brasses are oblong plates with bail handles or rosette knobs and oblong or oval keyhole escutcheons or inset keyhole surrounds.

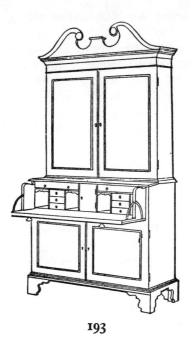

193

When there is a cupboard the door panels are faced with crotch-grain veneer and the keyhole fittings match those of doors in upper section. The interior of this lower cupboard has a single fixed shelf of full width and depth. Secretary has a narrow base molded to match the cornice and is supported by either scrolled bracket feet or turned and reeded legs. Total height varies from seven to eight feet. Made in cities and larger towns in all sections of mahogany with crotch-grain veneering. *Ca. 1800–1820.* YY to YYY

194

194. Secretary with Pull-Out Writing Shelf

Upper section varies in width from 36 to 42 inches and has either a low shaped pediment or a flat, slightly overhanging molded cornice generally faced with crotch-grain veneer. Beneath are a pair of solid doors with crotch-grain panels or, less frequently, glazed with geometric-shaped panes set in a latticework of interlocking muntins. Doors are fitted with small oblong keyhole escutcheons or keyhole surrounds of brass. Interior of bookcase has two or three adjustable shelves with rounded or molded front edges above a tier of six to eight pigeonholes with one or two rows of small drawers underneath that are plain and fitted with brass or wooden knobs.

At top of lower section is a pull-out writing shelf also fitted with small knobs. Beneath are three full-width graduated drawers, faced with crotch-grain veneer. They have cock-bead edges and their brasses are oblong plates with bail handles or rosette knobs with oval or oblong keyhole escutcheons or keyhole surrounds. The skirt is usually faced with crotch-grain veneer and is valanced. Is supported by four turned and reeded legs with small ball-shaped feet. Total height varies from five to six feet. Made in all sections of mahogany with crotch-grain veneer, cherry without veneering, maple with bird's-eye veneer or, in parts of New England, sometimes of birch. *Ca. 1800–1820.* Y to YYY

195. Schoolmaster's Desk

Has a deep, slightly overhanging lid, 20 to 28 inches wide, that slopes at about a 30-degree angle. It is hinged to a narrow flat top of equal width which generally has a plain strip about two inches high at its back and sides. Well under lid is eight to 10 inches deep at rear and four to six inches deep at front. It is usually without pigeonholes or drawers. Beneath it is generally a full-width drawer four to six inches deep. It has a plain front fitted with either brass or mushroom-turned wooden knobs and sometimes an inset keyhole surround.

Lower edge of carcase is straight and plain. Is supported by four slightly tapering legs, either square or

195

turned with ring-turning at upper and lower ends, terminating in small ball feet. Made in all sections of East and Middle West with legs of maple or other hardwood and carcase and lid of pine or other softwood. Usually was painted or finished in red filler. A late example is sometimes made of black walnut. *Ca. 1800–1850.* X to XX

196. Writing Box or Traveling Desk

Is indirect revival of the seventeenth-century writing box (*see No. 164*) but differs in construction, divides into two parts and has an elaborately fitted interior. It measures 12 to 20 inches long, eight to 12 inches wide and four to eight inches high. The two parts are hinged at the back and their sides are cut on a diagonal so that the open box provides a sloping writing surface. This consists of the baize-covered, center-hinged flaps of both parts. Behind the upper flap is space for writing paper and beneath the lower one, compartments for other writing materials and frequently toilet accessories. Beyond this is a shallow compartment fitted for ink bottle, sand

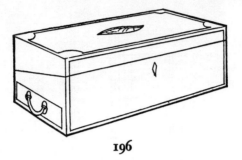

196

shaker and pens. Sometimes the concave pen tray is removable and has a secret compartment beneath.

With a larger box, the lower section has a false bottom which provides space for a shallow full-width drawer inserted from right side. Drawer is equipped with an inset brass handle with folding bail. Box edges are finished with narrow rounded brass strips and at the corners there are quarter-round brass insets. The front is fitted with an inset brass keyhole escutcheon and the top generally has a small centered brass plate, inset and designed to be engraved with the owner's initials. Sometimes these brass fittings are simulated by gilding. Made in all sections of crotch-grain mahogany veneer on pine or sometimes of rosewood or black walnut veneer. *Ca. 1800–1840.* X to XXX

AMERICAN EMPIRE

197. Slant-Front Bureau Desk

Is much like the bureau desk made in the Queen Anne period (*see No. 172*) in construction and general design. Its added details include columns or pilasters

197

and either carved paws or turned feet. Has a narrow oblong top from 36 to 44 inches wide. The slant-front has
a thumb-molded, overlapping edge and is fitted with an
oblong brass keyhole escutcheon or an inset brass keyhole surround. The interior is simply compartmented.
Generally there are from six to 10 pigeonholes above or
below three to five small drawers, each twice the width
of a pigeonhole. Sometimes the central pigeonholes and
corresponding drawer are replaced by a locker, with or
without a door. Pigeonhole dividers are plain as are the
drawer fronts, which have brass or wooden knobs.

Beneath the writing compartment are four full-width
graduated drawers with thumb-molded edges and fronts
plain or faced with crotch-grain veneer. They are fitted
with brass rosette, pressed glass or mushroom-turned
wooden knobs and either oblong keyhole escutcheons or
inset keyhole surrounds. Columns at the front corners
of the carcase may be plain, slightly tapering and crotch-
grain veneered, or turned in a vase shape combined with

ring-and-ball turnings. If there are pilasters instead, they may be simply turned, spirally reeded or acanthus-leaf carved. Desk is supported by carved feet at the front and turned ones at rear or by four ring-and-ball turned tapering legs. Height varies from 44 to 48 inches.

Made in all sections of the East and in the older parts of the Middle West, especially the Ohio River Valley. Woods used are mahogany with crotch-grain veneer, cherry, maple, birch and sometimes of assorted native hard and soft woods finished with red filler. *Ca. 1820–1840.* XXX to Y

198. Secretary with Writing Flap

Construction is chiefly like that of Sheraton secretary (*see No. 192*). The main differences are: writing flap is supported by top full-width drawer instead of pull-brackets and there are columns or pilasters at corners of lower section.

The upper section, 36 to 42 inches wide, is surmounted by a lift-off cornice, faced with crotch-grain veneer, that is either a flaring, overhanging bevel or an ogee-molded band four to six inches deep. Beneath it is a frieze also faced with crotch-grain veneer. The pair of bookcase doors generally overlap the sides of the upper carcase and have rounded outer edges. They have full-width glass panes, sometimes Gothic-arched.

The fold-over writing flap at top of lower section is slightly sloping. At its rear when open may be a compartment for pens and ink bottles, otherwise it is located inside the supporting drawer. Front of latter is sometimes ogee-molded with finger grips on lower edge. Below are three full-width graduated drawers faced with crotch-

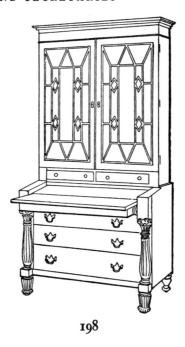

198

grain veneer, with or without banding. Some are fitted with mushroom-turned wooden or pressed glass knobs and inset brass keyhole surrounds. Columns at front corners of carcase are plain, crotch-grain veneered or reeded; pilasters are either reeded or acanthus-leaf carved. Is supported by carved paw feet at front and short turned legs at rear or by four turned legs about six inches long that are plain or reeded. Made in all sections, mostly by cabinetmakers in cities and larger towns, of mahogany with crotch-grain veneering. *Ca. 1820–1840.* XXX to YY

EARLY VICTORIAN

199

199. Drop-Front Secretary

Is the only secretary built in one piece. In design and
construction it is copied from the French *secrétaire à
abattant,* widely made during the Napoleonic period.
At the top is a frieze surmounted by a cove-molded
cornice. This and the carcase have rounded front corners. A hinged, counterbalanced writing flap, about 30
inches wide by 24 inches deep, drops to the middle of
the piece and gives it its name. It has a large fabric or
leather panel veneer-banded. Interior is compartmented
and has a double tier of small drawers below an arcaded open area that is frequently flanked by two small
locker cupboards. This writing interior is generally
satinwood veneered with rosewood banding. The small

drawers are fitted with brass, ivory or rosewood knobs.

The lower part of the carcase contains a cupboard enclosed by a pair of solid doors. These have cartouche-shape panels formed by applied carved and scrolled molding that match a larger panel on the drop-front. All are fitted with scrolled brass keyhole escutcheons and keys serve as handles. Secretary has a wide banded base with a slightly scrolled skirt above low plain or carved bracket feet.

Made of rosewood veneer with interior done in satin-wood mostly by cabinetmakers in the larger cities. A considerable number were made in New Orleans and shipped up the Mississippi River. Later examples were made sometimes of walnut and occasionally three drawers replaced the cupboard. *Ca. 1840–1865.* XXX to YY

Highboys, Lowboys, Chests-on-Chests and Linen Presses

THE highboy is an architectural variation of the tall chest of drawers. Made for only a short time in England, ending before 1715, it developed at the hands of American cabinetmakers into one of the finest and most decorative pieces of furniture ever produced here. The first American-made ones appeared just before 1700 and for about seventy-five years were in considerable demand. The styles that influenced them were the William and Mary, Queen Anne and Chippendale, the latter being the high point of American design and craftsmanship.

The base of the highboy was similar to its companion piece, the lowboy, which resembled a low chest on legs or a table with drawers and was made during the same years. Often, but not always, matching pieces, the climax in their decorative detail and fine carving was reached in Philadelphia during the Chippendale period.

Two variants of the highboy appeared during the last twenty years of its making and remained in favor until the early part of the nineteenth century. They were the chest-on-chest and the linen press. As the name of the former connotes, it consists of two chests of drawers, one surmounting the other. It was made until about 1800 and was especially popular with New England cabinetmakers. Those working in the Connecticut River Valley in or near Hartford made some fine and highly ornamental examples.

The linen press was a utilitarian piece with cupboard top, especially designed for storage of household linens. With Hepplewhite or Sheraton details, it continued in favor for a decade longer.

Special Comments on Highboys and Lowboys and Their Construction

All highboys are two-part pieces. The upper one is from four to six inches narrower and from two to four inches shallower than the lower part. This base has a raised and slightly overhanging molding into which the upper section fits.

A decorative broken pediment sometimes surmounts the upper section. It may be either in silhouette or enclosed. The enclosed type or bonnet top is formed by a pair of balancing molded cyma curves with upper ends frequently terminating in carved rosettes, three to five inches in diameter. In the break between these curved elements is a molded plinth, generally surmounted by a turned or carved finial, with or without matching ones at the corners. The sides have flat cornices which continue the molding of the front curved pieces. The backboards are shaped to conform to the front and the top is enclosed by thin boards shaped to conform. Behind the central finial on either side of the break, other boards are placed vertically and complete the enclosing, thus giving it the shape of a bonnet with a deep central crease.

Other construction details are like those of a chest of drawers (*see Section VII, page 175*).

A highboy base is like a lowboy in construction and decorative detail but larger in every dimension. General measurements are from 44 to 48 inches wide, 20 to 24 inches deep and from 34 to 38 inches tall. Lowboys are from 30 to 36 inches wide, 16 to 18 inches deep and from 26 to 30 inches tall. Therefore what may seem to be an overlarge lowboy is a highboy base with its raised molding finish replaced by a table top.

This was apt to occur in family divisions of heirlooms. At the same time feet would be added to the upper part, making it a chest of drawers. This also can be deduced by studying dimensions since the base will be too large for an original lowboy and the upper part too small for a standard chest of drawers.

Legs of highboys and lowboys have extensions that form the stiles to which fronts and sides are joined by mortice and tenon joints. These are generally pinned by small dowels with ends visible on close inspection.

Legs braced by stretchers occur only with William and Mary highboys and lowboys. They are either box-shaped or X-shaped with flat members, cyma-curved.

Construction details of lowboy drawers and backboard are the same as with chests of drawers (*see Section VII, page 175*).

WILLIAM AND MARY

200. Scroll-Leg Highboy

Upper section has oblong top from 40 to 46 inches wide with slightly overhanging molded edge. Contains four tiers of graduated drawers, the top one half-width drawers and the balance full-width. Drawers are sur-

· **200**

rounded by single arched moldings. Their fronts are plain and fitted with brass teardrop handles and cartouche-shaped or square, diagonally set keyhole escutcheons.

Lower section has plain skirt containing a full-width drawer fitted with same brasses as above. It is supported by five short Flemish-scroll legs, plain or carved, with one placed in the center of the front. They are braced by a flat concave box stretcher and terminate in ball or bun feet. Total height varies from four feet to four feet six inches. Made in Massachusetts and Connecticut of cherry, maple or of either wood combined with pine. Not numerous. *Ca. 1690–1700.* YYY to ZZ

201. Trumpet-Leg Highboy

Upper section has flat oblong top, 36 to 42 inches wide, with slightly overhanging edges that form either a simple molded cornice or a deeper one with a wide

201

cove or torus molding which generally masks a full-width secret drawer about two inches deep. The carcase contains four tiers of graduated drawers. Top tier is either a pair of half-width or three drawers of equal width. Those below are full width. All are framed by single or double arched moldings. Drawers in both upper and lower sections are fitted with brass teardrop handles and cartouche-shaped pierced keyhole escutcheons or square ones diagonally set. When the highboy is of walnut, the drawer fronts are frequently faced with burl walnut or ash or crotch-grain walnut veneer with herringbone banding.

The skirt of the base is deeply valanced with a triple arch done with balancing scrolls, of which the central arch is the most pronounced, or with three nearly semicircular arcs. The lower edge of the skirt is either plain or finished with a narrow cock-bead molding. Sometimes the entire skirt is faced with burl veneer matching that of the drawer fronts. The skirt contains either a full-width drawer or, more generally, three to five narrow drawers. With this the usual arrangement is a central shallow drawer flanked by narrower ones twice as deep if there are only three drawers, and a tier above containing two half-width drawers if five are present.

The base is supported by six turned legs, four of them at the front. They are either trumpet-shaped, surmounted by inverted cups or trumpet-and-vase turned and are braced by a flat scrolled or concave box stretcher shaped to conform to the arched outline of the skirt. Legs terminate in amply turned ball or bun feet. A few of these highboys have only four trumpet-and-inverted-cup legs. These are braced by a flat scrolled X-stretcher and terminate in ball feet. Total height varies from five feet four inches to five feet 10 inches. Made in all sections, usually of walnut, with or without burl veneering, maple, maple and pine, maple and butternut, beech and pine or of basswood or tulipwood painted and grained to simulate walnut. *Ca. 1700–1720.* YYY to ZZ

202. Trumpet-Leg Lowboy

Design is the same as lower part of the foregoing highboy but noticeably smaller. Has rectangular top, 32 to 34 inches wide, with square corners and thumb-molded edge. It overhangs body about three inches at each end and half that at front. The skirt of body is deeply valanced in a triple arch done in balancing scrolls with the central one the most pronounced. Lower edge of skirt is usually finished with a narrow cock-bead molding and has two turned pendent finials. Sometimes faced with burl veneer, it contains three narrow draw-

202

ers, the central one shallow and flanked by deeper draw-ers.

Drawer openings are framed by arched moldings and the fronts are fitted with brass teardrop handles. Legs are either trumpet-and-inverted-cup or trumpet-and-vase turned. They are braced by a flat cyma-curved X-stretcher and terminate in ball or bun feet. Some ex-amples are made with six trumpet legs braced by a flat scrolled box stretcher and terminating in ball feet. Height varies from 28 to 30 inches. Made in all sections, generally of walnut but occasionally of maple. Not as numerous as highboys of the same period. *Ca. 1700–1720.* YY to Z

QUEEN ANNE

203. Flat-Top Highboy

Design and construction are similar to that of the William and Mary highboy except for the legs. These are cabriole, four in number, terminate in Dutch feet and are *not* stretcher-braced. The upper section, 36 to

203

44 inches wide, has either a simple, slightly overhanging molded cornice or a deeper one in which the lower cove element may mask a shallow full-width secret drawer. Carcase contains from four to six tiers of graduated drawers. The two upper tiers may be half-width or narrower, and flank a central drawer of double depth decorated with an incised carved fan or sunburst. The balance of the drawers are full-width.

Drawer fronts are either plain and framed by arched moldings or slightly overlapping with thumb-molded edges. If piece is of walnut, they may be faced with burl ash or walnut or crotch-walnut veneer and banded. Drawers of both sections are fitted with either brass teardrop handles and pierced cartouche-shaped keyhole escutcheons, or bat's-wing plates with bail handles and matching keyhole escutcheons.

The front corners of both sections are sometimes chamfered and fluted. The base has the usual triple-arched valanced skirt with or without two turned pendent finials at lower ends of its central arch. Drawer arrangement may be (1) three narrow drawers of equal depth, (2) a central shallow drawer flanked by two double-depth drawers or (3) a full-width drawer above three of medium depth with front of the central one carved to match the corresponding drawer of the upper section.

With a walnut highboy, the skirt is sometimes faced with veneer to match that of drawer fronts and its lower edge may be either plain or cock-beaded. Total height varies from five feet eight inches to six feet eight inches. Made in all sections of walnut, plain or curly maple, walnut and maple combined, cherry, applewood and sometimes pine with hardwood legs and finished with red filler. *Ca. 1720–1750.* YY to Z

204. Bonnet-Top Highboy

Upper section, 38 to 44 inches wide, is surmounted by a bonnet top and contains five tiers of graduated drawers. The top one consists of a deep central drawer, with front sunburst inlaid or carved in a sunburst or shell motif, flanked either by shallow drawers or by deeper ones with upper edges sloping towards the sides in cyma curves. Below this are four full-width drawers.

Drawer fronts in both sections are slightly overlapping with thumb-molded or cock-bead edges and are fitted with either brass bat's-wing or willow plates with bail handles and matching keyhole escutcheons. The skirt of the base is valanced, usually with triple arches, and contains either a full-width or two half-width shallow drawers above three deeper ones of equal width, the

204

central one either carved or inlaid to match similar drawer of upper section. When made of walnut, all drawer fronts may be faced with crotch-grain veneer Total height varies from seven feet to seven feet 10 inches. Made in all sections of walnut, maple and sometimes cherry. *Ca. 1730–1750.* Z to ZZZ

205. Lowboy

Frequently made to match a highboy with either flat or bonnet top. Decorative details identical but always from one fifth to one quarter smaller than highboy base. Has rectangular top from 30 to 36 inches wide that overhangs two to three inches at each end and less than two inches in front. Edge is molded or beveled and corners are rounded or incurved. Skirt is valanced, gen-

205

erally with cyma-curved triple arches with or without two pendent acorn turned finials. Lower edge is sometimes finished with cock-beading.

Skirt generally contains either a full-width or two half-width drawers above a tier of three narrower drawers. These are all of medium depth with the central one frequently either decorated with an inlaid sunburst or carved in sunburst or shell motif, or the central drawer is shallow and those flanking it are of double depth. All drawers have either slightly overlapping thumb-molded edges or are framed with single or double arched moldings. Their fronts are fitted with either bat's-wing or willow plates and bail handles and corresponding keyhole escutcheons.

Walnut pieces may have drawer fronts and skirt faced with crotch-grain veneer and banding. The front corners of the body are sometimes chamfered and fluted. The four slender cabriole legs terminate in Dutch, drake or Spanish feet. Height varies from 29 to 32 inches. Made in all sections of walnut, maple, plain or curly, or cherry. *Ca. 1720–1750.* YYY to Z

CHIPPENDALE

206

206. Flat-Top Highboy

Upper section, 44 to 46 inches wide, has generous molded cornice, sometimes with corners chamfered to match those of the carcase. The latter contains five tiers of graduated drawers with upper one or two sometimes divided into two or three narrower drawers of equal width. All drawer fronts are slightly overlapping with thumb-molded edges. Brasses are plain or pierced willow plates with bail handles and matching keyhole escutcheons.

The skirt of base is scroll-valanced and contains from one to three tiers of drawers. With the one tier, there is a full-width drawer of about the same depth as that of the lowest one in the upper section. When there are two or three tiers, the top one or two have full-width shallow drawers with narrower ones below, the central one often shallower than those that flank it. Piece is supported by four cabriole legs of medium length with knees sometimes shell-carved and terminating in claw-and-ball or drake feet. Total height varies from five feet six inches to six feet nine inches. Made in all sections of mahogany, walnut, plain or curly maple, cherry or infrequently of assorted hard and soft woods, finished with red filler. *Ca. 1750–1770.* YYY to ZZ

207

207. Bonnet-Top Highboy

The upper section, 40 to 46 inches wide, is surmounted by bonnet top and generally contains five tiers of gradu-ated drawers. The top tier is composed of a central deep drawer that is fan-carved and flanked by shallow, narrow ones. Beneath this are four full-width drawers flanked by either fluted pilasters or inset quarter-round reeded columns. These are sometimes repeated on the lower section.

All drawer fronts of both sections have either overlapping thumb-molded or cock-bead edges and are fitted with either bat's-wing or willow plates with bail handles and matching keyhole escutcheons of brass. The skirt of the lower section is valanced with a triple arch and contains a full-width shallow drawer above three narrower and deeper drawers, the central one fan-carved. Piece is supported by four cabriole legs, sometimes with scroll or foliage carved knees, which terminate in boldly done claw-and-ball feet. Height varies from seven to eight feet. Made in all sections, with exceptionally fine ones of New England provenance, of mahogany, cherry, maple or walnut. *Ca. 1750–1775.* Z to ZZZ

208. Philadelphia Highboy

Upper section, 41 to 46 inches wide, is surmounted by an elaborate broken pediment that is either silhouetted or enclosed to form a bonnet top. The central plinth supports a cartouche-shape finial either of scrolled openwork or with a central kidney motif. It is flanked at the corners by square molded plinths with carved flame and urn-turned finials. A shaped frieze is carved with a balancing design or rococo foliage scrolls done in relief.

The carcase contains five tiers of graduated drawers, sometimes surmounted by a frieze drawer ornamented by a carved shell medallion with or without flanking foliage scrolls. The top tier consists of three narrow drawers, the next of two half-width drawers and the remaining three are full-width. Drawers of both sections have overlapping fronts with thumb-molded edges. They are faced with crotch-grain veneer and fitted with plain

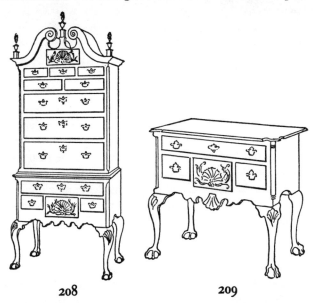

208   209

or diamond-pierced willow brasses with bail handles and matching keyhole escutcheons. The front corners of both sections have quarter-round reeded columns or are chamfered and fluted.

The skirt of the base is valanced in balancing scrolls flanking a central pendant carved with either a foliage scroll or a shell motif. Drawer arrangement includes a full-width top drawer with three narrower ones beneath. The central and widest one has an incised carved shell generally framed by balancing foliage scrolls carved in relief. The base is supported by four cabriole legs of medium height with foliage or scroll-carved knees that terminate in boldly done claw-and-ball feet. Total height varies from seven feet six inches to eight feet. Made of mahogany by the leading Philadelphia cabinet-makers, such as Savery, Gostelowe, Affleck and their contemporaries. *Ca. 1760–1770.* All are highly esteemed rarities. Q to QQQ

209. Lowboy

Has oblong top, 32 to 36 inches wide, with molded edge. Occasionally front corners are notched with balancing ogee curves. Top overhangs body two to three inches at each end and one or two inches at front. Skirt is valanced in a triple arch with pair of pendent turned acorn finials or has a scrolled outline with a pendent carved shell sometimes present at center.

Skirt generally contains a full-width shallow drawer above three narrower, deeper ones with that at center sometimes fan-carved. If made to match a Philadelphia highboy, the front of this narrow central drawer is carved with an incised shell flanked by foliage volutes carved in relief. Drawer fronts are overlapping with thumb-molded edges and fitted with plain or pierced willow brasses with bail handles and matching keyhole escutcheons. The fan or shell-carved drawer has either a small brass knob or a pendent loop handle placed at the axis of the carving. The front corners of the body may be plain, chamfered and fluted or have inset quarter-round fluted columns. Is supported by four cabriole legs of medium height with knees plain or carved in foliage or scroll motif and terminating in boldly carved claw-and-ball feet. Height varies from 29 to 31 inches. Made in all sections of mahogany, walnut or, in parts of New England, of cherry. Those of Philadelphia provenance, made by outstanding cabinetmakers such as Savery, Gostelowe or Affleck, are highly esteemed rarities. *Ca. 1750–1775.* YYY to Q

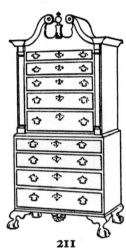

210   **211**

210. Flat-Top Chest-on-Chest

Is a variation of the highboy but differs in that both sections are chests of drawers and base has short bracket feet. Upper section, 40 to 50 inches wide, has a deeply molded flat cornice with front corners sometimes chamfered. It contains from four to five tiers of graduated drawers. Top tier frequently consists of two or three narrower drawers. Those below are full-width. Drawer fronts in both sections are slightly overlapping, have thumb-molded edges and are fitted with plain or pierced willow brasses with bail handles and matching keyhole escutcheons.

Front corners of both sections are frequently chamfered and fluted or have inset quarter-round reeded columns. Lower section contains two to four full-width drawers. Base of the lower section is molded and supported by four bracket feet. An early example has plain bracket feet; a later one, either molded and scrolled bracket feet or short cabriole brackets terminating in claw-and-ball feet; and still later, Hepplewhite French feet with valanced skirt. Total height varies from six to seven feet. Made in all sections of mahogany, walnut, cherry or curly maple. *Ca. 1750–1790.* YYY to ZZ

211. Chest-on-Chest with Broken Pediment

Has same structure and form as the foregoing but is surmounted by a broken pediment that may be either a frontal silhouette or an enclosed bonnet top. The design is of two kinds — molded cyma curves, plain or terminating in rosettes, or triangular gable form. With the first, finials, when present, may be either three carved and turned flames with urn bases or a central carved openwork cartouche flanked by turned urns at the corners. With a triangular pediment, the central finial may be either urn-shaped or a carved figure with or without flanking urns. The pediment may also have a horizontal matching molding and a carved frieze.

The upper section contains five tiers of graduated drawers with upper one consisting of three narrower drawers of which the center one is frequently deeper and fan-carved. All drawer fronts are either framed by cock-bead molding or are slightly overlapping with thumb-molded edges. They are fitted with willow brasses, plain or pierced, with bail handles, and have matching keyhole escutcheons. Drawers of upper section may be flanked by fluted pilasters or corners of both sections may be either chamfered and fluted or have inset quarter-round reeded columns. Base is supported by plain scrolled or molded and scrolled feet or by short cabriole brackets terminating in claw-and-ball feet. Total height varies from seven to eight feet. Made in all sections of mahogany, walnut, cherry and curly maple. Those designed and carved by Samuel McIntire of Salem, Massachusetts, are especially fine and such rarities that less than six examples are known. *Ca. 1760–1795.* Z to QQQ

Special Comments on the Linen Press and Its Construction

Is always a two-part piece. Consists of an upper cupboard section and a base which is a chest of drawers. The upper section is slightly narrower and shallower than the base and fits within the raised molding of its top.

Front of the cupboard section is enclosed by a pair of solid doors with large, slightly sunk panels. Door frames are joined by mortice and tenon joints, pinned by small dowels, the ends of which are visible.

The doors are usually hung with H-shaped or butt hinges. The right-hand door is fitted with a plate lock set in a mortice cut in the inner side of the stile and the other door is fitted with catches or sliding bolts.

Cupboard interior may have either shelves or sliding

trays. Other construction details of both sections are like those of a chest of drawers (*see Section VII, page 175*).

212

212. Linen Press

Upper section, 44 to 52 inches wide, has flat cornice that is usually boldly cove-molded but may have a more elaborate arcaded frieze. Door panels may be plain, arched at top or faced with crotch-grain veneer with inlaid oval sunbursts in light-colored wood. Doors are often hung with H-shaped brass hinges and inner stiles are fitted with either brass scrolled keyhole escutcheons or inset keyhole surrounds. Doors are sometimes flanked by reeded pilasters or the corners of section are chamfered and fluted.

Lower section contains three full-width drawers. Fronts are slightly overlapping, have thumb-molded or cock-bead edges and are fitted with willow brasses or small rosettes with bail handles and either small oval keyhole escutcheons or inset brass keyhole surrounds.

Has molded base without skirt and is supported by plain scrolled, molded bracket feet or by short cabriole brackets terminating in claw-and-ball feet. Made in all sections, especially Pennsylvania, New Jersey, New York and Connecticut, of mahogany, maple, walnut, cherry, pine or an assortment of hard and soft woods finished with red filler. *Ca. 1770–1810.* YY to QQ

Block-Front and Bombé Furniture

Two very different furniture designs were used by a limited number of American cabinetmakers between 1740 and 1775 for certain unusual and sophisticated pieces now known as block-front and bombé or kettle-base.

Block-front furniture takes its name from the triple formation of the front in which outer projecting blocks flank a central recessed one. This divides it into three vertical panels of equal width which are continuous with molded base, bearer strips and drawer fronts all shaped to conform to this convex-concave-convex line. The more elaborate pieces also have large carved shells capping the panels, done in relief when the panels project and incised when they are recessed. The finest of these shell-carved block-front pieces were the work of the Goddard-Townsend family of Newport, Rhode Island. Plain block-fronts, with the exception of some few knee-hole bureau tables made by an unidentified craftsman working in New York, were all produced within the limited area of southeastern Massachusetts, Rhode Island and Connecticut from the Connecticut River Valley east.

Bombé or kettle-base furniture is so named from the resemblance of the outcurved shaping of the lower front and sides of a piece to that of a large squat copper tea-kettle. This design of Italian-French origin was widely used in the Low Countries and somewhat less so in England by way of which it eventually reached America. Apparently it met with no great favor here as only a few cabinetmakers, working in or very close to Boston, are known to have made any bombé furniture.

Special Comments on Block-Front Furniture and Its Construction

The block-front is found on five case pieces — chest of drawers, knee-hole bureau table, slant-front bureau desk, slant-front secretary and chest-on-chest.

There are two kinds of block construction, plain and shell-carved. With the plain, the projections are more pronounced; the shell-carved are less so and each of the three vertical panels is surmounted by a somewhat flattened carved scallop shell of the same width, having from 11 to 13 rays. The shells that cap the outer projecting panels are carved in relief separately and then applied; the one above the recessed central panel is incised and carved as part of the panel.

The feet used for block-front pieces are of five kinds. They are (1) plain scrolled bracket, (2) molded bracket, (3) molded bracket with pronounced scrolls at each side, (4) short cabriole bracket with plain or foliage-carved knee terminating in a claw-and-ball foot and (5) a turned ball foot.

Drawer fronts are cut either from extra-thick pieces of wood or the projecting blocking is accomplished by applied pieces. Both methods were used but not combined on the same piece.

Other details of construction are the same as with similar case pieces (*see Section VII, page 175, and Section VIII, page 217*).

BLOCK–FRONT FURNITURE

213   **214**

213. Plain Chest of Drawers

Has rectangular, slightly overhanging top from 34 to 36 inches wide with front shaped to conform to blocking and cove-molded edge. Carcase contains four full-width graduated block-fronted drawers fitted with brass willow plates with bail handles and matching keyhole escutcheons. Narrow molded skirt, sometimes with central cyma-curved pendent finial. Supported by plain scrolled or molded bracket feet. Height varies from 30 to 36 inches. Made in New England of mahogany or walnut. Rare. *Ca. 1760–1775.* YYY to Z

214. Shell-Carved Chest of Drawers

Oblong top, 36 to 42 inches wide with straight front and cove-molded edge, has little overhang. Carcase contains either four full-width, graduated block-fronted drawers or three of equal depth. The front of top drawer is carved with scallop shells (outer ones in relief and central one incised). Drawer fronts are fitted with either willow brasses or small rosettes with bail handles and small oval keyhole escutcheons. Single or double cove-molded conforming base is supported by either molded brackets with pronounced scrolls on sides or short cabriole brackets terminating in claw-and-ball feet. Made at Newport, Rhode Island, of mahogany or sometimes of walnut, maple or applewood. All high-priced rarities. *Ca. 1760–1775.* ZZ to QQ

215   216

215. Knee-Hole Bureau Desk

Rectangular top, 32 to 36 inches wide with shaped front and cove-molded edge, overhangs case about two inches on sides and an inch at front. Carcase contains single full-width block-fronted drawer of medium depth. Its interior is sometimes equipped with pivoted writing flap and compartments for pens, ink bottle and sand shaker. Its front is fitted with a pair of willow brass plates with bail handles and matching keyhole escutcheon. Beneath it is a central knee-hole recessed six to eight inches and backed by a door having a panel that is either chamfer-arched or incised and surmounted by a carved scallop shell, also incised. Door is sometimes hung with H-shaped brass hinges and fitted with either a small brass knob or a brass keyhole escutcheon. This door gives access to a cupboard, with or without shelf, which may have shallow secret drawer at top with concealing scroll-carved front. At top of knee-hole there is usually a shallow full-depth drawer of same width as knee-hole with concave valanced front, not fitted with brass handle. Two tiers of three narrow graduated drawers with projecting blocks flank the knee-hole and in turn may be flanked by reeded pilasters. Their fronts are fitted with single willow brasses, sometimes pierced with keyholes. The shaped double- or triple-molded base is supported by six feet. These may be plain scrolled or molded brackets or turned ball feet. Total height varies from 30 to 34 inches. Made of mahogany or sometimes of walnut in New England and occasionally in New York City. Not numerous. *Ca. 1740–1775.* ZZZ to Q

216. Shell-Carved Knee-Hole Bureau Table

Has rectangular top with straight front 34 to 36 inches wide with slightly projecting molded edge. Construction is the same as the plain block-front table just described. Top drawer front has three carved scallop shells, the outer ones in relief and the central one incised. Its interior may be equipped with a writing flap and compartments for writing materials. Central knee-hole is backed by incised paneled and shell-carved door but lacks top shallow drawer usually found with the foregoing table. All drawer fronts are fitted with willow brass plates, with or without pierced keyholes. The shaped double-molded base is supported by six molded bracket feet with pronounced scrolls at sides. Height varies from 31 to 34 inches. Made of mahogany at Newport. *Ca. 1765–1775.* A high-priced rarity. Q to QQQ

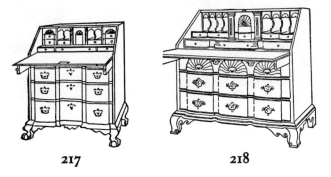

217   **218**

217. Slant-Front Bureau Desk

Construction is like that of other slant-front bureau desks except for the block formation of the carcase front (*see No. 172*). The slanting front sometimes has three carved fan-motif plaquettes, the outer ones raised and the center one incised.

Writing compartment is handsomely fashioned with four arched pigeonholes above a double or triple tier of small drawers on either side of central locker, flanked by document boxes with pilastered or molded fronts. Fan carving of slanting front is generally repeated on the locker door as well as on the arching of each pigeonhole, which can mask shallow secret drawer. Slanting front is fitted with a willow brass keyhole escutcheon and matching brasses appear on drawer fronts. The double-molded base, with or without cyma-curved central pendent finial, is supported by short cabriole brackets terminating in claw-and-ball feet. Height varies from 46 to 50 inches. Made in New England of mahogany or occasionally of walnut. Not numerous. *Ca. 1760–1775.* YYY to ZZ

218. Shell-Carved Bureau Desk

Is similar in construction to the foregoing. The raised and incised shells capping corresponding panels when present on the carcase front limit the full-width drawers to three. If there are four drawers, the front blocking is continued upward and includes the slanting front with the raised and incised shells occurring there instead.

In the writing compartment these raised and recessed panels with corresponding carved shells are repeated on the fronts of the outer small drawers and on the locker door. As a variation the locker door sometimes has a raised panel and shell and the fronts of the very shallow drawers at the top of the flanking pigeonholes have incised carved shells.

The slanting front when plain is fitted with a centered willow brass keyhole escutcheon, but if paneled and with carved shells, it has two smaller oval brass keyhole escutcheons placed above the narrow spacing on either side of the central panel and shell. The fronts of all full-width drawers are fitted with willow brasses. Has a double-molded base and is supported by four molded bracket feet with pronounced side scrolls. Made in Newport, Rhode Island, of mahogany or walnut. Always an expensive rarity. *Ca. 1760–1775.* ZZZ to QQ

219. Block-Front Secretary

Like other secretaries is in two parts (*see Nos. 174, 175, 179 and 180*). The block-fronted lower section can be either plain or shell-carved. Upper section is surmounted by a bonnet top. With the plain block-front, this upper section has two doors with shaped panels.

The shell-carved type has three doors which repeat the projecting and recessed blocking of the lower part and are surmounted by corresponding carved shells. This same block and shell motif decorates the slanting front

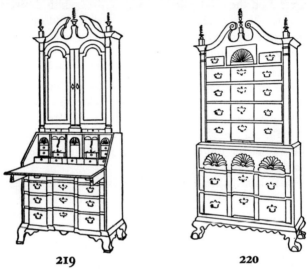

219　　　　　　　**220**

of the lower section. Secretary is supported by four molded brackets or by short cabriole brackets terminating in claw-and-ball feet. Dimensions vary from 44 to 48 inches in width and from eight to nine feet in height. Made of mahogany or sometimes walnut in New England. Shell-carved examples always high-priced rarities. *Ca. 1760–1775.* ZZZ to QQQ

220. Block-Front Chest-on-Chest

Construction is the same as with other like pieces (*see No. 210 and No. 211*), except for blocking of front.

Majority of these pieces have this formation only on front of lower part. They are usually of the plain block-front type though a few examples have the raised and incised shell carvings. Bonnet-topped upper section usually has no blocking. In the few exceptions there is the consistent repetition of the triple block panels surmounted by carved scallop shells to match the lower section.

With the plain upper section, the five or six tiers of drawers are frequently flanked by reeded pilasters and the top tier is composed of three narrow drawers, the center of double depth with its front shell or sunburst carved. The rest of the drawers in both sections are full width and graduated. Carved drawer fronts are fitted with brass knobs; the others with willow brasses. Base, either shaped and molded, frequently with central pendent finial, or straight and valanced, is supported by four plain scrolled brackets or short cabriole brackets terminating in claw-and-ball feet. Dimensions vary from 38 to 44 inches wide by seven feet six inches to eight feet 10 inches high. Made only in Massachusetts, Rhode Island and Connecticut of mahogany, cherry or walnut. Not numerous. *Ca. 1760–1775.* ZZZ to QQ

BOMBÉ OR KETTLE-BASE

Special Comment on Bombé Furniture and Its Construction

The bombé or kettle-base occurs with three case pieces —chest of drawers, slant-front desk and slant-front secretary.

The curved sides were always cut in one piece from

thick planks. The outcurved fronts of the three lower drawers were also made from plank-thick wood and their sides shaped to conform to the bombé curve of the carcase. This resulted in a considerable waste of wood and made such pieces expensive.

Other construction details are the same as with similar case pieces (*see Section VII, page 175, and Section VIII, page 217*).

221

221. Bombé Chest of Drawers

Has a rectangular, slightly overhanging top with molded edge, from 36 to 40 inches wide. Front and sides of the carcase are boldly curved, starting just below the top drawer and returning above the molded base. There are four full-width drawers. The front of the top drawer is plain and those of the three lower ones are shaped to conform to the kettlelike shape of the carcase. All fronts have cock-bead edges and are fitted with willow brasses. The triple-molded base, with or without a central scrolled pendent, is supported by four short cabriole brackets with plain or foliage-carved knees that terminate in carved claw-and-ball feet. Height varies from 35 to 37 inches. Made only of mahogany in or near Boston. *Ca. 1765-1775.* Z to ZZ

Bombé Bureau Desk

Structurally is like the bombé chest of drawers just described. Writing section has a slant-front supported by two pull-brackets and the interior is compartmented with the usual pigeonholes, central locker and small drawers. Desk is from 40 to 46 inches wide and from 44 to 48 inches tall. Made only of mahogany in or near Boston. *Ca. 1765-1775.* ZZ to ZZZ

Bombé Secretary

The lower section is the same as the bombé desk. It is surmounted by a cupboard with broken pediment top having turned urn and flame finials. The front is enclosed by a pair of solid doors with scroll-outlined, slightly sunk panels that are sometimes flanked by reeded pilasters. In the base of this upper part are a pair of pull-out candlestick shelves with molded overlapping fronts fitted with small brass knobs. Total height varies from seven feet two inches to eight feet four inches. Made only of mahogany in or near Boston. Is the finest and rarest of the bombé furniture. *Ca. 1765-1775.* ZZZ to QQ

Sideboards, Hunt Boards, Sugar Chests

AMERICAN-MADE sideboards are of three types — the long or standard sideboard, the New England short sideboard and the hunt board. All date within the span of a little more than a half-century, or from 1785 to 1840.

The long sideboard came first and, with variations, was made in three styles: Hepplewhite, Sheraton and American Empire. The short sideboard was peculiar to New England. It always has a simpler arrangement of drawers and a single central cupboard. Made during the quarter-century, 1800 to 1825, it is similar in outline to a chest of drawers and is Sheraton in style, save for a few examples that are Hepplewhite in feeling.

The hunt board was made only south of the Mason and Dixon Line. A long-legged piece that combined the attributes of a serving table and a sideboard, it was designed for the convenience of hungry hunters who came direct from the chase. The earliest type consisted of a slab of yellow pine, four or five feet long, that rested on four legs and stood about four feet high. From it evolved the more conventional but still simple piece with drawers and central cupboard. Never part of the dining room furniture, it was put in the back hall of the main house or in one of the detached plantation buildings where an after-the-hunt meal was served buffet style.

Special Comments on Sideboards and Their Construction

Most sideboards are supported by six slender tapering legs, four at the front, that are square or turned and usually from 18 to 22 inches long. The upper extensions of them are the stiles to which the sides and front of the carcase are joined by mortice and tenon joints.

Cupboard doors are generally flush, veneer-faced and hung with brass butt hinges. Those of hunt boards may be either plain or have slightly sunk panels.

The sideboard carcase is usually faced with mahogany and has satinwood or curly maple panels and banding for decorative contrast. Where there is stringing, holly or boxwood is used.

Both sideboards and hunt boards have slightly overhanging top and some have an ornamented backboard or gallery.

Other construction details are like those of the chest of drawers (*see Section VII, page 175*).

HEPPLEWHITE

222. Serpentine-Front Sideboard

Has oblong top, five to seven feet long with boldly serpentined front. Generally the edge is faced with crotch-grain veneer with or without inlaid stringing. The extensions of the four front legs form pilasters that divide the front into a wide central section which is convex and flanking ones that are concave. These pilasters have oval or oblong panels outlined by stringing. Sometimes the two interior legs and their upper pilaster extensions are set diagonally and all four pilasters are stringing-outlined. The central section of the carcase contains a wide shallow drawer with convex front to conform to the shaping of the top. Beneath it is a slightly

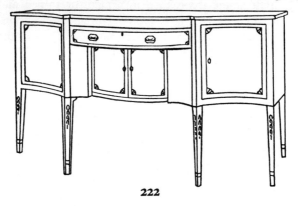

222

recessed cupboard of equal width that is enclosed by a pair of balancing concave doors, veneer-faced and generally with veneer panels and stringing.

The narrower end sections each have either a single-doored cupboard or a cupboard with a shallow drawer above. Both drawer fronts and cupboard doors are concave to conform to the top. Sometimes what appears to be a cupboard door in an end section is the front of a deep drawer fitted for bottles. Drawer fronts and doors are faced with crotch-grain veneer, frequently with inset oval panels outlined by stringing or with rectangular panels having fan-motif inlays at the corners. Drawer fronts are fitted with oval brass plates with bail handles and oval brass or inlaid diamond-shaped keyhole escutcheons or inset keyhole surrounds.

Fronts of the six supporting legs are outlined with stringing and frequently have either inlaid bellflower or pendent husks done in light wood as well as crossbanding to simulate feet. Sometimes the legs terminate in small spade feet. Height varies from 40 to 44 inches. Made in all sections of mahogany with liberal use of crotch-grain veneer, satinwood inlay and holly or box stringing, or of cherry with curly or bird's-eye maple veneer panels. *Ca. 1790–1800.* YYY to Q

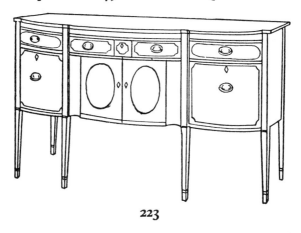

223

223. Bow-Front Sideboard

Is similar to the foregoing, but top and front have a slightly convex continuous curve. Total length is from five feet to six feet two inches. Central section of carcase contains a wide shallow drawer with conforming front above either a slightly recessed cupboard with a pair of doors that conform to the line of top or a second wide drawer with arched skirt beneath. The end sections contain shallow drawers with conforming fronts above (1) single cupboards, (2) a cupboard at one end and a cellaret drawer at the other or (3) a cellaret drawer at each end. Drawer fronts and doors are faced with crotch-grain veneer paneled with stringing. Drawers are fitted with oval brass plates and bail handles and either diamond-shaped inlaid keyhole escutcheons or inset brass keyhole surrounds. Doors have like keyhole fittings.

Carcase is supported by six tapering square legs paneled with stringing. Sometimes there is the added decoration of bellflower inlays and crossbanding to simulate feet. Height varies from 38 to 42 inches. Made in all sections of mahogany with crotch-grain veneer, satinwood panels and stringing. Not as numerous as the serpentine-front sideboard. *Ca. 1790–1800.* YYY to ZZ

224. Half-Moon Sideboard

Takes its name from its semi-elliptical shape of top and carcase and is about a foot shorter than other sideboards. Top is from four feet four inches to five feet six inches long. The edge is finished with either crotchgrain veneer or checkered inlaid fillet. The pilaster extensions of the four interior legs divide the front into three sections flanked by convex ends. The central section contains a top drawer and beneath it either a matching drawer and arched skirt or an arched knee-hole with recessed single-door cupboard. The sections on either side contain two drawers or a drawer with cupboard beneath. The convexed ends have two false drawer fronts that match the others.

All drawer fronts and cupboard doors are faced with

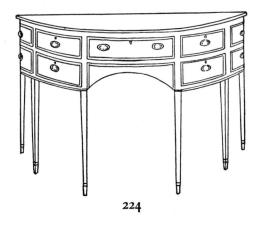

224

crotch-grain veneer paneled with stringing or banding and have cock-bead edges. Drawer fronts are fitted with brass oval plates with bail handles. These and the doors have either oval brass or inlaid diamond-shaped keyhole escutcheons or brass keyhole surrounds. The carcase is supported by six square tapering legs that are sometimes inlaid with bellflower or husk inlays and crossbanding simulating feet. Height varies from 38 to 42 inches. Made in all sections of mahogany, sometimes with rosewood banding. Not numerous. *Ca. 1790–1800.* YYY to Z

225. Straight-Front Sideboard

Has rectangular top, four feet six inches to six feet 10 inches long. Edge is faced with either crotch-grain veneer or a checkered band of inlay. The upper extensions of two interior legs divide front into three sections. The central one contains a wide shallow drawer with a flush or slightly recessed double-door cupboard below. The end sections each contain either a shallow drawer with cupboard below or only a cupboard. Drawer fronts and cupboard doors are faced with crotch-

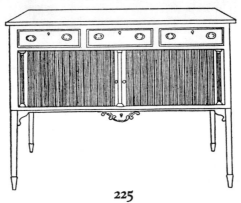

225

grain veneer paneled with stringing, sometimes with inlaid fan-motif medallions at corners, and have cock-bead edges. Pilaster extensions of the legs are either plain or have oval inlays or mock fluting. Drawer fronts are fitted with brass oval plates with bail handles. Drawers and doors have either inlaid diamond-shaped keyhole escutcheons or brass keyhole surrounds. Carcase is supported by six tapering square legs, sometimes with bell-flower or husk inlays and crossbanding simulating feet.

With some examples with four or six legs, vertical tambour slides replace the cupboard doors. Sometimes made of alternate strips of mahogany and satinwood, they are flanked by reeded or plain pilasters. Below are one or two scrolled pendants containing locks and fitted with brass keyhole surrounds. With this variation, the carcase is supported by only *four* legs terminating in spade feet.

Straight-front sideboard with six legs, inlaid, is largely of Baltimore or Philadelphia provenance; that with tambour work and four legs is of Boston origin. Made in all sections of mahogany with crotch-grain veneer, satinwood inlay and sometimes rosewood banding. Not as numerous as sideboards with shaped fronts. *Ca. 1780–1800.* YYY to Q

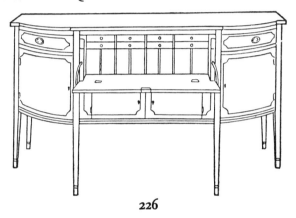

226

226. Break-Front Sideboard

Has rectangular top, five feet two inches to six feet four inches long, with a central straight section projecting about two inches and flanked by narrower convex ones. Edge of top is either banded with crotch-grain veneer or inlaid with stringing. The front of the carcase is divided into sections conforming to shape of the top. Central one usually contains a wide, deep fall-front drawer that pulls out halfway and is supported by

quadrant brass brackets. It has a writing interior compartmented at rear with six to eight pigeonholes above
or below small drawers fitted with either small brass or
turned wooden knobs. This construction detail is like
that of the fall-front desk and of the break-front secretary (*see No. 183 and No. 185*).

When sideboard is without this butler's desk, there
are two shallower drawers instead of a cupboard with
double doors, sometimes flanked by narrow bottle drawers.

The convex end sections each contain a shallow
drawer above a cupboard with conforming front. All
drawers and doors are paneled with veneer and stringing or banding and have cock-bead edges. Drawer fronts
are fitted with brass oval plates with bail handles. Keyholes of both drawers and cupboard doors have oval
brass or inlaid diamond-shaped escutcheons or brass surrounds. The pilasters above the legs are plain or paneled
with stringing. Carcase is supported by six tapering
square legs, sometimes with stringing and bellflower
inlays, and are crossbanded to simulate feet. Made in
all sections of mahogany with crotch-grain veneer, satinwood inlay and box or holly stringing, or of cherry or
curly maple without inlay or banding. About as numerous as serpentine-front sideboards. *Ca. 1790–1800.*
YYY to ZZ

SHERATON

227. Bow-Front Sideboard

Has a rectangular top, four feet eight inches to five
feet nine inches long with front bowed from end to end

in a continuous curve. Edge is either banded with crotch-grain veneer or has inlaid stringing. The carcase front conforms to shaping of top and is divided into three sections by plain or string-paneled pilasters above

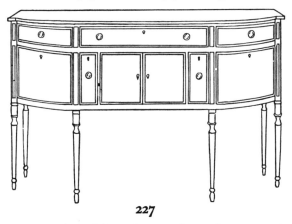

227

the interior legs. The pilasters above the corner legs are either flush and matching the others or are outset, three-quarter round and reeded.

The wide central section contains a full-width, medium-deep drawer with conforming front above a double-doored cupboard which is flanked by a pair of bottle drawers. The end sections each have a shallow drawer above a cupboard with single door. All drawer fronts and doors are faced and banded with crotch-grain veneer and have cock-bead edges. The drawers are fitted with brass rosette knobs and both drawers and doors have brass oval or oblong keyhole escutcheons or inset keyhole surrounds. The carcase is supported by four or six slender turned and reeded legs. Height varies from 36 to 42 inches. Made in all sections of mahogany with crotch-grain or satinwood veneer inlays, cherry with curly maple inlays, or curly maple, either plain or with crotch-grain mahogany inlays. *Ca. 1800–1820.* YY to Z

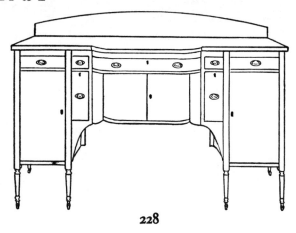

228

228. Break-Front Sideboard

Has rectangular top, five feet six inches to six feet six inches long, with wide central section projecting about two inches. This is either straight or slightly curved and is flanked by narrower straight-front sections. Sometimes has an arched backboard or gallery. Central section of carcase contains a shallow wide drawer with conforming front that is frequently flanked by a pair of narrow shallow cutlery drawers. Beneath it is a double-door cupboard with plain or conforming doors that are usually flanked by a pair of narrow bottle drawers. The end sections each have a shallow full-width drawer at top with a tall single-door cupboard beneath. All drawer fronts and cupboard doors are faced with crotch-grain veneer, have cock-bead edges, and are sometimes paneled with banding. Drawers are fitted with either oval brass plates with bail handles or brass rosette knobs. These and doors have brass inset keyhole surrounds.

The carcase is supported by six turned and reeded legs. Height, including gallery, varies from 42 to 52 inches. Made in all sections of mahogany with liberal use of crotch-grain veneer and sometimes rosewood banding, or of cherry or curly maple, with or without crotch-grain mahogany veneer. *Ca. 1800–1820.* YY to ZZ

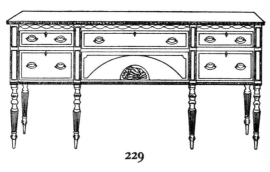

229

229. Straight-Front Sideboard

Has oblong top, five feet two inches to six feet four inches long. Edge is banded with either crotch-grain veneer or inlaid stringing. Front of carcase is divided into three sections by pilasters above interior legs. The wide central section contains a full-width shallow drawer above either a deeper drawer with arcaded front or a tall double-door cupboard. The end sections each have either a shallow drawer above a deeper one or a tall single-door cupboard. Drawer fronts are faced with either satinwood or crotch-grain veneer, have cock-bead edges and are fitted with oval brass plates with bail handles or brass rosette knobs and oval brass or diamond keyhole escutcheons or brass keyhole surrounds.

Cupboard doors are crotch-grain veneered and banded or may have slightly sunk panels faced with crotch-grain veneer. They are fitted with brass keyhole escutcheons or brass keyhole surrounds. Carcase is supported by six turned and reeded legs. These are short when tall cupboards are present. Height varies from 42 to 46 inches. Made in all sections of mahogany with crotch-grain, satinwood or curly maple veneer, or sometimes all of cherry or fancy-grained maple. *Ca. 1800–1820.* YY to ZZ

230. New England Short Sideboard

Has oblong top, 36 to 48 inches long with front either straight or bowed and front corners square or three-quarter round outsets. The edge is faced with crotch-grain veneer, has stringing or is plain. Carcase front conforms to the shaping of the top and contains a cupboard with double doors flanked by bottle drawers located either above or below one or two full-width drawers. Doors and drawer fronts are straight or shaped to conform to the top, usually faced with satinwood or bird's-eye maple veneer and often veneer-paneled and banded. Drawer fronts and doors have cock-bead edges.

Drawers are fitted with oval or oblong brass plates with bail handles, brass rosette or mushroom-turned wooden knobs. Keyholes on doors and drawers have oval or oblong brass or inlaid diamond escutcheons or brass inset surrounds. The bottom of the carcase is straight or has an arched valanced skirt, sometimes with a pendent central plaquette faced with satinwood or bird's-eye maple veneer. The front corners of the car-

230

case frequently have three-quarter round pilasters either reeded, with capitals of wide bands of satinwood or bird's-eye maple veneer, or ring-turned. They terminate in turned and reeded legs, eight to 12 inches long with matching ones at back.

If the corners are square, the carcase is supported by four slender turned and plain or reeded legs. An early example will have slender square tapering legs. Height varies from 36 to 42 inches. Made only in New England. Mahogany with satinwood veneer used for more sophisticated examples; others of cherry with bird's-eye maple veneer, or fancy-grain maple or birch with crotch-grain mahogany or cherry veneer. Finest examples are of Boston or Salem provenance. *Ca. 1795–1825.* YY to ZZ

AMERICAN EMPIRE

231

231. Straight-Front Sideboard

Has oblong top, four to six feet long, with half-round
crotch-grain veneered edge and a shaped gallery, arched
or with voluted corners. The upper part of the front is
an overhanging deep frieze containing either two half-
width drawers with torus-molded or ogee fronts that
sometimes have finger grooves on the underside instead
of handles, or two tiers of full and half-width drawers
with flat veneered and banded fronts fitted with mushroom-turned wooden knobs. Beneath the frieze are
either two wide cupboards flanking two tiers of narrow bottle drawers or a double-door cupboard flanked
by single-door cupboards. Doors are faced with crotch-
grain veneer and have slightly sunk square or oblong
panels. They are fitted with oval or oblong brass keyhole escutcheons or brass keyhole surrounds.

These cupboards are flanked either by acanthus-leaf carved pilasters or by columns, plain or spirally reeded, which support the overhanging frieze. The ends of the carcase have large oblong, slightly sunk panels that are crotch-grain veneered. Has a plain base faced with crotch-grain veneer, outsquared at the corners to form plinths for the columns or pilasters above. It is supported either by carved paw feet with acanthus-leaf carved knees at front and turned rear legs or by four stout ring-turned legs terminating in small ball feet. Height, including gallery, varies from four to four feet eight inches. Made in all sections with liberal use of crotch-grain veneer. *Ca. 1820–1840.* XXX to YYY

232

232. Southern Hunt Board

Has oblong top, four to six feet long, with square corners and plain edges. Front of carcase is straight and contains (1) a central cupboard flanked by two deep drawers, (2) two shallow central drawers flanked by cupboards or (3) two half-width drawers of medium depth. Drawer fronts are plain or sometimes have cock-bead edges and are fitted with plain brass or turned wooden knobs and brass keyhole surrounds. Doors have plain or slightly sunk panels with tops sometimes arched, and are fitted with brass pendent ring handles, turned wooden knobs or keyhole surrounds. Carcase is supported by four or six long tapering legs, square or ring-and-baluster turned. Height varies from 42 to 52 inches. Provenance from Virginia south and as far west as Kentucky. Are mostly simple plantation-made pieces of walnut or southern hard pine. *Ca. 1790–1830.* XXX to YYY

233

233. Sugar Chest

A southern plantation piece, made when sugar was a luxury and used to keep it under lock and key along with coffee, tea, spices and other scarce and costly items.

Has a rectangular, slightly overhanging lid, 32 to 44 inches wide, which either is hinged at the back or is in two pieces with rear one fixed and front one hinged to it. Beneath it is a well about 14 to 16 inches deep that is divided into compartments or bins, the larger for sugar and smaller ones for coffee, tea and spices. Front of well is plain and centered at top is a simple brass keyhole escutcheon or an inset keyhole surround.

Below the well the carcase contains a full-width drawer, eight to 12 inches deep, with overlapping thumb-molded edges. It is fitted with brass, glass or mushroom-turned knobs and brass keyhole matching that of well. Ends of carcase are either plain or stile and rail constructed with large rectangular, slightly sunk panels. Is supported by turned and reeded, vase-turned or square tapering legs. Height varies from 34 to 38 inches and depth from 18 to 20 inches.

Made only south of the Mason-Dixon line, mostly by plantation carpenter-cabinetmakers, of walnut, cherry or other native hardwoods. Is an interesting example of a piece made for a specific purpose. Not collected outside of the South. Examples dating before 1800 are unusual. *Ca. 1750–1840.* XXX to YY

Cupboards and Dressers

CUPBOARDS are of two kinds, the triangular corner cupboard and the rectangular one that stands against the wall of a room. In the latter group, along with the open-face and closed-front dressers, can be included the ornamental seventeenth-century court and press cupboards and the Dutch kas, all of which are door-enclosed furniture for storing household accessories.

As the term indicates, the *cup board* began as a shelf for cups and other dishes. Increasing the number of shelves, putting them within a supporting frame and adding enclosed closet space resulted in a piece of furniture large enough to hold a quantity of tableware and related items. It was first made in America about 1660 and continued for close to two centuries. The examples which collectors see most frequently are the corner cupboard and the dresser with upper shelves either open or enclosed by double glass doors. As one-piece built-in fixtures, they were the work of house carpenters while the movable ones in two parts were generally made by cabinetmakers.

Very simple corner cupboards were made as early as 1675 and there were probably crude dressers too, but none have survived. The earliest of the rectangular cupboards still extant are the court and press cupboards. Both are architectural Puritan Span furniture and look more like cabinets than the general concept of a cupboard.

Judging from the numbers that are available to collectors today, corner cupboards and dressers must have been popular and made in considerable numbers in all sections from 1740 onward. Court and press cupboards and kases date earlier. The former are distinct rarities, seldom seen outside a museum, and the wardrobe-like kas, peculiar to Americans of Holland descent and the Pennsylvania Dutch who migrated here from the Rhine Valley, is not popular because of its size.

Special Comments on Corner Cupboards, Dressers and Kindred Pieces and Their Construction

Corner cupboards and dressers occur as one- and two-part pieces. The one-part, built-in type was the work of house carpenters. Except for their doors, they have only plain butt joints fastened with hand-wrought or cut nails. Glazed or paneled doors have mortice and tenon joints and the ends of the muntins which hold the small panes of glass are morticed into the frames. Plain solid doors have nailed batten strips on the inner sides. Doors are hung with H-shaped or rat-tail exposed hinges or plain butt hinges, and are fitted with turned wooden knobs and wooden turn buttons. These pieces are without molded base or feet and rest directly on the floor.

Two-part movable corner cupboards and dressers were the work of cabinetmakers. The upper part of a corner cupboard is slightly smaller and fits behind a raised molding at the top of the lower part. With a dresser, the narrower recessed upper part rests on the counter top of the lower section and the ends of its sides have tenons that fit into mortices cut in counter top. Both pieces are supported by short bracket feet.

Mortice and tenon joints are used for joining members on fronts of two-part cupboards and dressers; sides, tops and bottoms are more frequently nailed butt joints than dovetails. Backboards are smoothly planed on the front, left rough on the back and nailed in place. Doors have the same construction details as those of built-in pieces but are usually fitted with locks, brass knobs and key-hole escutcheons.

Upper sections of dressers are recessed a third to half the depth of the lower sections whether they are in one or two parts.

With the closed-front dresser, the upper section is generally raised from four to six inches above the counter top and supported by extensions of the sides. The backboards also rest on the counter top, making an open space between the two sections that is enclosed at sides and back.

Shelves in upper part of both cupboards and dressers fit into grooves cut in the sides and are not adjustable. They are straight in dressers and generally have sixteen or more notches in which silver or pewter spoons can be hung. Shelves in corner cupboards are either straight or deeply concave. Some of the latter have an ample half-round central projection.

Drawers have the same construction details as those in chests of drawers (*see Section VII, page 175*).

Court and press cupboards have the stile and rail construction of other seventeenth-century pieces. Mortice and tenon joints are used throughout for stiles and rails. They are pinned with small dowels, the ends of which are visible. Extensions of corner stiles serve as feet.

With both types the upper part is recessed and its overhanging cornice is supported at the corners by columns or has turned pendant finials. Backs as well as fronts and sides are paneled but not as smoothly finished.

In addition to carved ornamentation, done in low relief, applied split turnings and bosses are used. These and the wooden knobs are generally painted black and the background of the carved panels is sometimes painted red.

Drawers have the same construction details as in chests, except that alternating wide and narrow dovetails are used (*see Section VII, page 175*).

The kas is also stile and rail constructed except for its base. Here the corners are dovetailed and clearly visible.

234. Built-in Corner Cupboard

Has diagonal front, 34 to 40 inches wide, sometimes flanked by plain canted returns four to 10 inches wide. Cornice is flat or simply molded. Carpenter-made, cupboard is in one piece without molded base. Handwrought nails are used throughout. Contains two cupboards. Upper one, a third to a half taller than lower, has open front framed by scroll-cut sides and top and is fitted with two or three concave shelves, sometimes boldly outrounded at center.

Lower cupboard is enclosed by single solid door, plain

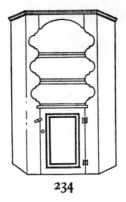

234

or paneled. It is fitted with a pair of plain, H-shaped, butterfly or strap wrought-iron hinges, a turned wooden knob and a wooden turn button. It generally contains a single shelf with straight front. Height varies from six to seven feet. Made in all sections of pine or other native woods and finished with red filler or paint. *Ca. 1675–1750*. Y to Z

Survival Examples

Were made for farmhouses seventy-five years longer. Are generally without scrolled framing and shelves of upper cupboard are either straight or only slightly concave. Nearly always crudely made of an assortment of softwoods and painted. *Ca. 1750–1825*. XX to Y

235. Architectural Built-In Corner Cupboard

Construction is same as foregoing but diagonal front is from 40 to 58 inches wide. Ornamental details are architectural and match design of room trim. Has flat, overhanging, molded and denticulated cornice, fre-

235

quently supported by plain or fluted pilasters that flank upper and lower doors. Upper cupboard has arched opening and is enclosed by single or double doors. When glazed, glass at top is of small panes that conform to semicircular arch, with those beneath rectangular. The muntins which retain the small panes of glass form a geometric pattern. The interior is fitted with three concave shelves having boldly outrounded centers. At the top there is often a shell-shaped dome of carved wood with alternating incised and raised rays. This dome is sometimes supported by interior fluted pilasters or colonnettes.

The lower cupboard contains a single plain shelf and is enclosed by either single or double doors with flush, bevel-edged rectangular panels. Doors are hung with butt or H-shaped hinges and fitted with either small brass knobs or pendent loop handles and sometimes scrolled brass keyhole escutcheons. Cupboard is without molded base and rests directly on floor. Height varies from six feet 10 inches to eight feet two inches. Made in all sections of pine or other softwood and painted. *Ca. 1720–1800.* Y to YYY

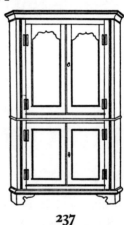

236   **237**

236. Movable Corner Cupboard with Glazed Doors

Is made in two parts, otherwise construction is similar to that of built-in cupboard. Diagonal front of both sections is from three to over four feet wide and has either canted returns or fluted pilasters flanking upper and lower doors. Upper section is surmounted by a flat molded cornice or, with a more elaborate example, a broken arch pediment with balancing scrolls in silhouette and turned or carved finials. Cupboard beneath is enclosed by a single glazed door or by a matching pair that are either rectangular or have an arched top. With the latter, the upper muntins and panes are shaped to conform to this semicircular arch. Interior contains two or three concave shelves outrounded at center.

Lower section frequently has a tier of one to three shallow drawers placed above the single or double paneled doors which enclose the lower cupboard. This is fitted with one or two plain shelves. Drawer fronts have either bat's-wing or willow brass plates with bail handles or small brass knobs. Has molded base and rests on plain or molded bracket feet. Total height for flat-top cupboard varies from seven to eight feet and for broken pediment type from seven feet 10 inches to nine feet two inches. Made in all sections of walnut, maple, cherry, sometimes of mahogany and frequently of pine and painted. *Ca. 1730–1800.* Y to YYY

237. Movable Corner Cupboard with Paneled Doors

Like foregoing with similar construction, it is usually in two parts. Details are either simple or architectural. The diagonal front is from 44 to 58 inches wide, has a flat, slightly overhanging molded cornice and either canted returns or flat fluted pilasters. Upper part is enclosed by double doors with slightly sunk panels, scrolled or arched at top. Interior contains two or three fixed shelves. Lower part sometimes has a tier of one to three shallow drawers placed above the pair of rectangular, plain paneled doors. Those of both sections are hung with either butt or H-shaped hinges and are fitted with scrolled brass keyhole escutcheons. Drawer fronts have bat's-wing or willow brass plates and bail handles or small brass knobs. Molded base rests on plain or molded bracket feet. Total height varies from seven to eight feet. Made in all sections of walnut, cherry, plain or curly maple and less frequently of pine, painted. *Ca. 1750–1800*. Y to YYY

238

238. Court Cupboard

Takes its name from the French word *court* and designates a short or low cupboard. Made in two parts, the upper one has a flat top 46 to 52 inches wide and 22 to 24 inches deep with simply molded edge. Below it is a cornice frieze, four to six inches high, that is either molded or carved in low relief and has centered applied bosses. It is supported at corners by baluster-turned columns, ebonized. The front beneath this is recessed about six inches and consists of a central door that gives access to a full-width cupboard flanked by sharply canted fixed sections. They are of about equal width and have slightly sunk panels framed by moldings in geometric patterns with applied ebonized bosses. The door has an elongated turned wooden knob and the stiles flanking it have applied and ebonized split baluster turnings.

The lower section on which this upper cupboard part rests has a slightly overhanging top with molded edge. Beneath it are two half-width drawers with sunk panel fronts which are framed by geometrically arranged moldings and have bosses and knobs to match those above. Drawers are flanked by applied split baluster turnings also like those in upper section. The space below is open and the supporting corner stiles at the front are replaced by columns matching those of the upper section with molded stiles at back. Just above the feet is a full-width shelf with molded edge that rests on molded rails connecting the square extensions of the large turned and ebonized feet at front and the rear stiles. Total height varies from 56 to 62 inches. Made only in Massachusetts and Connecticut of oak with pine top and bosses and split turnings of native hardwoods. Most examples are in museums or fine private collections. About six have been included in important auction sales during the past twenty years. Always a high-priced rarity. *Ca. 1670–1690.* Q to QQQ

239. Press Cupboard

A companion piece to the court cupboard, it is in two parts. The upper section has flat top, 46 to 54 inches wide and 20 to 22 inches deep with molded edge. Beneath it is a plain or flatly carved frieze with either baluster-turned columns at the corners or turned pendent ball finials.

Cornice overhangs full-width cupboard, 12 to 16 inches high, which is recessed from three to six inches. Front of cupboard is composed of two nearly square paneled doors, flanking a central fixed panel. These three elements have either plain raised panels framed by simple moldings or sunk panels decorated by molding set in geometric patterns and applied bosses. The doors are equipped with elongated turned wooden knobs, and sometimes keyhole without escutcheon.

239

Lower section has a slightly overhanging top with molded edge in front of the recessed upper part. Beneath it may be (1) three full-width drawers, (2) two half-width drawers above cupboard space with single door or (3) cupboard space with a pair of doors. Drawer fronts are paneled with moldings in geometric designs and fitted with elongated turned wooden knobs. Single door is flanked by fixed panels, and wide stiles flank a pair of doors. All either have raised panels framed by simple molding or are sunk and carved in low relief with formalized tulips and foliage or a strapwork floral motif. Doorknobs match those in upper section.

Stiles of both upper and lower sections may be plain or have applied split balusters singly or in pairs. Ends of both sections have plain sunk panels, sometimes with applied bosses. Supported either by ball feet at front and stiles at rear or by stiles front and rear. Total height varies from 56 to 60 inches. Columns, split balusters, bosses and sometimes drawer and doorknobs are ebonized.

If of New England provenance, cupboard is of oak with pine top. Elsewhere is made of oak and walnut combined. All press cupboards are rarities but elaborate New England type is rarest and highest priced. Most of the latter are now in museum collections. *Ca. 1660–1700.* ZZ to QQQ

240

240. The Kas

Is from six to eight feet wide, 24 to 30 inches deep, and from six to over seven feet tall. Except for base, is largely panel-constructed. For aid in moving it, front, sides, back and top are held together with removable wooden pins. The cornice is deeply molded with a decided outward splay that overhangs the body of the piece from six to eight inches. Below it is an unusually narrow molded frieze. The front has two tall rectangular doors with large oblong raised panels. They are flanked at center and ends by wide stiles, each frequently bearing two oblong molded surrounds that frame insets of fancy-grained contrasting woods. Central stile is usually fitted with a scrolled brass keyhole escutcheon.

The interior contains three or four plain shelves of full width and depth. The base is from 10 to 14 inches high and has a medium cove molding at top and a heavier one at the bottom. It contains a full-width drawer with front frequently molding-paneled to simulate half-width drawers flanked by diamond-shaped molded surrounds and insets matching those above. Drawer is fitted with turned wooden knobs or small rosettes with bail handles. Kas is supported by large ball feet at front and at the back by stiles.

Made in and around New York and sometimes by the Pennsylvania Dutch of walnut, maple or such softwoods as gum, basswood or pine. When of the latter and without raised panels, it was painted with fruit, flower and foliage medallions copied from contemporary European prints. Not numerous and, because of size, not popular. *Ca. 1680–1750.* XXX to YY

241. Open-Face Dresser

Is in two parts. Upper part has flat, slightly overhanging molded cornice or hood, 46 to 60 inches wide, sometimes with narrow flat frieze below. This section contains three to four full-width shelves, either of the same or of graduated depth, with plain or rounded edges. They either have a framing of narrow scrolled pieces at sides and top or the supporting sides are scrolled or slightly tapered.

The lower section has a counter top from 16 to 22 inches deep with a rounded front edge. Below it the usual arrangement is a tier of two or three drawers, four to five inches deep, above a full-width cupboard with single or double doors that may be plain or paneled. These are flanked by wide stiles and sometimes a central

241

one, all plain, reeded or paneled. Drawer fronts are plain and fitted with turned wooden knobs. The doors are hung with H-shaped or butt iron hinges and fitted with either knobs matching those on the drawers or small wooden turn buttons. The interior has a single fixed shelf of full width and depth. Generally has a simple molded base supported by four plain bracket feet. If dresser is of the one-piece, built-in type, it rests directly on the floor. Height varies from five feet 10 inches to seven feet.

Made in all sections of maple, cherry, walnut or birch or of various softwoods and either painted or finished with red filler. Many found in antiques shops are of early nineteenth-century Pennsylvania provenance. *Ca. 1730–1840.* XXX to YYY

242

242. Closed-Front Dresser

Similar to the foregoing dresser except for the glazed doors that enclose the upper shelves. Upper section has a flat, slightly overhanging molded cornice, 44 to 58 inches wide with narrow plain frieze below. Space beneath is enclosed by a pair of glazed doors with from six to nine rectangular panes of glass with straight muntins. Doors are flanked at center and sides by narrow plain stiles or wider ones, reeded, and are hung with H-shaped or butt hinges and fitted with small turned wooden knobs. Interior usually contains two full-width and full-depth shelves.

Sides of section are raised four to six inches above counter top of lower part and lower edge of front is finished with a simple molding, sometimes downcurved at ends. Space between sections is open at front and enclosed at sides and back. Counter top has rounded or molded edges on front and sides. Below it is a tier of two or three shallow drawers above a cupboard which is equipped with a pair of plain or paneled doors. Drawers and doors are fitted with wooden knobs that match those in upper section as do the door hinges. Has molded base and is supported by plain or molded bracket feet. Total height varies from six feet to seven feet four inches. Made in all sections, especially rural Pennsylvania, of walnut, maple or cherry but more often of pine or other softwoods and painted. *Ca. 1780–1860.* Y to YYY

Day Beds, Sofas and Settees

Day beds, sofas and settees are all enlargements of the chair. With a seat nearly six feet long by two feet wide, multiple legs and an open back rest at one end, either fixed or adjustable, it was called a day bed. This lounging piece was made from about 1690 to 1760 and re-appeared in the early nineteenth century as the Grecian couch, a sophisticated version inspired by the French chaise longue and first shown by Sheraton in his second book, *Designs for Household Furniture,* issued in 1812.

Sofas and settees are patterned after the armchair form but with seat wide enough to accommodate two or more people. The sofa, an all-upholstered piece, is closely related to the wing chair. It was first made in America toward the close of the Queen Anne period and the resemblance was marked, but it became less so during the Chippendale years. The sofa attained real popularity in the Hepplewhite period and from about 1800 through the Early Victorian period was such an important household piece that no American parlor was considered properly furnished without one.

The settee, previous to 1720, was an enlarged wainscot chair with solid seat and back. Beginning in the Queen Anne and continuing into the Sheraton period, it followed the pattern of the various designs for the open armchair, with or without upholstered seat, and was made in limited numbers. Its day of wide public favor coincided with the advent of the painted fancy chair. Painted and stencil-decorated like the chairs it matched, this form of the settee was attractive, relatively inexpensive and widely made by chair makers even after furniture began to be factory-produced. With the finer pieces, the seat was of rush or cane and of solid wood for the simplified later settees.

Special Comments on Day Beds and Their Construction

Day beds have the same construction features as the turned chairs after which they are patterned (*see Section IV, page 46*).

Where the back rest is adjustable, the ends of its lower cross rail are round and fit into sockets bored in the uprights that support the back. The top rail is free and has short lengths of chain that hook on the uprights just below the finials. With a fixed or stationary back rest, the ends of the top and lower cross rails are short tenons set into mortices cut in the uprights and pinned with dowel-like pegs from the rear.

The seat frame can be (1) turned members socketed into the legs and covered by woven rush, (2) square members morticed and tenoned at the corners and either bored for cane work or grooved for a breadth of heavy canvas or (3) heavier square members likewise morticed and tenoned at the corners and bored for a rope lattice like that of a four-post bed (*see Section XIV, page 364.* If the back rest has a cane panel, the inner edges of its frame are also bored and the caning holes are spaced about a half inch apart, the same as the seat.

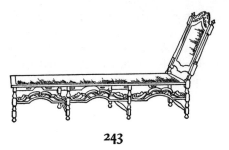

243

243. Restoration Day Bed

Has the same carved details and panels of woven cane as the Restoration chair (*see No. 9*). Back rest is of medium height and has a pronounced cant (about a 20-degree angle). The uprights are baluster-turned, terminating in small urn-shaped finials, and support an arched top rail which is surmounted by a handsomely carved and pierced molded cresting, done in either Flemish scrolls or lunettes and foliage. The lower cross rail is shaped to match the top rail and molded.

The elongated seat is supported by eight legs. These are either knob-turned with blocking and terminate in small ball feet or are carved in Flemish scrolls and have short vase turnings at their upper ends. They are braced on sides and end by arched stretchers, carved and pierced to match the top rail cresting, and by three transverse stretchers that are baluster-turned. Seat rails are plain or with slight bead molding. Back rest is from 40 to 44 inches high and the seat measures 22 to 24 inches wide by five feet to five feet six inches long.

Made in all sections, most frequently of walnut but sometimes of maple which may be combined with other

native hardwoods. Rarest of all American day beds, it is
sometimes found with cane back and seat covered with
or replaced by upholstery. *Ca. 1675–1710.* Z to Q

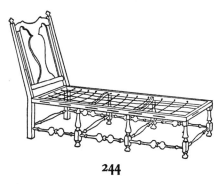

244

244. William and Mary Day Bed

Resembles the vase-splat chair in shaping of uprights
and splat, also leg and stretcher turnings (*see No. 14*).
The slightly lower back rest has a less pronounced cant
and is sometimes adjustable. The uprights are square
with molded fronts and terminate in small ball or vase-
shaped finials. The top rail is yoke-shaped and surmounts either an ample vase-shaped splat or three smaller
ones. The lower rail is plain.

The elongated seat is supported by eight legs. The
two which are continuations of the back rest uprights
are square posts; the other six are either vase-and-ring
turned with blocking and terminate in knob or Spanish
scrolled feet or are vase-and-cylinder turned and terminate in small ball feet. They are braced on the sides and
sometimes at the end by stretchers with boldly done
ring-and-ball turnings and by three or four transverse

stretchers with simple bobbin turnings. The seat rails
are either square or turned. If square they are either
rope-hole bored like some bed frames (*see No. 263 and
No. 264*) or grooved for heavy canvas. With turned
rails, the seat is of rush. With some examples a very
early replacement of the rushing with hand-woven linen
is found. Back rest measures 38 to 42 inches high, seat
from 22 to 24 inches wide by five feet to five feet six
inches long.

Made in all sections, most frequently of maple but
sometimes of walnut combined with other native hardwoods for rails and transverse stretchers. *Ca. 1710–1720.*
YYY to ZZ

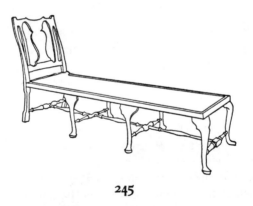

245

245. Queen Anne Day Bed

Is similar to vase-splat chair with cabriole legs (*see
No. 15*). Back rest has slight cant, may be adjustable.
The uprights are square with slight cyma curve and
generally terminate in small knob finials. The panel

of the back rest consists of top rail with pronounced yoke shaping, flat sidepieces and a molded lower cross rail which frame a large vase-shaped splat.

The seat is supported by eight legs. Those at the back rest are square, chamfered extensions of the uprights; the others are cabriole, generally with uncarved knees, and terminate in Dutch feet. They are braced by four vase-and-ring turned stretchers that are connected by three central bobbin-turned stretchers. The rails are square, plain and grooved for heavy canvas on which the seat cushion rests. With some examples of the early Chippendale period, the back-rest splat is pierced in a strapwork or lozenge design, the top rail has a cupid's-bow shaping with voluted ends, the cabriole legs terminate in claw-and-ball feet and the underside of the rails is slightly valanced in the manner of an early Georgian chair (*see No. 19*). The back rest is 40 to 46 inches high, the seat 23 to 25 inches wide by five feet six inches to six feet four inches long.

Made in all sections of walnut, plain or curly maple, cherry and sometimes with later examples of mahogany. *Ca. 1720–1760.* YYY to ZZZ

Special Comments on Sofas and Their Construction

The legs and exposed parts of the frame are made of walnut, mahogany, rosewood or, infrequently, of cherry. The framework concealed by upholstery is generally of pine or other softwood. Where extra strength is required, some of the parts are of maple, birch or chestnut.

Sofa construction in general is the same as that of an upholstered chair, particularly the wing chair (*see Section IV, page 48*).

With long sofas, the seat frame is usually strengthened by two slightly concave cross braces so spaced as
to divide the area into three sections.

Use of coil spring in the seat did not become standard
practice until about the middle of the American Empire period. Previous to that, the basis of the seat was
tightly stretched canvas padded with curled hair or
other material. With some sofas, the upholstery of back
and ends is tacked directly to the frame; with others,
there are removable panels or frames over which the
padding and upholstery material is stretched. Such panels are held in place by concealed screws.

246

246. Queen Anne Sofa

Has upholstered body with stuffed back, seat and
arms similar to wing chair but with wing detail omitted
(*see No. 17*). The high back has a pronounced triple
arching and boldly outrounded corners. The enclosed
flaring arms curve downward slightly from the back to

a vertical scroll and have an outward roll at front. The seat is deep and slightly flaring with straight front, ample quarter-round corners and a conforming exposed seat rail about two inches high.

Sofa is supported by five legs. Those at the front are cabriole, terminating in Dutch or drake feet, and the knees are sometimes shell or scroll carved. The three back legs are square, plain and canted. Length varies from four feet eight inches to five feet six inches and back is from four feet four inches to four feet 10 inches high. Made of walnut, chiefly in Philadelphia and New York. Rare. *Ca. 1740–1750.* Z to ZZZ

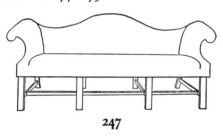

247

247. Chippendale Sofa

Upholstery completely encloses frame above legs. Back is of medium height and top has a bold serpentine outline terminating in a pronounced roll of the out-scrolled ends. These slope forward slightly and have a flaring roll with pronounced overhang. The seat is deep with straight front. Sofa is supported by six to eight legs. The front ones are square, with or without molded outer sides; the rear ones are square, plain and canted. Legs are braced by a box stretcher placed three to four inches from the floor. It has plain straight members with front ones recessed about four inches. Where there are six legs, those at front are cabriole, terminate in claw-and-ball feet and have scroll or foliage-carved knees with wings. The rear legs are square and canted. Stretchers are not present.

Back is from 32 to 36 inches high and length varies from six to eight feet. Some with cabriole legs were made in love-seat size, about four feet long. Made of mahogany in Boston, New York, Philadelphia and other leading cabinetmaking towns. Sofas with cabriole legs are rarer than those with square, stretcher-braced legs. Not numerous. *Ca. 1750–1775.* YYY to ZZZ

248. Hepplewhite Sofa

Has an upholstered body with top rail of back and ends either exposed or enclosed. Back is slightly arched in undulating curves that extend into the slightly down-curved ends. When exposed, the top rail is molded or sometimes carved, forming a banding of alternating rosettes and fluting, and is surmounted by a central carved cresting. Back and ends join in a quarter-round curve and the exposed top rail continues in a downward curve to join supports molded or carved to match. The front of the deep seat is serpentined or slightly bowed to match the outline of the top and the conforming seat rail is covered by upholstery material.

Sofa is supported by eight legs, frequently castered. Those at the front are slender, square and tapering. Their fronts may be plain, molded, inlaid with pendent husks or bellflowers or carved in low relief with sprays of husks. A further decoration on the outer legs may be acanthus-leaf carved medallions above the husk sprays.

Sometimes the front legs terminate in small spade feet. The rear legs are square and canted. In the smaller size, this sofa frequently has only three front and two rear legs. Back is from 29 to 31 inches high and length varies from five feet four inches to seven feet six inches.

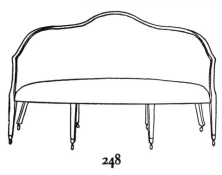

248

Made of mahogany in all sections. Especially fine examples with carved details are of Salem provenance; those with satinwood inlay on front legs are of Baltimore or Philadelphia origin. *Ca. 1785–1800.* Z to ZZZ

249. Sheraton Eight-Leg Sofa

Except for variations and simplifications, it follows the sofa design shown in Sheraton's *Cabinet-Maker and Upholsterer's Drawing-Book*. Has a rectangular body with frame either exposed or enclosed by upholstery. There are six variations in the treatment of the back. They are: (1) straight enclosed top rail. (2) Exposed top rail, four or five inches high, divided into three to five plain panels, sometimes faced with satinwood veneer. (3) Same top rail, carved in low relief with (*a*) drapery festoons on center panel and bowknotted arrows or thunderbolts or bowknotted heads of wheat on flanking panels, (*b*) cornucopias on central panel and drapery festoons on the flanking ones. Sofas thus ornamented are generally attributed to Duncan Phyfe. (4) A shaped top rail consisting of a central rectangular panel, carved

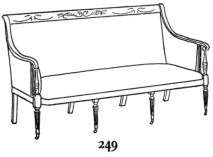

249

in low relief with either a basket of flowers or two drapery festoons, with superimposed spread eagle, flanked by half cupid's-bow volutes, laurel sprays or festoons. Punchwork stippling forms background of panel. Sofas with this top rail are attributed to Samuel McIntire of Salem, Massachusetts. (5) Top rail is slightly bowed and enclosed. (6) Exposed, slightly bowed top rail, is either very narrow and reeded or about four inches high and faced with satinwood veneer. The latter is of Philadelphia or Baltimore provenance.

Sofa ends have either a concave or a downward cyma curve and are supported by free-standing, vase-shaped columns. These are continuations of the outer legs and are either turned and reeded or foliage-carved. When frame is exposed, the upper surface of the ends is reeded or carved with alternating rosettes and fluting or with the water-leaf motif. The deep seat is straight and generally projects slightly with rounded corners. The seat rail, when exposed, is horizontally reeded.

The four front legs are tapering, turned and reeded, terminating in simple turned feet, cup casters or brass paw feet. If seat rail is exposed, the upper ends of the outer legs have either carved dies or small oblong panels of satinwood veneer. The four rear legs are always square and canted. The back is from 36 to 38 inches tall and sofa varies in length from six feet to six feet 10 inches. Was occasionally made in love-seat size, four feet to four feet six inches long, with three front and two rear legs.

Made in all sections of mahogany, sometimes with satinwood veneer. The simpler examples were work of village cabinetmakers; the more elaborate ones were produced by their contemporaries in cities and important cabinetmaking towns. Although fairly numerous, this sofa is in such demand that examples are high-priced. (Some excellent copies of the Phyfe type sofa have been made in the past thirty years. They measure about five to under six feet long, lack the indications of age and frequently buzz-saw marks can be seen on seat braces and other structural parts. Not deliberate fakes but copies made in a smaller and more convenient size.) *Ca. 1800–1810.* Z to QQQ

250. Lyre Sofa

Is so named because of the lyre-shaped ends and reflects the Directoire style. Has a rectangular body with exposed frame. Top rail of back is straight with slight backward roll and quarter-round concave ends. It may be plain or have three panels carved in low relief with drapery festoons at center flanked by bowknotted thunderbolts or with cornucopias at center flanked by drapery festoons. The fronts of the lyre-curved ends are reeded and terminate in small carved rosettes. These ends may have upholstered panels, shaped to conform to lyre

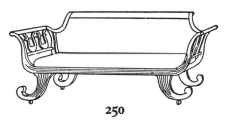

250

curve, or are open and have two lyre-shaped silhouette splats each with strings simulated by slender brass rods. The seat rail is reeded in a continuation of reeding on the ends. The four legs are either cornucopia-shaped, with reeded fronts and fitted with plain casters or castered brass paws, or are simulated animal legs with carved paw feet, furred ankles and feathered wings, sometimes gilded. Back is 36 to 38 inches high and length of sofa varies from six feet three inches to seven feet 10 inches.

Made of mahogany, chiefly by Phyfe and contemporary cabinetmakers working in New York City. *Ca. 1815–1820.* Z to ZZ

251. American Empire Sofa

Has same construction as the foregoing but decorative details are either typical carving of the period or liberal use of crotch-grain mahogany veneer as facing. Back has either a straight or a shaped top rail with downcurved ends. If straight, may (1) be about five inches high, slightly rolled with a single panel of crotch-grain veneer outlined by a fine bead molding and terminating in concave ends, (2) have three-quarter round applied crest terminating in rosette-centered volutes or (3) be

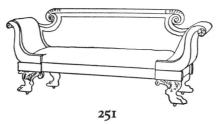

251

ogee-molded and faced with crotch-grain veneer. If shaped, may (1) have a short central oblong reeded panel flanked by twice as long cyma curves or (2) be molded and inversely arched with high central section horizontally reeded and terminating in carved sunburst rosettes.

The lyre-curved ends are upholstered and faced with balancing swan-neck uprights that are (1) plain and faced with crotch-grain veneer, (2) reeded or (3) carved with acanthus-leaf, cornucopia or dolphin motifs and terminate in carved or brass rosettes. The deep seat has a straight front and below it is an unvalanced skirt that is (1) plain and generally faced with crotch-grain veneer, (2) water-leaf or acanthus-leaf carved, (3) a deep torus molding faced with crotch-grain veneer or (4) ogee-molded and veneer-faced.

Sofa is supported by four brackets with casters. These are (1) animal legs with foliage-carved knees or feather-carved wings terminating in either carved paws or eagle's-heads, (2) melon-turned with bold ribbings or (3) large downcurved scrolls faced with crotch-grain veneer. Back is from 31 to 35 inches high and length of sofa is from six feet six inches to eight feet. Made in all sections of mahogany with liberal use of crotch-grain veneer. *Ca. 1820–1840.* YY to Z

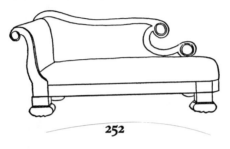

252

252. Grecian Couch

This variation of the sofa with a high headrest at one end and either a low footrest or none at the other end reflects Sheraton's concept in his *Designs for Household Furniture*. It is also known as a *Récamier* sofa from the David portrait of Madame Récamier which depicts her half reclining on a backless couch of this type.

The American version of the Grecian couch has a curved back that joins a headrest of equal height at one end and at the other a much lower footrest or none at all. It has a shaped top rail, generally not the full length of the piece, that terminates at the foot in a bold volute with rosette or in a deep concave curve. The decorative treatment of the rail may be (1) three panels carved in low relief with thunderbolts at the center flanked by drapery festoons, (2) reeded or (3) plain and faced with crotch-grain veneer. The headrest is boldly rolled and faced with a swan-neck carved piece terminating in a rosette matching that of the back. The footrest, when present, is either a bolsterlike roll or a lower curve balancing that of the headrest. Below the seat is a reeded or carved rail or a deeper unvalanced skirt faced with crotch-grain veneer.

The couch is supported by (1) cornucopia brackets terminating in brass paw feet, (2) animal-leg brackets terminating in carved paw feet with carved winged knees, (3) large downcurved scrolled brackets faced with crotch-grain veneer or (4) rectangular plinths above block feet, bowed at bottom. Back is 34 to 40 inches high and couch varies in length from six feet to seven feet six inches. Made in all sections, chiefly in the large cities and important cabinetmaking towns. A considerable number are of Philadelphia or Baltimore provenance but some fine examples were made by Phyfe. McIntire of Salem also designed and carved a few. Not as numerous as the corresponding sofas. *Ca. 1815–1835.* YY to Z

Survival Example

Made in the Early Victorian period and known as a *lounge,* it is all-enclosed by upholstery and has plain outcurved scrolled feet, generally faced with crotch-grain mahogany or cherry veneer. There is a convex headrest but no footrest. The shaped back has a sweeping cyma-curved outline, high where it joins the headrest and low at the foot. Made in all sections by the early furniture factories. *Ca. 1840–1865.* X to XX

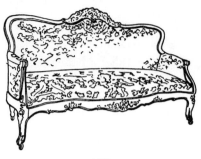

253

253. Early Victorian Sofa

Reflects revival of French style of Louis XV. Has a medium tall back with scroll-arched rail, deeply molded and surmounted at center by a cresting of carved fruits and flowers with foliage. The ends are boldly rounded and extend downward to the arms which are molded, scrolled and supported by arm stumps which are upper extensions of the front legs. The seat has rounded corners at the back and a serpentined front. Below it is a scroll-valanced conforming skirt with central carving that matches the cresting of the back. The front legs are molded cabriole brackets, foliage-carved at the knees, and terminate in rudimentary feet, castered. The back legs are plain and canted. Back is 40 to 48 inches high and length of sofa varies from five feet to six feet eight inches.

Made of rosewood, black walnut or sometimes, with early examples, of mahogany, chiefly by city cabinetmakers or those working in furniture-making towns as far west as the Ohio River Valley. Made also in New Orleans and shipped up the Mississippi. *Ca. 1840–1865.* XXX to Y

Special Comments on Settees and Their Construction

Settees have the same construction as contemporary open armchairs.

Mortice and tenon joinings are used consistently with the early solid-back settee; socketed joints are usual with the painted settees.

If a settee has a rush seat, the rush is woven over the seat rails, concealing them as with the early type of painted fancy chair; with a cane seat the caning holes are spaced about half an inch apart on the inner edges of the rails and a solid wooden seat is of pine, in one piece, with the six or eight legs socketed into the seat as with a Windsor chair or Boston rocker.

The ends of turned stretcher members are socketed into the legs; if flat, the ends fit into mortices cut in the legs. Many settees have a flat front stretcher and turned ones at ends and back.

Backs of painted settees consist of either spindles, with ends socketed into the top rail and seat, or horizontal splats, mortice-and-tenon joined to the back uprights. Some settees have both.

254. Wainscot Settee

Design and construction are similar to that of wainscot chair (*see No. 2*) but the back is plain, made of three wide boards, deeply canted, with straight unmolded upper edge, and extends nearly to the floor. Square-shaped uprights are present with some examples. The arms are square with slight downward slope and have rounded ends or are slightly cyma-curved, terminating in rolled handgrips. They are supported by extensions

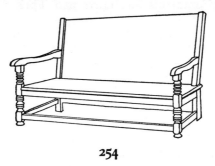

254

of the front legs which are either ring or knob turned with blockings at seat and stretcher level and terminate in small ball or button feet. The solid seat has flush edges or is slightly overhanging with edges plain or molded. Legs are braced by a plain three-quarter box stretcher or an H-shaped one placed just above the feet. Back and seat are sometimes covered with leather un-padded and trimmed with round-headed brass nails. Length varies from six feet three inches to over seven feet.

Made of walnut, chiefly in Pennsylvania, with extreme simplicity of decorative detail. Very rare. Not over four examples have been in important collections dispersed at auction in the past twenty years. Most of these are now in museum collections. *Ca. 1700–1725.* Z to ZZZ

255

255. Queen Anne Settee

Construction, design and ornamentation are same as open armchairs of period (*see No. 15 and No. 19*). Back has double yoke-shaped or serpentine top rail and two solid or pierced back splats. Has an unvalanced seat rail and is supported by five legs. At the front are three cabriole legs with knees sometimes shell-carved and terminating in Dutch or drake feet. Back legs are plain and canted. Width varies from four feet four inches to four feet eight inches.

Made of walnut in all sections, especially Philadelphia and Newport, Rhode Island, or elsewhere in New England, of maple. Rarer than the corresponding armchairs. *Ca. 1720–1750.* Z to ZZ

256. Chippendale Settee

Similar to ladder-back chair in construction, design and ornamental detail (*see No. 22*). The open back is formed by three characteristic ladder-backs. Voluted ab-

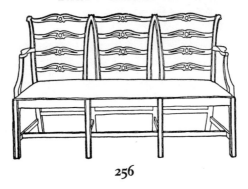

256

breviated arms are supported by incurved arm stumps
attached to seat rails just behind front legs. Is supported
by eight legs. Those at the front are square and molded
and at rear, plain and canted. They are braced by a box
stretcher with plain members and front ones are recessed.
Width varies from four feet four inches to five feet two
inches. Made of mahogany chiefly in Philadelphia and
New York. Rarer than corresponding armchair. *Ca.
1760–1775.* Z to ZZZ

257

257. Hepplewhite Settee

Like shield-back chair in construction, design and decorative detail (*see No. 25*). The double or triple back is formed by two or three connected shield-shaped backs which frame typical openwork splats with fronts carved in low relief. Settee with double back is supported by four slender square and tapering legs not braced by stretchers; with triple back, has eight legs braced by a triple H-shaped stretcher. Width of settee varies from three feet six inches to four feet 10 inches. Made of mahogany in all sections. Not as numerous as corresponding armchairs. *Ca. 1785–1800.* YY to Z

258

258. Sheraton Settee

Is like the Sheraton drawing-book armchair (*see No. 32*) in construction, design and decorative detail. Has double connected back formed of interlacing rectangles with inner one framing a carved tripod hung with drapery festoons and surmounted by carved Prince of Wales feathers. Settee is supported by four legs fitted with brass casters. The front ones are more often square and tapering than turned and reeded; the back ones are square and canted. Width varies from 40 to 44 inches. Made in all sections of mahogany. Much less numerous than corresponding armchair. *Ca. 1800–1820.* Y to YYY

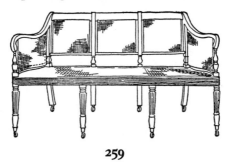

259

259. Phyfe Settee

General construction and design is similar to Sheraton eight-leg sofa (*see No. 249*) but with cane instead of upholstery for back, ends and seat. Has triple back consisting of three almost square cane panels surmounted by a rolled and paneled top rail. The panels are carved in low relief with the center one either of cross laurel sprays or bowknotted wheat ears and the flanking panels bowknotted thunderbolts or drapery festoons.

The ends are framed by cyma-curved and reeded top rails. They are supported by free-standing, vase-shaped turned, reeded columns that are continuations of the outer legs. The deep cane seat is bowed at the front with seat rail horizontally reeded. Settee is supported by eight castered legs. Those at the front are turned and reeded and the rear ones square and canted. Back is from 36 to 38 inches high and length of settee varies from six feet to six feet six inches. Was frequently made with four or six matching side and armchairs.

Made of mahogany by Duncan Phyfe and other New York cabinetmakers. Although fairly plentiful, is in such demand that examples are always high-priced. *Ca. 1800–1820.* ZZ to ZZZ

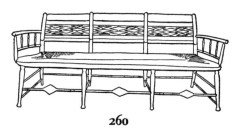

260

260. Painted Fancy Settee

Like painted fancy chair in construction, design and decorative detail (*see No. 39*). Has a triple connected back with each section consisting of a wide flat top rail and either vertical or horizontal cutout back splats, placed between top and bottom rails. The wide, deep seat, generally slightly bowed and with rounded corners, is of rush woven as a unit. Settee is supported by eight legs. Those at the front are decorated with ring or bamboo turnings and terminate in small ball or knob feet. The rear ones are plainly turned and canted. Legs are braced by a triple box stretcher with front members decoratively turned or flat.

Settee is generally painted black, but examples in

lighter colors are found, and decorated with striping and stenciling in gilt and contrasting colors. Length varies from six to seven feet. Made in all sections by fancy chair makers of maple and other close-grained native hardwoods. *Ca. 1800–1820.* XX to Y

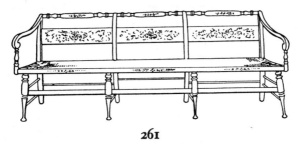

261

261. American Empire Settee

Is like the Hitchcock chair in construction, design and decorative stenciling (*see No. 42*). The top rail of the triple back either is turned with vase-and-ring elements or is flat. The rest of the back consists of horizontal splats or spindles or the two combined. The arms have a downward cyma curve, sometimes terminating in rolled ends. They are screwed to the back uprights and are supported at the front by turned arm stumps. Between each back upright and arm stump are usually two simple spindles, matching those of the back.

The seat is (1) rush, woven as a unit, (2) cane or (3) solid wood and slightly body conforming. Is supported by eight turned legs, the front ones tapering and ring-turned, braced by a triple stretcher of turned members except at the front where they are flat strips about an inch wide. Sometimes this settee has only four legs and is mounted on rockers. It is painted a reddish brown, to simulate rosewood, or black and is stencil-decorated in conventional floral and foliage designs and striped with yellow or gilt.

A settee bearing the Hitchcock stenciled label on the back of the solid wooden seat is most desirable. Made chiefly of maple or other close-grained native hardwoods and with solid seat of pine in a number of chair shops located in New England, New York and Pennsylvania. *Ca. 1820–1850.* XX to Y

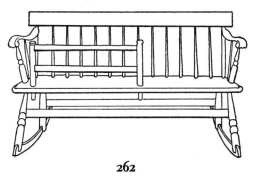

262

262. Hitchcock Settee Cradle

Construction and lines are the same as the foregoing. The back always has a wide top rail and about twelve slender spindles. The arms are like those of a Boston rocker (*see No. 43*). The solid seat is of pine and slightly body conforming. At right, the front of the seat has two one-inch holes into which fit the ends of the cradle fence which consists of two turned uprights and two flat horizontal slats. Settee has four turned legs, the front ones vase-and-ball turned and the rear ones plain, mounted on short narrow rockers. Legs are braced by a box stretcher with front and back members flat strips and end ones turned.

Piece was designed so that an adult could sit at one end while the infant slept behind the protecting fence. Occasionally a settee cradle is found with fences at both ends to accommodate twins. Length varies from 48 to 56 inches.

Made of maple with pine seat by Hitchcock and other chair makers. Painted black or other dark color and striped in yellow or gilt. *Ca. 1830–1840.* XX to Y

Beds

Beds contemporary with the carved oak chests and wainscot chairs of the Puritan Span have not survived but were probably very simple arrangements. America was a new country settled by plain people of simple tastes, small houses and lean purses. The bed frame of posts, rails and plain low headboard evolved by American craftsmen was a memory piece similar to the kind that had existed in the homes of the yeomanry in England long before the first emigrant crossed the Atlantic.

Plain in outline but of good proportions, these bed frames with slight refinements in post turnings and headboard shaping were common in average homes and in lesser rooms of the well-to-do for nearly a century and a half. Like the slat-back chairs that equaled them in longevity, such beds were little affected by changing styles but remained unassuming household pieces until nearly the middle of the nineteenth century.

A variation was the slaw or folding bed that stood in the main living room for the use of guests. It too was simple. Two tall headposts supported a frame from which hung curtains of decorative crewelwork. The side rails were hinged in ingenious fashion so that the bed could be raised and concealed behind the curtains.

During the Queen Anne and Chippendale periods, more impressive beds with tall posts, a full-size tester frame and fine hangings were made for wealthier households. But the first real break with simplicity in American bed design came with the tent or field bed which appeared about 1780 in Philadelphia and from there spread to the various northern sections. It was Hepplewhite in design and during that and the two following periods a considerable number of handsome bed frames were produced.

With the advent of the American Empire period, more developments in bed construction and design materialized than in all the preceding furniture styles combined. In addition to tester beds, there were the three-quarter high-post bed without tester, the low four-poster and the sleigh bed, an American version of the French Napoleon bed. During these years also, the concealed bed catch of iron was invented by John Hewitt, a New York cabinetmaker, and eventually replaced the bed screw. Other improvements were springs and mattresses which began to be substituted for the latticework of rope and tick stuffed with feathers or straw on which rich and poor alike had rested previously.

Finally, the Early Victorian brought in elaborately carved beds with high headboards and footboards as well as spool-turned bedsteads made in quantities as inexpensive cottage furniture and especially favored by readers of *Godey's Lady's Book*.

Special Comments on Beds and Their Construction

Beds made previous to about 1825 are frames consisting of four posts, two side and two end rails and a headboard. General overall dimensions are six feet four inches to six feet eight inches long by four feet to four feet six inches wide. Height of rails from floor ranges from 18 to 30 inches. Headboards, 12 to 24 inches wide, are generally in one piece and made of pine or other softwood stained to match the wood of the posts.

Posts were turned from lumber three to four inches square. Width and thickness of rails match the size of posts. All bedposts have a square section where the rails fit. There are mortices cut on inner side of each post about half its thickness. Into them fit the tenons at ends of the rails.

With many bed frames these mortice and tenon joinings of posts and rails are made fast by countersunk bed screws that pass through the posts and thread into nuts morticed into the rails.

The rails either have holes bored through them six to 10 inches apart or are fitted with small turned knobs. Originally a rope was threaded through the holes or wound around the knobs and drawn taut to form a lattice on which a feather or straw tick was placed. For a frame without bedscrews, this roping was stretched so tightly that it held posts and rails firm. To achieve it, a rope wrench or wooden lever about two feet long was used.

The head posts also have mortices into which the ends of the headboard fit. For a headboard with scrolled or rounded ends, there are two extensions at each end that serve as tenons and fit into the post mortices.

Posts and rails of a bed frame are marked with chisel-cut Roman numerals to identify matching mortices and tenons. Running from I to VIII, they are found on the rails just inside the projecting tenons and on the posts generally under the mortices. Usually they start with Roman I at the right-hand head post and continue around so that the other mortice in this post is marked VIII. These markings were done with a flat chisel, one half to an inch wide. They have the usual irregularities of spacing typical of handwork. If posts and rails are original, the chisel numbering will be as alike as handwriting.

The canopy of a tester bed consists of wooden strips, an inch and a half wide and three quarters of an inch thick, lap-joined at the corners and held in place by iron pins about a quarter of an inch in diameter that are inserted in the ends of the posts. Frequently posts and canopy frame are surmounted by urn-shape finials which are bored and slip over the iron pins.

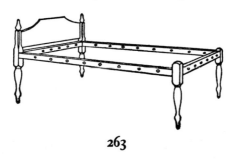

263

263. Early Under-Eaves Bed

Has short head posts, low headboard and rail-high foot posts. Length varies from six feet to six feet six inches long; width is four feet to four feet four inches; and height from top of rails to floor is 18 to 20 inches. The plain headboard is 10 to 14 inches high with upper edge either straight or slightly arched in a continuous flat curve and lower edge is about two inches from top of end rail.

Head posts are 28 to 36 inches tall. Above rail joinings they may be turned, square with chamfered edges or octagon and terminate in button or ball turnings or in flat or slightly rounded ends. They taper slightly below the rails and conform to shaping above. The foot posts vary in height from 20 to 24 inches and extend one to three inches above rails, terminating in rounded ends or button turnings. Shaping below rails matches that of the head posts. All posts are from two and a half to three and a half inches square where rails fit and are without bed screws. Rails are as wide as posts and either square or slightly thinner than wide. They are bored for rope holes.

Made in all sections of assorted hard and soft woods. The most frequent combinations are posts of maple or birch and headboard of pine, basswood or tulip. Originally left natural or finished with red filler. *Ca. 1690–1775.* XX to XXX

Survival Type

Made for nearly seventy-five years longer, is of same size and construction. With some examples the head posts terminate in cone-shape turnings and posts below rails are vaselike in shaping. The upper edge of the headboard is more studied in outline, sometimes with concave curves flanking a flat central section. Posts tend to be heavier, four inches square at rail level. The four-inch square rails have either bored rope holes or small turned rope knobs.

Made of assorted hard and soft woods in all sections

and as far west as Indiana and Kentucky. Finished with red filler or painted with such colors as mahogany red, bottle green or Amish blue. *Ca. 1775–1840.* X to XX

264

264. Folding or Slaw Bed

Slaw is corruption of the sixteenth-century word *slough,* meaning clothed, hence a bed clothed with curtains. Has tapering three-inch square bedposts from six feet two inches to seven feet tall. These support a tester frame about 24 to 30 inches from front to back on which a pair of wide curtains were hung. It consists of plain strips, about an inch wide and three quarters of an inch thick, braced by two short diagonals mortice-joined to the head posts. The low headboard, 10 to 14 inches high, has a straight upper edge, sometimes in-curved at the ends. The rails are 16 to 20 inches from the floor and bored for rope holes. Side rails have wooden knuckle-joint hinges, located 20 to 24 inches from the head posts, with simply turned tapering legs beneath that match the foot posts. The latter extend two or three inches above the rails and terminate in button turnings or with ends slightly rounded or flat.

This bed was always equipped with curtains and matching coverlet of linen, usually embroidered with colored woolen yarn called crewelwork. When not in use, the lower part folded back behind the drawn curtains. Dimensions of bed are six feet to six feet six inches long by four feet to four feet four inches wide. Made chiefly in New England of native hardwoods, mostly maple with original finish red filler. Not numerous. *Ca. 1690–1760.* XXX to YY

Early Tester Bed

Has same simple lines as the foregoing but side rails are not hinged and foot posts are same height as head posts. The four posts support a full-size tester frame. Was originally equipped with four enclosing bed curtains and may have stood in corner of living room or have been placed in the single small bedroom on the ground floor. Made in New England and elsewhere of native hardwoods, mostly maple and finished with red filler. Not numerous. *Ca. 1690–1760.* XXX to YY

265. Queen Anne-Chippendale Tester Bed

Posts are from seven to eight feet tall and support a full-size tester frame. The foot posts are tapering and turned above the rails. Legs below are cabriole, terminating in either Dutch or carved claw-and-ball feet,

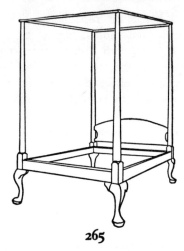

265

or are square with block feet. The head posts are generally square and tapering with slightly chamfered edges and square plain legs or they may match the foot posts. The headboard is not over 24 inches high with upper edge either slightly arched or straight. Top of rails are from 20 to 24 inches from floor. Bed is six feet four inches to six feet eight inches long by four feet four inches to five feet wide. Made in the larger cities and important towns of walnut or mahogany with headboard occasionally of same wood. Always a sophisticated piece. Rare. *Ca. 1740–1775.* YY to ZZ

266. Hepplewhite Tester Bed

Structurally is like the foregoing with full-size tester. Posts, slender and tapering, are from seven to eight feet six inches tall. Foot posts are turned with urn shaping surmounted by a tall vase element and finely

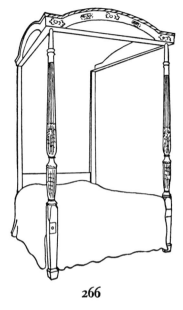

266

reeded. Sometimes they are partially carved as well in
a water-leaf, palm-leaf or acanthus-leaf motif. Below
the rails, which are 18 to 20 inches from the floor, posts
are square, slightly tapering and may terminate in
spade feet. Head posts, designed to be concealed by
curtains, are plain, square and tapering. They are like
the foot posts below the rails but without spade feet.

Tester frame either consists of plain strips of wood
or is a decorative cornice. This is molded, slightly arched
and painted with flower, leaf and other motifs and
surmounts the tester valances. The headboard is 14
to 20 inches high with upper edge straight or slightly
arched. Bed is six feet four inches to six feet 10

inches long by four feet four inches to five feet wide.

Made in cities and important cabinetmaking towns of mahogany or sometimes cherry with headboard of same wood or of pine stained to match. Pine is also used for painted cornice. Not numerous. *Ca. 1785-1800.* YY to ZZ

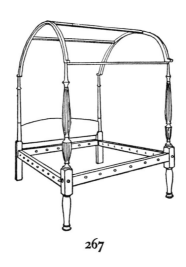

267

267. Field or Tent Bed

Takes name from its resemblance to an army officer's tent with arched roof. This bed, especially popular in America, was made longer and in greater numbers than in England where Hepplewhite included it in his *Cabinet-Maker and Upholsterer's Guide.*

Posts are from five to six feet tall and are surmounted by an arched tester frame. Its side members may be shaped in (1) a continuous curve, (2) two balancing cyma curves or (3) a low serpentine curve. With the latter it is repeated in the shaping of the crosspieces at head and foot. Otherwise the tester crosspieces are plain and flat. The arched sidepieces are always in two parts, butt-hinged at the center. With replacement frames, the sidepieces generally have less arching and are each in one piece.

Treatment of posts differs. With a simple example all four are alike and turned in a plain or slightly vase-shape taper. In a more elaborate bed, the foot posts have an urn shaping above the rails surmounted by a vase-shape element and are reeded, sometimes with a spiral twist for the upper part. Below the rails the posts are square with bead-molded edges, sometimes terminating in box feet, or vase-and-ring turned with simple peg feet. A late example has all four posts turned in vase-and-ball shapings with ring turnings between. They are also vase-shape below the rails and terminate in turned peg feet.

Height of rails from floor is generally from 24 to 28 inches. Rails have either bored rope holes or rope knobs. Headboard is 14 to 18 inches high with upper edge either straight or slightly arched. A late bed may have a matching footboard. Dimensions are: height of tester arch, six to seven feet; length of bed, six feet to six feet six inches; and width, four feet to four feet four inches. Infrequently made in single-bed size, 32 to 36 inches wide.

Made in all sections with differences of decorative style details throughout Hepplewhite, Sheraton and American Empire periods, especially in New England. Woods used are mahogany, plain or curly maple, cherry or birch with headboard of same wood or of pine stained. Is one of the most popular beds with collectors. *Ca. 1785–1830.* Y to Z

268

268. Sheraton Tester Bed

Closely resembles Hepplewhite tester in construction and design (*see No. 266*). The differences are: (1) Turned foot posts have slightly less taper; the urn elements, in addition to reeding and ring turnings, are usually carved in foliage or festoon motifs, and above the reeded vase elements are small capitals formed by single or double ring turnings placed just below the tester valances. (2) Head posts may be either square and tapering or turned to match foot posts, with or without reeding and carving. (3) All posts below rails may be vase-shape, frequently with ring turnings the entire length. (4) Posts are fitted with casters.

The headboard is 14 to 18 inches high. Its upper edge is either flat with incurved corners or arched, sometimes resembling a broken pediment in outline. Tester frame may be plain strips of wood or an ornamental cornice handsomely carved and sometimes gilded. It may also have central carved and gilded plaquettes at foot and sides.

Made in larger cities and important cabinetmaking towns of mahogany with headboard either of same wood or of stained pine. Especially fine examples were made by Phyfe in New York and in Salem, Massachusetts, designed and carved by McIntire. *Ca. 1800–1820.* YYY to ZZ

AMERICAN EMPIRE

269. Tester Bed

Construction is the same as the foregoing but posts are a little heavier with very slight taper. They are (1) vase, baluster and ring turned, (2) urn-shape with stout vase shaft above, either acanthus-leaf carved or spirally reeded, and turned simulated capitals 12 to 16 inches below upper ends, or (3) crotch-grain veneered columns about three and a half inches in diameter with block simulated capitals. Posts vary in height from seven to nine feet and support a tester frame of plain strips of wood. If posts are vase, baluster and ring turned, the legs are vase or baluster shape and terminate in peg feet; if carved or reeded, legs match and terminate in carved paw feet, castered, and if columns, legs are four inches square and fitted with large casters. Rails are 18 to 20 inches from floor.

269

Headboard is 16 to 20 inches high with upper edge either flat with voluted ends or surmounted by a foliage-carved cresting matching that of the posts. An example with column posts usually has a headboard 30 to 36 inches high that is paneled with a shaped upper edge. It may also have a footboard 12 to 16 inches high, plain or paneled with molded upper edge. Made in all sections of mahogany, maple, cherry or birch. *Ca. 1820–1840.* Y to Z

270. Three-Quarter High-Post Bed

Is without tester and all posts are alike. They measure from four feet six inches to five feet eight inches tall and are either vase-and-ring turned, terminating in ball, urn or cone-shape finials, or acanthus-leaf carved and terminate in urn or pineapple-carved finials. Below rails they are turned in vase shape, are either plain or leaf-carved and terminate in small peg feet.

270

Headboard, 16 to 20 inches high, has either a straight upper edge with voluted ends or a carved and pierced cresting. Matching footboard may be present. Rails are generally 26 to 28 inches from floor. Made in all sections of mahogany, maple, cherry or birch. *Ca. 1820–1840.* XX to YY

271. Low-Post Bed

Has same construction as other post and rail beds. The four posts are of same height, which varies from three feet eight inches to four feet two inches. They are turned above rails in vase-and-urn or baluster shaping with ring turnings and terminate in simple peg feet. Sometimes the vase-and-urn elements are acanthus-leaf carved. Headboard is 16 to 20 inches high, either one piece or paneled. Upper edge is either flat with voluted ends or slightly arched. Foot posts may be connected by a vase, ring and ball turned element known as a blanket rail. Less frequently bed has a matching footboard. Rails are from 20 to 26 inches from floor.

271

Made in all sections and as far west as Indiana, Kentucky or western Tennessee of maple, cherry, birch or other native hardwoods, sometimes of pine combined with other softwoods and less frequently of mahogany. Many were work of country cabinetmakers and originally finished with red filler. *Ca. 1820–1850.* XX to Y

272. Sleigh Bed

Is so named because of similarity in outline to a horse-drawn cutter or sleigh. The American version of elaborate French Napoleon bed, it has headboards and footboards of equal height, 36 to 44 inches, with outcurved top rails and sidepieces that have distinct flaring cyma curves. Headboard and footboard sections practically rest on floor. Each has two or three oblong, full-width panels, the upper ones being about 20 or 24 inches high; supported by four low, shaped block feet, sometimes castered. Headboards and footboards are 44 to 52 inches wide and are connected by straight sidepieces 10 to 14 inches high. They are held in place by concealed iron catches that project tenonlike from ends

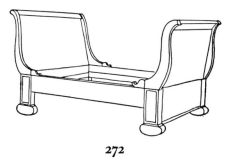

272

of the sidepieces and fit into slots in edges of head and footboard sections.

Bed varies in length from six feet four inches to six feet eight inches and in width from four feet six inches to five feet. Made in larger cities and important cabinetmaking towns of mahogany and frequently crotch-grain veneered wherever possible. Tends to be a ponderous piece. New Orleans antiques dealers make a specialty of sleigh beds. *Ca. 1820–1835.* Y to YY

EARLY VICTORIAN

273. Spool Bed

Takes its name from knobby spool turnings on headboards and footboards and is sometimes referred to as a *Jenny Lind* bed since it was in vogue during her American concert tours. Head and footboards are of equal height, 36 to 42 inches, and are of two types. One has spool-turned posts terminating in urn-shape or small ball-and-ring turned finials connected by two spool-turned cross rails which support four to seven spool or spool-and-vase turned spindles, 12 to 14 inches tall. The other and

273

later type has shorter spool-turned posts surmounted by quarter-round turned segments, the upper ends of which join the spool-turned top rail. The bottom cross rail is either spool-turned or flat and space between the two generally contains four spool or spool-and-vase turned spindles.

Headboard of bed with finials may have spindles or be a one-piece board 18 to 20 inches high surmounted by a spool-turned cresting with ends that match finials. Sometimes headboard is four to six inches higher than footboard. Headboards and footboards are connected by sidepieces six to eight inches wide that are made fast by either four countersunk bed screws or concealed iron catches. Inner sides always have applied strips at lower edge into which fit the slats on which bedspring rests.

Bed varies in length from six feet four inches to six feet eight inches and width is four feet six inches. Made in large quantities by early furniture factories of maple, birch or other native hardwoods with pine headboard and frequently painted or stained to simulate black walnut or rosewood. Numerous. *Ca. 1840–1865.* XX

274

274. Belter Bed

Has headboard about twice as tall as footboard. Both have bold quarter-round corners and tops are arched in balancing cyma curves ornamented by deep bands of pierced carving done in leaf-and-tendril motif with central cartouches carved in high relief. Footboard is somewhat serpentined and so deep that lower edge is close to floor. Both are supported by quarter-round molded block feet, sometimes castered. Has wide outboard sidepieces with upper edge concave and lower one straight that are held in place by concealed iron catches. Dimensions are six feet eight inches to seven feet four inches long by five feet to five feet four inches wide. Made of laminated rosewood by John Henry Belter, leading New York cabinetmaker of this period. Not numerous. *Ca. 1844–1865.* Y to YY

Mirrors

WHAT few mirrors hung on the walls of American homes in the closing years of the seventeenth century were small and set in simple protecting frames. Until 1673, all mirror glass current in England and the American colonies came from Venice and was scarce and costly.

That year, at Lambeth, a glassworks across the Thames from London and close by the Vauxhall Gardens, the first English-made mirror glass was produced. The venture was successful and Vauxhall glass was used by English and American cabinet and frame makers for about a century. For about fifty years it was made in comparatively small sheets, 16 to 20 inches wide by not over 30 inches high. Consequently mirrors of the William and Mary period, though larger than earlier ones, were still of no great size.

The Queen Anne style brought in a long narrow frame in which two panels of glass were used. The lower one was 14 to 18 inches wide and about 19 to 27 inches high. The overlapping panel above was only half as high, generally had an arched top and was decorated with wheel cutting or etching, done in a stylized pattern of flowers and sprays. Some of the frames for this type were made in America, for by 1715 there were craftsmen advertising themselves not only as importers of mirrors but as repairers and frame makers.

Silvered glass unframed was also being imported in increasing amounts. So more and more cabinetmakers began to make the necessary frames and of course followed the style current in England.

Beginning with the Queen Anne and continuing through the American Empire periods, American cabinet and frame makers produced some eleven designs. The silvered glass for them was all imported until about 1790. Likewise mirrors complete with frames continued to be imported for wealthy Americans. This is high-lighted repeatedly by eighteenth-century newspaper advertising in which our craftsmen either complain of lack of patronage or announce receipt from London of the newest styles of framed mirrors. In fact, it is often difficult to decide whether the frame of a Queen Anne or Chippendale mirror was made here or imported and sold by the frame maker whose label it may bear. About the best one can do is to consider it as a mirror of a style and type current in America at that time.

During the Hepplewhite period, there were many more frame makers working in the United States and at least part of their supply of silvered glass was produced here. Since many of these mirrors have an upper panel decorated with a patriotic emblem or scene and makers' labels include phrases like "looking glass manufactory," it is clear that from about the turn of the nineteenth century the majority of mirrors were made by craftsmen working in America. Some of these, like the Del Vecchios, father and son of New York, and Cermenati and Bermarda of Salem, Massachusetts, were of Italian origin; others, like Kidder and Carter of Boston and the earlier John Elliott of Philadelphia, were either native-born Americans or frame makers out of London.

Special Comments on Mirrors and Their Construction

The thickness of the glass in mirrors varies. In general, the original glass in William and Mary, Queen Anne and early Chippendale frames is from three sixteenths to a quarter of an inch thick with bevels reducing the edges to an eighth of an inch or less. This glass can be identified by passing one's finger tips along a bevel. It will feel uneven and slightly wavy. The bevel on replacement glass is always smooth. Further, the bevels on an original glass are noticeably narrow, about half an inch; those on most replacement glass are from three quarters of an inch to an inch wide.

Glass in most Chippendale mirrors is about an eighth of an inch thick. In Hepplewhite, Sheraton and American Empire mirrors it is from three thirty-seconds to just under an eighth of an inch thick, most of it being the latter. Some sheets, however, are almost paper-thin and feather-light.

The upper panel of mirror glass in a two-panel Queen Anne frame consistently overlaps the lower one about a quarter to half an inch. In Hepplewhite and later mirrors the upper panel, whether painted or silvered, is always separated from the lower panel by a wooden strip from a half to an inch wide. The frame is rabbeted on the sides, top and bottom to retain the glass.

The glass in all mirrors is protected by thin backboards that are tacked onto the frame. They are generally of pine or other softwood, are about a quarter to half an inch thick and left rough, showing the marks of the ripsaw. Some have slightly beveled edges roughly done with a large plane.

Rectangular mirror frames either have mitered joints at the corners or top and bottom pieces are butt-joined to the sides. Either type of joining is made fast with glue and countersunk nails. The four or more pieces of a circular or oval frame are either tongue-and-groove or lap-joined. The lines of such joinings are concealed by the gilded finish but are visible on the back.

Gilded or veneered mirror frames are always of pine, visible at the back. Where a veneered frame has a cresting, it is formed of a thin piece of wood of the same kind as the veneer and is sometimes strengthened by small strips of pine glued on the back. If there is a skirt, it is of the same wood as the cresting.

Chippendale fret-carved mahogany mirrors have narrow frame pieces of solid mahogany about an inch thick. Cresting, skirt and corner volutes are generally scroll-saw cut from mahogany under a half inch thick. These are glued to the frame pieces and reinforced by blocks glued on the back. Sometimes cresting and skirt are faced with crotch-grain veneer for decorative effect but more often are of solid wood with straight or slightly figured grain.

Many of the shaped mirror frames faced with either walnut or mahogany veneer also have raised and gilded decorative scrolls and the like. These are of a puttylike composition, pressed in molds and glued to the face of the frame before gilding.

The columns, pilasters and split baluster turnings of Hepplewhite, Sheraton and American Empire mirror frames are made fast with glue and sometimes with countersunk nails. The same method is used for the corner blocks.

The method of gilding all frames, either partially or wholly, was the same. It was done only with gold leaf prepared in sheets about two by three inches in size. All gold leaf was made of pure gold, beaten tissue thin between leather skins with heavy mallets. A gilding compound applied paintlike with a brush was never used. Such gold paints have no real gold in their mixture and are a mid-nineteenth-century invention.

For gold leafing, the portion to be gilded is first coated with gesso (whiting and glue mixed in water) to make the surface smooth. When dry, it is painted with a light coat of "tack" varnish which makes the gold leaf adhere readily. After the leafing is finished, the frame is rubbed with small bats of lamb's wool which tightens the bond of gold leaf and tack and removes loose, overlapping fringes of the metal sheets. Finally, the parts intended for a bright finish are burnished.

Old mirror glass frequently has spots of discolored silvering or peeled patches. Provided there is no corrosion, it can be resilvered, but it is expensive and risky. The glass is brittle from age and often breaks in the process. For practical purposes it is better to replace it with modern glass, packing the original away safely so it can be returned to the frame later if it is to be sold. Frames with original glass, especially if beveled, naturally are more valuable from an antiquarian point of view.

275

275. William and Mary Mirror

Has a rectangular frame, three to four inches wide, and is mitered at the corners. Is surmounted by an arched or lunette-shaped cresting. The cresting is either fret-carved in foliage arabesques or inlaid in a flower-and-leaf design done in light-colored wood. The frame has a boldly done convex-shaped molding flanked on both sides by narrow matching channel-molded elements. It is faced with walnut veneer, frequently burl. The rectangular glass generally has slightly beveled edges.

Majority of these mirrors were imported complete with frames. Some of the simpler frames may have been made in America to replace those broken in transit or use. All are rare. Size varies from 42 inches high by 26 inches wide to 48 inches high by 30 inches wide. *Ca. 1690–1700.* XXX to YY

QUEEN ANNE

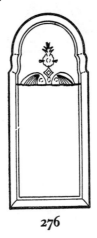

276

276. Arched Queen Anne Mirror

Has a tall, narrow frame, arched at the top. This arching is either semicircular with short cyma-curved elements or consists of balancing ogival curves with or without a slight central peak. The frame is about two inches wide with a convex molded face and is bead-molded on the outer edge. It is faced with fancy-grain walnut veneer. The glass is in two panels, the lower one rectangular and the upper one arched and slightly overlapping the lower panel. Both have beveled edges. The upper panel is generally decorated by a wheel-cut or engraved conventionalized design consisting of a combination of floral, star and bird motifs. The size varies from 36 inches high by 16 inches wide to 48 inches high by 18 inches wide. *Ca. 1710–1730.* Y to YYY

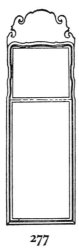

277

277. Crested Queen Anne Mirror

Is like the foregoing save for a cresting, four to eight inches high, of thin wood with scrolled outline, either plain or edged with gilding to emphasize the formalized foliage design. At the center, there is frequently an incised standing scallop shell, carved and gilded. The size varies from 36 inches high by 16 inches wide to 56 inches high by 24 inches wide. *Ca. 1725–1750.* Y to YYY

Survival Example

Because of the popularity of this design, it was made until about 1770 in the same tall, narrow proportions but without wheel-cut or engraved decoration in the upper panel. Frequently the glass is in one piece, reflecting the Chippendale influence. Frame is faced with walnut veneer, mahogany veneer for later examples, or may be lacquered in the Chinese manner. Some of the latter are of pier-glass size, measuring about 60 inches high by 35 inches wide. *Ca. 1750–1770.* Y to YYY

CHIPPENDALE

278   279

278. Fret-Carved Chippendale Mirror

Has an oblong frame with cresting and apron fret carved in an outline or rococo scrolls and conventionalized foliage. The cresting is from four to 10 inches high and generally has a triple arch. It may be plain or have a centered medallion, usually a falcon or an eagle, carved and gilded. Sometimes the cresting has a broken pediment outline, surmounted by a gilded bird finial, with the sides of the frame flanked by pendent flowers and leaves, also gilded. The valanced apron is shallower

than the cresting and is fret-carved to match it in pendent scrolls. The oblong mirror glass is in one piece,
sometimes has beveled edges, but more often does not.
Surrounding frame is either plain or molded and may
have a gilded inner fillet and inlaid stringing.

The size varies from 18 inches high by 10 inches wide
to 60 inches high by 30 inches wide. Made in all sections
of mahogany. Some fine examples of Philadelphia provenance have the label of John Elliott, printed in both
English and German. *Ca. 1750–1800.* XXX to YYY

279. Chippendale Architectural Mirror

Also known as a *Constitution mirror,* which is a
trade misnomer since its design antedates the Constitution of the United States by three or four decades. Its
design reflects early Georgian architecture. The oblong
frame has a broken pediment top with balancing cyma
curves that are carved and gilded and terminate in
rosettes. At center is a carved and gilded falcon or
spread eagle mounted on a plinth. Beneath the pediment is a frieze with gilded moldings top and bottom.
The lower one is continued and outlines the shaped
frame with its valanced apron which is either outrounded
or scrolled. The frame is frequently flanked at the sides
by gilded pendent flower or foliage swags. The one-
piece mirror is outlined by an inner gilded fillet.

Size varies from 45 inches high by 21 inches wide to 71
inches high by 26 inches wide. Frame is faced with
mahogany or sometimes burl walnut veneer. Made
chiefly in Philadelphia. Examples bearing the English-
German label of John Elliott are known. *Ca. 1760–1770.*
YY to ZZ

HEPPLEWHITE

280   281

280. Hepplewhite Mirror with Urn Finial

Has an oblong frame with broken pediment cresting and valanced apron. The cresting has gilded balancing molded cyma curves that terminate in gilded rosettes. At the center is a plinth surmounted by a gilded urn with flowers on wirework stems. The cresting is from eight to 14 inches high and frequently has a centered inlaid medallion or an urn or shell. The base of the cresting is defined by gilded molding or an inlay fillet, and the frame surrounding the glass is outlined on one or both edges by inlay or gilded fillets.

The valanced apron frequently has a centered inlaid medallion matching that on the cresting. The oblong mirror glass is frequently surmounted by a glass frieze panel. It is decorated in stencil gilding with a patriotic eagle or other motif on a white background or with an imaginary landscape done in gold leaf and black on a light-colored background. The sides of the frame are hung with pendent sprays of flowers and leaves done in gilded composition and mounted on wirework supports. Made in the larger cities, especially New York, of mahogany with applied detail of gilded composition. *Ca. 1785–1800.* YY to Z

281. Hepplewhite Gilded Filigree Mirror

The molded oblong frame is carved in fine beading and surmounted by a classic filigree cresting. This consists of a central urn or jardiniere containing either flower and leaf sprays or wheat ears. From it also are draped foliage festoons that hang down the sides of the frame. All are of molded composition and gilded. At the base of the frame there is a corresponding festoon of flowers and leaves.

The size varies from 47 inches high by 19 inches wide to 68 inches high by 34 inches wide. Some examples are found with the frame intact but with filigree cresting and base festoon missing. Made of gilded pine, chiefly by mirror makers in New York City, Boston, Philadelphia, Salem and Portland, Maine. Rare when complete and unrestored. *Ca. 1790–1810.* YY to Z

Hepplewhite Oval Gilded Mirror

Is of the same design and construction but frame and glass are oval and the festoons hung from central urn of the cresting have a cyma-curved line to conform to

shaping of oval frame. Examples sometimes lack cresting and bottom festoon. Size varies from 46 inches high
by 18 inches wide to 60 inches high and 26 inches wide.
Rare when complete and unrestored. *Ca. 1790–1810.* YY
to Z

282

282. Hepplewhite Mantel Mirror

Has an architecturally designed oblong frame, carved
and gilded, and surmounted by a molded and slightly
overhanging cornice, sometimes decorated with about
forty small pendent spheres. It is supported by four fluted
columns with capitals and plinths. These columns separate the large central panel of mirror glass from the
two narrower ones that flank it. Beneath the cornice is
a painted glass frieze, also in three panels, decorated
with jardinieres of flowers and symmetrical foliage
sprays done in gold against a white background.

Later examples are of the same design but have
either Sheraton or American Empire details. They sometimes include American scenes or patriotic emblems in
the frieze decoration and have split baluster turnings
with corner rosettes in place of the columns. These man-
tel mirrors vary in size from 50 to 60 inches wide by 24
to 30 inches high.

Made of pine, gilded, by frame makers, especially in Boston, Providence, New York and Philadelphia, who shipped their mirrors to practically all sections of the country. *Ca. 1790–1830.* Y to Z

SHERATON

283

283. Sheraton Architectural or Tabernacle Mirror

Is popularly known as a *tabernacle mirror* because the frame with its pilastered sides and decorative frieze panel somewhat resembles the glazed door of a niche in a large display piece of furniture. Has a flat molded cornice, generally with projecting breaks at the corners, and may have thirteen to seventeen pendent spheres. There are single or double columns or pilasters, reeded or plain, with or without capitals. The base of the frame is molded to correspond to the cornice and its square corners form the plinths beneath the columns or pilasters.

The oblong frieze panel is either of painted glass or of wood with decoration carved in high relief. The painted glass panel is more usual and may have (1) a spread eagle or other patriotic symbol as a central medallion done in gold leaf against a white background, (2) a painting of one of the naval engagements of the War of 1812, (3) an imaginary landscape done in gold leaf and black or in colors, (4) a vase or basket of flowers or fruit. The solid frieze panel with carved decoration is found only with a gilded frame; the painted glass panel is used with either a gilded or a mahogany frame. The proportions are generally about twice as high as wide and the size varies from 30 inches high by 16 inches wide to 68 inches high by 32 inches wide.

Made in all sections of either pine gilded or of mahogany by the increasing number of frame makers. A considerable number of these mirrors have been found with maker's label. The names are frequently Italian and furnish the first indication that craftsmen of this nationality were working in the United States. *Ca. 1800–1820.* XXX to YYY

284. Carved and Gilded Convex Mirror

Circular frame has concentric elements that are (1) leaf-carved, (2) bead-molded, (3) a ring of small spheres or (4) an inner fillet of ebonized reeding. It is surmounted by a pediment consisting of a spread eagle perched on a rockery flanked by acanthus-leaf scrolls. At base of frame is a pendent finial of carved foliage.

The frame is sometimes equipped with scrolled or twisted metal and carved wood arms which terminate in candle sockets. The circular mirror glass is convex

284

and about 24 inches in diameter. Size varies from 48 to 56 inches in height and 30 to 34 inches in width. Always an elaborate piece with carving boldly done. Made of pine and gilded by frame makers and carvers, chiefly in New York, Boston, Philadelphia. Not numerous. *Ca. 1800–1810.* YY to Z

AMERICAN EMPIRE

285. American Empire Tabernacle Mirror

Has an oblong frame, usually without a cornice. In place of it, top, bottom and sides have applied half-round pilasters that are (1) spirally reeded, (2) acanthus-leaf carved, (3) vase-and-ring or vase-and-cylinder turned. At the corners are square projecting blocks trimmed with either composition or stamped brass rosettes. The upper glass panel is generally deep enough to be nearly square and is painted with a landscape, a naval engagement or an urn containing flowers or fruits, generally in colors. Sometimes this upper panel is of mirror glass, probably an early replacement of the orig-

 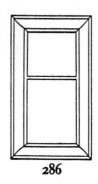

285   **286**

inal painted one. The lower panel is usually about twice
as high as it is wide. The frame is two to three inches
wide and the size varies from 20 inches high by 10
inches wide to 60 inches high by 26 or 28 inches wide.

Made by frame makers in all sections of gilded pine
or mahogany. When gilded and with baluster-turned
pilasters, the vase or cylinder sections are frequently
painted black. *Ca. 1820–1840.* XX to XXX

286. American Empire Ogee-Molded Mirror

Has an oblong frame, mitered at corners, and generally a single panel of mirror glass. Frame is about five
inches wide, has inch-wide flat banding on both edges
with a three-inch wide ogee molding between. It is
usually faced with crotch-grain mahogany but is sometimes coated with gesso and painted to simulate either
mahogany or rosewood. Then the flat inner and outer
bandings are replaced by simple gilded moldings. Made
in all sections. *Ca. 1830–1850.* X to XX

Dressing Glasses

287

287. Hepplewhite Dressing Glass

Has a small oval or shield-shaped swivel mirror supported by curved uprights decorated with small applied rosettes. These surmount a base with bowed, serpentine or half-moon shaped front. It contains a tier of three small drawers and is supported by small molded bracket feet. The central drawer is wider and generally has an inset diamond-shaped keyhole escutcheon. The narrower drawers flanking it are fitted with small brass or turned wooden knobs. The drawer fronts are frequently outlined with stringing or may be faced with satinwood banded with mahogany. Size varies from 22 to 26 inches high and from 16 to 18 inches wide. Made in all sections of mahogany veneered on pine with boxwood stringing and sometimes satinwood facing for drawers. *Ca. 1790–1800.* XXX to Y

288

288. Sheraton Dressing Glass

Construction is the same as the foregoing. Has a small oblong swivel mirror in a molded or stringing outlined frame, supported by turned or square uprights. These surmount a base with straight or bowed front containing one full-width or three narrow drawers. The drawer fronts are faced with crotch-grain veneer, sometimes outlined with stringing, and fitted with small wooden knobs. The base rests on six small ball feet or four molded bracket feet. Made in all sections of mahogany veneered on pine. *Ca. 1800–1830.* XX to Y

289. Courting Mirror

So named because such small mirrors were widely given to young women by their suitors. Has a small frame, generally with an arched top that encloses a geometrically shaped painted glass panel. The frame consists of fine bead moldings along inner and outer edges with bands of painted glass between. The size is from eight to 12 inches high by six to eight inches wide. Originally this type of mirror was fitted into a protecting wooden box. With cover removed, the mir-

289

ror was hung on the wall inside its box. Many of these courting mirrors were made in China for export, and are of camphorwood; others were made along the Atlantic seaboard of maple, cherry or pine. The latter have molded frames without the inset panels of glass. *Ca. 1790–1830.* X to XX

SECTION **XVI**

Pennsylvania Dutch Furniture

THE settlers from the German Palatinate, known as Pennsylvania Dutch, came early, stayed put on the fertile farmlands of the six counties north and west of Philadelphia and, clinging to their South German dialect, were content to be a people apart with a minimum of intercourse with their English-speaking contemporaries. Although the first of them arrived in 1673, even before Penn had laid out Philadelphia, they were set in their ways and held tenaciously to their homeland folk arts from generation to generation until after furniture making ceased to be a handcraft.

Consequently their furniture has its own distinct characteristics. Pieces made of walnut or other native hardwoods are sturdier and ampler; those of softwoods are painted in strong colors and, in addition to color, symbolism plays a major part in the decoration, notably of their dower chests.

Special Comments on Pennsylvania Dutch Furniture and Its Decoration

Decoration and, to a degree, proportion distinguish Pennsylvania Dutch furniture from other American pieces.

There are very few differences in construction. Of these the most outstanding are paneled headboards with four-post beds and wide pull-brackets with slant-front desks.

Such pull-brackets are often three to four inches wide since they serve the double purpose of a bracket and a long narrow drawer. Being drawer constructed, the sides and ends are dovetailed. There is frequently a sliding top that fits into grooves cut in sidepieces and front. Access to the interior is gained by sliding this top back.

Their walnut furniture is decorated with narrow, stringlike lines of inlay, done in a light-colored wood, such as maple or holly, or with striping of yellow paint. This decoration is mostly found on chests of drawers and some dower chests and includes the initials of the original owner and a date. With a chest of drawers, the valanced skirt is sometimes outlined with inlaid stringing or with painted striping. Some of the finer chests are decorated on the front with three inlaid asterlike flowers on long stems rising from an urn-shaped vase, done in outline.

Their painted furniture is made of pine, tulipwood, poplar or of assorted softwoods. Much of it, including such large pieces as dressers and corner cupboards, is painted in a single color, Amish blue, cypress green, reddish brown, chrome yellow or, with some of the later examples, gray. A piece with graining to simulate black walnut or golden oak means still later work done sixty to eighty years ago. An expert restorer can sometimes remove it without damaging the original paint beneath.

Most of the painted decoration is concentrated on the fronts of dower chests and consists of two or three elaborately designed panels in which flowers, hearts, stars, birds and animals occur. Each is symbolic. For example, the heart is for happiness, the star for luck, the turtledove for peace, rampant unicorns for maidenly virtue and a mounted horseman for chivalry. On some of the chests, done between 1800 and 1830, the designs include the spread eagle and other patriotic symbols. Colors used in these designs, besides the three primary ones, are light and dark shades of green, rose tints, orange, a reddish brown against either a black or cream-colored background.

Usually the designs include the name or initials of the bride for whom the dower chest was made and the date of her marriage. German lettering is always used. The best of the designs were painted by men who made a specialty of this work and traveled from village to village doing it. Some of them, like Christian Selzer or Johann Rank, signed their work. These signed chests are the rarest and most desirable. They date from about 1770 to 1810.

Some of the chests of drawers, made from about 1800 to 1830, have stylized medallions of small birds, flowers, hearts and sometimes angels at the center of the four drawer fronts beneath the keyhole escutcheons. Star symbols are usually found on the paneled ends of the carcase. The same range of color is used in the designs as on the dower chests and the top drawer front may bear the bride's name in German lettering and the date of her marriage.

290. Plain Chest

Has one-piece lid with slightly overhanging molded edges or rounded ones that overhang the width of the cleats at ends. It is attached to the carcase by wrought-iron hinges. These may be shaped strap, butterfly, snipe or plain butt hinges. The carcase is generally made of one-piece boards and is dovetailed at the corners. The front is fitted with a centered keyhole escutcheon of scrolled wrought iron or brass of bat's-wing, willow or oval plate pattern.

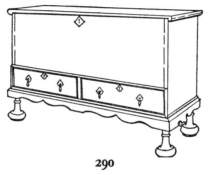

290

The well is 14 to 16 inches deep and may have a small built-in till at one end just below the top. It is four to eight inches deep with a pivoted, slightly overhanging lid. With some of these tills, the front is movable and slides up when pressed slightly, disclosing two secret drawers about two inches deep beneath a false bottom.

Sometimes there are two half-width or three narrower drawers below the well. They are either framed by arch molding or have slightly overlapping thumb-molded edges. Their handles and keyhole escutcheons reflect the various styles from William and Mary to American Empire.

The molded base may (1) be plain, (2) have a shallow valanced skirt or (3) a scrolled pendent finial, centered. Is supported by plain bracket feet or ball or bun-shaped turned feet. Dimensions vary from 40 to 56 inches in length, 22 to 32 inches in height and 22 to 24 inches in width. Made of pine, tulipwood, poplar or other softwood. Exterior originally finished with oil and wax or painted Amish blue, cypress green or brown. Interior always left in the natural. *Ca. 1700–1825.* XX to Y

291

291. Inlaid Walnut Chest

Design and construction are the same as the foregoing but this is made of walnut and lid has applied molded edge, matching the base. Front is decorated with inlay done in holly or other light-colored wood. The design is generally a central cartouche-shaped panel, often lettered with the two initials or name of the original owner, flanked by two stylized floral sprays. The usual design is that of three petaled flowers without foliage on long slender stems rising from a heart or urn-shaped vase. This with a woman's name, inlaid, indicates that it is a marriage chest. It generally has two half-width drawers fitted with brass bat's-wing or willow plates and matching keyhole escutcheons. Is usually supported by large plain brackets. *Ca. 1730–1775.* Y to YY

292

292. Painted Dower Chest

Has elaborate painted decoration on a background of Amish blue, reddish brown or cypress green that is either plain or stippled. The decoration is usually concentrated on the front and consists of two or three panels. Shaping of panels and design detail vary according to the county in which chest was made: (1) Berks County, arched panels enclosing or flanked by a pair of unicorns, rampant among tulips and pomegranates; (2) Dauphin County, square panels filled with flower sprays rising from a vase; (3) Lancaster County, arched panels enclosing parrotlike birds with tulips and fuchsias; (4) Lebanon County, arched panels having vase motif with tulips and five-petal flowers upright in center; (5) Lehigh County, large circular medallions overlaid with six-pointed stars, generally flanking an arched central panel lettered with the bride's name and (6) Montgomery County, square panels with tulips and carnations.

Lid either is plain or has large shaped central panel decorated with flower-and-foliage design. If chest is

lettered and dated, this usually appears in the central
panel or in the space between two panels. Inscriptions
vary, from the usual bridal one such as "Elizabetha
Bambergeri Anno 1784" to that on a chest obviously
non-dower and inscribed "John Kesler, dem 16 Junius
1814 in Under Mahantango Taunschip Schul County."
Dates on these chests range from 1760 to 1830. Some
are signed by the painter. Some of the later chests are
decorated with rectangular panels showing town scenes
or patriotic emblems. Made of pine or other softwood.
Not numerous and in such demand that they are always
high-priced. *Ca. 1760–1830.* YYY to ZZZ

293

293. Early Chest of Drawers

Has oblong top 36 to 42 inches wide with applied
molded cornice. Carcase contains five tiers of graduated

drawers. The top tier has either two half-width or three narrower ones. Those below are all full-width. Drawers have slightly overlapping thumb-molded edges and are fitted with either brass bat's-wing or willow plates and matching escutcheons. Has a slightly molded base with tall, large scrolled bracket feet and a skirt with a deeply scrolled central pendent finial. Brackets and skirt are outlined with painted striping that simulates inlaid stringing. There is also a date painted on the pendent finial that matches two initials on the front of the central top drawer.

Chest of drawers is from four feet six inches to five feet tall. Made of walnut. Not numerous. *Ca. 1730–1760.* Y to YY

294. Painted Chest of Drawers

Has slightly overhanging oblong top, 42 to 48 inches wide, with straight front edge. Carcase contains four graduated drawers with overlapping thumb-molded edges. They are fitted with brass rosette or mushroom-turned wooden knobs and either oblong brass keyhole escutcheons or inset brass keyhole surrounds. Ends of carcase are stile-and-rail constructed with large sunk panels.

The body color of cypress green or reddish brown is overlaid with an elaborate design done in tones of yellow, red, green and blue. The drawer fronts are striped to simulate inlay with complementary quarter sunbursts at the corners of the panels. Beneath the inset keyhole are painted sprays of tulips and fuchsias flanked by small birds. The top drawer is frequently lettered with the initials of the original owner. The

294

stiles and rails of the carcase are decorated with small rosettes, done in alternating colors, and the end panels with large star motifs and quarter sunbursts. Piece is supported by four short, slender, baluster-turned legs. Height varies from 46 to 54 inches. Made of pine, tulip-wood, poplar or assorted softwoods. Not numerous. *Ca. 1800–1830.* Y to YY

295. Painted Rocking Chair

Has wide, boldly rounded hoop back with wide vase-shaped splat. The arms are downcurved, about two inches wide, and terminate in large convex scrolls. They are supported by short, simply turned arm stumps. The solid wooden seat is an inch and a half to two inches thick, rolled at front and upcurved at rear. Is

295

supported by four short turned legs mounted on rockers about 28 inches long. These are braced front and rear by single turned stretchers.

Body coat of brown or black is overlaid with clusters of flowers and shells on back top rail, splat and front of seat painted in polychrome colors, and is striped in gilt or yellow. Maker's name and date made may be painted on underside of seat. Construction and design somewhat resemble the Boston rocker but differ in treatment of back (*see No. 43*). Made of maple and assorted hardwoods with pine seat. *Ca. 1830–1870*. X to XX

Painted Side Chair

Color or body coat, overlaid painted decoration and chair design match the rocker. The solid seat is usually slightly saddled. Is similar to Hitchcock chair with wooden seat (*see No. 42*). Was made in sets of six side chairs and a rocker. *Ca. 1830–1870*. X to XX

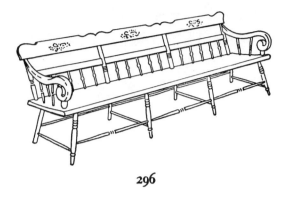

296

296. Painted Settee

Back has top rail, four to seven inches high, with slightly shaped upper edge and is supported by four turned and slightly canted uprights. About half the distance to the seat is a narrow horizontal splat in three sections. Beneath it are frequently twelve to fifteen short turned spindles with ends socketed into splat and seat. Has downcurved arms about two inches wide that terminate in large convex scrolls. Arms are supported by short turned arm stumps and spindles matching those of the back.

Has a solid wooden seat, 18 to 20 inches deep, that is slightly body conforming and has a rounded front edge. Is supported by either four or eight legs, the front ones with some ring turning and the rear ones plain. These are braced by a single or triple box stretcher composed of all turned members or front ones flat and about two inches wide. When settee has only four legs, it is generally mounted on rockers about two inches wide and

28 inches long. Body coat is brown or black. Decorations are polychrome flower-and-foliage medallions on back top rail and striping in gilt or yellow on back uprights, spindles, arms, legs and front stretcher members. Construction and design similar to American Empire settee (*see No. 261*). Made of maple or assorted hardwoods with one-piece pine seat. *Ca. 1820–1850.* XXX to YY

297. Open-Face Dresser

Is in two parts. Upper section has flat, slightly overhanging cornice, 56 to 66 inches wide and sometimes denticulated. Beneath it may be a slightly valanced frieze and scrolled sidepieces that frame the shelves. Contains two full-width shelves, with one notched for spoons. This section is recessed about half the depth of the lower one and rests on an 18 to 20 inch deep counter top.

The enclosed lower section contains drawers and cupboards. Their arrangement varies. Generally there is a tier of three shallow drawers above two paneled cupboard doors; sometimes there are six drawers of equal depth in the center, flanked by paneled cupboard doors. The drawers have overlapping thumb-molded edges and are fitted with (1) brass willow plates, (2) wrought-iron rings or (3) turned wooden knobs. The cupboard doors are hung with (1) wrought-iron rat tail, (2) H-shaped or (3) plain butt hinges and are fitted with either exposed wrought-iron latches or turned wooden knobs.

Piece rests on a simple molded base supported by short cylinder-turned legs or scrolled bracket feet or is without base and rests on three shoelike block feet. Construction and design similar to open-face dressers

297

made elsewhere (*see No. 241*). Made of walnut and
finished with varnish or oil and wax or of pine and
assorted softwoods and painted Amish blue, cypress
green or brown. Dresser of walnut is generally earlier,
larger and has finer workmanship. *Ca. 1750–1850.* YY
to Z

298. Painted Closed-Front Dresser

Upper section has a flat, slightly overhanging molded
cornice, 54 to 66 inches wide, with or without a narrow
frieze beneath. Cupboard is enclosed by a pair of
glazed doors, each with six to nine rectangular panes
set in straight molded muntins. Doors are flanked at
sides and center by narrow plain stiles or wider ones

298

that are either reeded vertically or in herringbone design. They are hung with butt hinges and fitted with
turned wooden knobs. Cupboard has two full-width
shelves, one of them notched for spoons. Is raised four
to six inches above counter top of lower section and
front lower edge is finished with a simple molding,
sometimes downcurved at ends.

Space between sections is open at front and closed at
sides and back. The counter top has rounded or molded
edges at front and sides. Beneath it is a tier of three
shallow drawers, the center one narrower than those
that flank it. Their fronts are reeded or have incised six-
pointed stars flanking reeded rosettes. They are fitted
with wooden knobs. Beneath them is a pair of paneled

doors enclosing the lower cupboard, with or without herringbone reeding. They are hung with butt hinges and fitted with wooden knobs matching those on the drawers. Has simply molded base and is supported by four plain or molded bracket feet. Made of pine and assorted softwoods and painted Amish blue, cypress green or brown. Construction and design similar to dresser made elsewhere (*see No. 242*). *Ca. 1785–1850.* Y to YYY

299

299. Kitchen Cupboard with High Counter Top

Has slightly overhanging top, 40 to 50 inches wide, surrounded at back and sides by a simple gallery three to five inches high that terminates in quarter-round ends. The carcase contains a tier of half-width drawers above a tall cupboard. The drawers are about four inches deep and have plain fronts fitted with mushroom-turned knobs. Cupboard is enclosed by two doors separated by a central stile three to five inches wide. The doors have plain vertical panels, are hung with butt hinges and fitted with knobs matching those above, or there are turn buttons, screwed to the central stile.

Sometimes there is a simple skirt with slightly curved lower edge. Instead of feet, the ends of cupboard extend to the floor and are cut in shallow curves that form flat arches six to eight inches high. Piece is from 46 to 54 inches tall. Made of pine or assorted softwoods and painted Amish blue, cypress green, brown, gray or left natural. Plentiful and inexpensive. *Ca. 1830–1870.* X to XX

300. Water or Bucket Bench

A kitchen piece, the pails of fresh water were kept on its broad counter shelf; milk pails and other buckets were stored in the cupboard below and dippers and basins were put on the narrow upper shelf. Is often used today as a buffet.

Has a recessed top shelf, 44 to 56 inches wide and six to 10 inches deep, surrounded at back and sides with a simple gallery, three or five inches high, that terminates in rounded ends. This is supported by scroll-cut end pieces. Beneath is a compartment, containing three shallow drawers of equal width and fitted with small wooden knobs, that is 18 to 20 inches above a full-width counter top, 20 to 22 inches deep, that is open at the back and has a slightly overhanging rounded edge.

The full-width cupboard below is 16 to 20 inches high and enclosed by a pair of plain or paneled doors hung

300

with butt hinges and fitted with knobs matching those above. On the central stile between are two wooden turn buttons. Ends of bench extend to the floor with lower edges cut to form flat arches six to eight inches high. Height of piece varies from 48 to 56 inches. Made of pine sometimes combined with other softwoods. Plentiful. *Ca. 1800–1860.* XX to XXX

301. Dough Tray or Kneading Table

A memory piece copied from a furniture form peculiar to the Rhine Valley homeland, it takes name from its use. Bread dough was set to rise in the trough and was kneaded on its flat removable top. This is rectangular, 36 to 54 inches long and 20 to 28 inches wide,

301

made in one or two pieces with cleated ends. It is either slightly larger than the trough or overhangs it six to 10 inches at the ends and four to six inches on the sides. The smaller-sized top has grooved cleats on its underside that secure it to the trough; the larger one lifts off.

The trough is from 10 to 14 inches deep with flaring sides and ends. It is supported by four canted, baluster-turned legs with simple ring turnings about four inches from the floor that simulate peg feet. Legs are connected by a deeply valanced skirt. Height varies from 27 to 31 inches. Examples with larger size of tray were also used as ordinary tables. Made of maple or walnut, sometimes with top of pine. Early examples are of walnut and not numerous. Later ones, dating after 1820, are generally of maple and plentiful. *Ca. 1700–1850.* XX to Y

Dry Sink

Used in farmhouse kitchens without plumbing connections, it is a simple rectangular cabinet, 40 to 48 inches wide and 18 to 20 inches deep. Has an inset top that is depressed five or six inches. Beneath it is a full-width cupboard with either single or double doors that are plain or paneled. They are fitted with butt hinges, wooden knobs and turn buttons. Instead of feet, the ends extend to floor with lower edges cut to form low flat arches. Height varies from 33 to 35 inches.

Made of pine or other softwoods with exterior left natural or painted Amish blue, cypress green, brown or gray. Plentiful and inexpensive. Are chiefly used to-day as plant stands, magazine tables or mixing stands. *Ca. 1830–1870.* X to XX

Shaker and Primitive Furniture

MAKING furniture bulked large with the Shakers. Their first community was started in 1776 at Watervliet, New York, on the Hudson River, just north of Albany. In less than twenty years twelve communities, where the core of belief was "dedication of their hearts to God and their hands to work," were thriving in Maine, New Hampshire, Massachusetts, Connecticut and New York. The men and women converts separated themselves from the world, shunned marriage, accumulation of private property, worldly pleasures and vanities and lived celibate lives in the manner of the medieval orders.

At the outset, men who had been woodworkers before their conversion concentrated on making the furniture for their communal residences and workshops. In 1789 the specialty of chair making was established at their New Lebanon, New York, community. The next year the Shakers were peddling their chairs to shopkeepers in surrounding towns and even as far away as Poughkeepsie. They were the first to start systematic production of slat-back rocking chairs.

These and their three-slat side chairs found such ready acceptance by worldly outsiders that Shaker communities at Harvard, Massachusetts, and Canterbury, New Hampshire, also established chair shops. The chairs were well made and cheap. During the first forty years of the nineteenth century, side chairs sold for seventy-five cents and rockers for a dollar each.

By 1815, the Shakers had over one thousand members living in eighteen communities and by 1850 some six thousand. It was during these years that chairs and other pieces of furniture which are now collectibles were produced. Beginning about 1860, their communities began to dwindle in size and number and making of their distinctive furniture declined in quantity and quality.

Chairs which they peddled through the countryside were their main products for outsiders, but for community use the Shaker cabinetmakers made about sixteen other furniture forms, such as tables, chests of drawers, blanket chests, desks, candlestands, writing boxes, washstands, sewing cabinets, mirror frames and occasionally a sideboard. All were austere in design. They also made tables, benches, spinning wheels, yarn reels, candlesticks and stools for use in their various workshops. This household and shop furniture was not often sold outside.

Pieces now available to collectors are those that passed from Shaker ownership when one after another of their communities were closed and surviving members transferred to the three that still remain.

Special Comments on Shaker Furniture and Its Design

Since the Shakers shunned ornament of any sort, their furniture has distinctive character because of its utter simplicity and absence of decorative details.

Their large tables are of three kinds, trestle, sawbuck and a simplified tavern type. Table legs are always simply turned, slightly tapering and without feet.

Chairs are all of the slat-back type and unornamented save for the acorn or knob finials of the back uprights. Splint was first used for the seats, with rush, cane and woven tape substituted later.

There are five kinds of Shaker rocking chairs — (1) scroll arm, (2) rolled arm, (3) front uprights with mushroom-turned upper ends, (4) back surmounted by a cross rail and (5) armless sewing rocker. Maple was the chief wood for turned uprights and slats but birch, cherry and butternut were also used. The turned stretchers and seat rails were made of ash, hickory or maple.

Case pieces, such as desks, chests of drawers, blanket chests, cupboards and various work benches, counters, and such, are rectangular and austere. Many are without feet and have plain molded bases that rest directly on the floor. If there are legs, they are plainly turned and taper slightly. Drawer fronts are plain and fitted with small turned knobs. Case pieces are consistently of pine throughout.

Although the Shakers disliked ornamentation on their furniture, they were not against painting it in various colors. A dark red was the standard color for their chairs and much of the furniture which the Believers made for their own use was painted red, orange, yellow or stained brown in tones ranging from cinnamon to russet.

Shaker furniture is of the same construction as that made by contemporaries outside their communities and the workmanship is of the best. Mortice and tenon or dovetail joinings are carefully cut and tightly fitted, the former securely pegged with wooden pins.

302

302. Trestle Table

Has plain rectangular two- or three-board top, 26 to 28 inches wide and five to eight feet long, with cross battens on underside just inside the supporting trestles, which are square with chamfered edges. They are joined by a plain stretcher, placed immediately beneath the top, and terminate in either low arched T-shaped tripods or slightly arched shoe feet that are about three inches wide and 24 inches long. The trestles, stretcher and tripods or shoe feet are secured by mortice and tenon joints and pegged with wooden pins. A rare communal dining table has a four-board top, 34 inches wide and 20 feet long, and is supported by three trestles terminating in high arched shoe feet. Made of maple or birch with larger tables generally of pine. *Ca. 1800–1860.* XXX to YY

Sawbuck Table

Has two stretchers placed below the crossings of the X-shaped trestles. Made as ironing board and for kitchen use. Top is from 28 to 34 inches wide and from 36 to 60 inches long. It closely resembles the nineteenth-century survival sawbuck table made elsewhere (*see No. 65*). Made of maple or birch with top sometimes of pine. *Ca. 1800–1860.* XX to XXX

Tavern Table

Has either square legs braced by box stretcher or plain tapering turned legs. Varies in size from a small table with top about 30 inches long to large work table with top 48 to 60 inches and one drop leaf at back. *Ca. 1800–1860.* XX to XXX

303. Slat-Back Rocking Chair

The turned front and back uprights are about an inch and a half in diameter with front ones vase-turned above the seat. Rear ones terminate in small acorn or knob finials. Some have a turned crossbar, instead of finials, over which a folded blanket or quilt might be stretched for the comfort of an ailing or aged Believer. The back has four slightly concave slats. These are about 12 inches long and two to two and a half inches wide with upper edges slightly curved. The chair has flat, shaped and slightly flaring arms that are socketed onto the front uprights and held fast by large button turnings.

Legs are braced by two box stretchers of plain turned members and are mounted on narrow rockers about 26 inches long with front ends quarter-rounded. Seat is of splint, rush or woven tape. Made of maple or less frequently of cherry, birch or butternut with stretcher parts

303

of ash, hickory or maple. Is generally plainer than other contemporary armchairs and always fitted with rockers (*see No. 5*). *Ca. 1800–1860.* XX to XXX

Slat-Back Side Chair

Is constructed like the foregoing but without rockers. Back has only three slats and uprights always terminate in acorn or knob finials. *Ca. 1800–1860.* X to XX

304. High Chest of Drawers

Has oblong top, 40 to 44 inches wide and usually 18 inches deep with a simply molded edge. Carcase contains two top tiers of half-width drawers and four below that are full width. Drawers are not graduated but have slightly overlapping thumb-molded edges and are fitted with small mushroom-turned wooden knobs. Piece is supported by simple bracket feet about six inches

304

high. Height varies from four feet eight inches to five feet two inches. Made of maple, birch or butternut. *Ca. 1810–1850.* XX to Y

Low Chest of Drawers

Is like the foregoing but carcase contains only one tier of half-width drawers and three that are full width. It varies in width from 24 to 32 inches and in height from 27 to 34 inches. *Ca. 1810–1850.* XX to XXX

305. Shaker Candlestand

Has rectangular one-board top 18 to 24 inches wide with cleated ends. This overhangs the bed six to eight inches on the sides and four to six inches front and

305

back. Bed contains a single drawer about four inches deep that has a plain front and is fitted with a small wooden knob. Stand rests on a slightly tapering shaft supported by three straight turned and canted short legs. Height varies from 18 to 25 inches. Made of maple, birch or butternut. *Ca. 1810–1840.* X to XX

PRIMITIVE FURNITURE

In addition to furniture made by trained cabinet-makers there is a small group of crudely fashioned but well-made pieces classed as primitives. Since most of them were discarded as soon as they could be replaced by professionally made ones, only a few examples have survived.

Dating a primitive is always difficult since its design is simple and lacks details characteristic of other pieces in the different style periods. The range is also limited. They are all pieces made to fill special needs, such as the fireplace settle, the wagon seat, the artisan's working candlestick and the earliest of the candlestands.

Further, there is a fine dividing line between a primitive and a country piece made by a farmer who was handy with woodworking tools. Settling this is a matter of personal opinion based on study of particular examples, but all primitives have characteristics similar to the four described here.

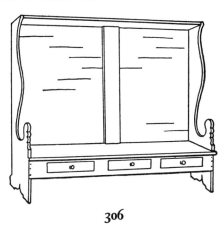

306

306. High-Back Settle

Placed at the side of the large fireplace, its solid back and wide sides provided protection from the cold drafts common to American homes of the seventeenth and early eighteenth century. Its design is a memory copy of the settles used in farm cottages in rural England. Has a solid back, five to seven feet long and from five feet to five feet six inches high, which is surmounted by a projecting hood. This is a plain board, eight to ten inches wide, with slight upward cant and is attached to the ends. The back is made of eight to twelve narrow boards nailed to the sides and frequently strength-

ened by a central batten, eight to 10 inches wide, placed
on the front and extending from seat to hood. The one-
piece ends above the seat have front edges shaped with
cyma curves that terminate in scrolled handgrips. Below the seat they are either plain or cut in low concave
curves and extend to the floor. The one-piece seat is
from 16 to 20 inches deep and has a rounded front edge
that is slightly overhanging. Beneath it is a plain skirt
about eight inches deep that sometimes contains a tier
of two or three drawers, of equal width and about four
inches deep, that are fitted with wooden knobs.

Made of pine, sometimes combined with other softwoods. Is always a well-proportioned but simply made
piece. Painted greenish blue, bottle green or finished
with red filler. Not numerous. *Ca. 1675–1775.* XXX to Y

307. Wagon Seat

Originally made in sets of two or three and used
in a farm wagon to convert it to a family conveyance.
Matching seats are seldom found today.

Is a low, double slat-back armchair. Generally has
three turned uprights, 33 to 37 inches high, terminating
in simple ball, knob or steeple finials. The double back
is formed by two or three slats that are slightly concave,
two to two and a half inches wide with slightly curved
upper edges. The front uprights are from 22 to 25
inches high and support the flaring turned or shaped
arms. The front and back central uprights are usually
about an inch greater in diameter than the end ones.
The seat, 14 to 15 inches deep, 32 or 33 inches wide and
14 or 15 inches from the floor, is of rush or splint.

An earlier example has seat in two sections with space

307

about an inch wide between them. With this, there are two extra seat rails socketed into the central front and back uprights. Legs are braced by either one or two double box stretchers with turned members about three quarters of an inch in diameter. Outside uprights frequently have somewhat flattened outer sides. This was done so the seat would fit inside the wagon box. General design and construction are the same as the slat-back armchair (*see No. 5*). Always simple and somewhat crudely made of maple and assorted hardwoods. *Ca. 1790–1825.* XXX to YY

308. Peg-Leg Screw Candlestick

Has a screw-threaded turned shaft rising from a plain round or square plinth about six inches across and two inches thick. This is supported by four short spindle-turned peg legs. Threaded onto the shaft is a crossarm with a candle socket at each end. Height can be adjusted by screwing candle arm up or down. Beneath this and adjustable in the same manner is a circular tray with bead-molded edge, about 18 inches in diameter. Such

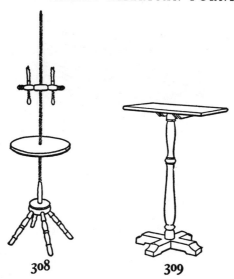

308   309

candlesticks were originally used by cabinetmakers, shoe-
makers, and the like, in their shops to get light close
to their work. Height varies from five feet to five feet
six inches. Made of maple, sometimes combined with
assorted hardwoods. *Ca. 1700–1800.* XXX to Y

309. Cross-Base Candlestand

Has plain top, 14 to 18 inches square, attached to a
baluster-turned shaft. This is socketed into a cross base
consisting of two chamfered shoe feet, lap-joined at center to form a right-angle cross. These feet are about 12
inches long, three inches thick and four inches wide.
Their upper edges are plain or slightly chamfered.
Made of assorted woods, generally with pine top, maple
shaft and oak feet. *Ca. 1700–1750.* XX to XXX

Hardware

NOTHING so enhances a piece of furniture as correct handles and other mounts. Nothing detracts from it more than wrong ones. But it is fairly common for a chest of drawers or similar piece, otherwise in excellent condition, to be lacking its original handles, due to wear, breakage or a natural tendency on the part of previous owners to bring the old piece up to date by substituting mounts of a later style. Fortunately there are excellent reproductions to be had which are faithful copies of antique originals. So for a piece with missing hardware or with the wrong kind, replacements of correct design and material are the solution.

There is more style consistency in drawer handles than with any other detail. Whether of brass, wood or glass, American cabinetmakers used only twelve different types during the two centuries in which furniture making was a handcraft. In the Puritan Span or Jacobean period, turned elongated wooden knobs were used consistently and appeared also on some of the early pieces in the William and Mary and Queen Anne periods. Then for about a century only brass fittings were in favor. These were made by the brass founders of Birmingham, England, in eight styles. The teardrop was used on William and Mary pieces, the bat's-wing for Queen Anne, rosettes with bail handle and willow designs for Chippendale, oval plate for Hepplewhite, oblong plate, lion's-head with pendent ring and embossed rosette with pendent ring in the Sheraton period and embossed rosette knob for the American Empire. During the two latter periods pressed glass and mushroom-turned wooden knobs were optional. For the early Victorian only wooden handles were used. These were carved ones with finger grips or, on the cottage pieces, mushroom-turned knobs which were holdovers from the American Empire.

There are slight variations of detail in these designs but each has definite characteristics that make it easy to place it as to period and there is also less overlapping of styles than in any other detail of furniture design.

For case pieces with doors or lids, there was the additional hardware of hinges. There were five designs made in wrought iron and two in brass. Those of iron were American made, being forged by the local blacksmith of the community where the piece was made. Brass hinges were imported as were the three types of brass feet used on tables, sofas and some chairs during the Sheraton and American Empire periods.

CABINET BRASSES

310. Teardrop Handles

Are found on highboys and lowboys with trumpet legs and on chests of drawers and desks with large ball or bun feet. They take their name from the shaping of the pendent handles. The plates behind them are either scroll-edged squares, set on the diagonal and decorated

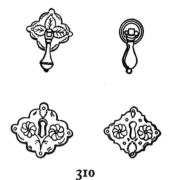

310

with simple chased designs, or circular with beaded rims. With the square plate the handle is one and a half to two inches long and the plate one and a quarter to one and three quarters inches across. With the round plate the handle measures one to one and a half inches long and the plate has a diameter of three quarters to an inch.

These mounts are fastened to the drawer by wirelike strips of metal called *tangs* in the following manner. With each, the tang is looped through the eye of the handle, its ends threaded through the central plate hole and the bored hole of the drawer front and then spread cotter fashion.

The keyhole escutcheons are of like design but with more elaborate chasing. They may be (1) scroll-outlined squares set on the diagonal, (2) circular or (3) cartouche shaped. At the corners or near the rim are four small holes for the bradlike brass nails with which they are attached. Are all of cast brass except the tangs. *Used ca. 1690–1720.*

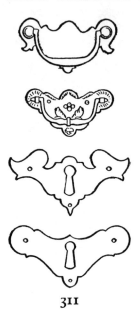

311

311. Bat's-Wing Mounts

Are found on highboys and lowboys with cabriole
legs terminating in Dutch, drake or Spanish feet, chests
of drawers and desks with scrolled brackets and desks
and tables with vase-and-ring or baluster-turned legs.
Take name from similarity in outline of plates and
escutcheons to a bat with outspread wings. The plates
are either plain or decorated with chased details and
the design varies from a simple outline to scrolled volutes
beneath the outcurved ends. They measure from two and
three fourths to three and one fourth inches wide by
two to two and a half inches high. They have bail

handles, held in place in early examples by tangs and in later ones by round-headed posts with threaded ends and small nuts.

The keyhole escutcheons have approximately the same outlines as the plates and are nailed in place by three small brads. Are of cast brass. *Used ca. 1720–1750.*

312

312. Willow Mounts

Are found on highboys and lowboys with cabriole legs terminating in claw-and-ball feet, some tables with claw-and-ball feet, chests of drawers, desks, secretaries, chests-on-chests with short cabriole brackets terminating in claw-and-ball feet and those with scroll bracket or molded bracket feet. Willow is an arbitrary name used to describe the baroque scrolled outline of the plates. It generally includes a triple arching at center of the top, scrolled volutes above the outrounded ends, and the lower edge is valanced, sometimes with a scrolled central pendant.

Solid plates belong on most of the furniture but with some of the elaborate pieces, plates that are pierced in intricate fretwork, strap or scroll patterns should be used. They have bail handles secured by round-head posts with the usual threading and nuts. Plates vary considerably in their design details. Sizes also vary but most of them are from three and a half to four and a quarter inches wide and from two and a quarter to three and three eighths inches high. For narrow drawers with only a single handle, a special plate with a centered keyhole is used.

The keyhole escutcheons match the plates and have nail holes at ends and bottom. Made entirely of cast brass. *Used ca. 1750–1775.*

313. Rosettes with Bail Handles

Are contemporary with the foregoing and found on the same pieces of furniture. They are of two kinds, plain and with design enhanced by French-inspired patterns of decorative scrolls done in relief on both rosettes and bails. The plain type is found on many Chippendale chests of drawers and desks and on some Hepplewhite pieces, where their use is a survival from the preceding period. The elaborate kind chiefly grace the fine Chippendale chests of drawers which were made in Philadelphia.

The rosettes are from an inch and a half to two inches across. Those of the plain type are round or oval with

313

beaded rims; the elaborate ones are foliage scrolled, the rim has a scrolled outline and the bail is also scroll ornamented. Posts with rounded or rosette heads hold them in place. A complete handle with rosettes and bail measures three and a half to four and a half inches wide.

The keyhole escutcheons with the plain type are either vertical ovals or are circular with small nailing holes top and bottom. The ovals are about an inch and a half high by an inch wide. The circular ones are about an inch and a half in diameter. With the ornate handles, the keyhole escutcheons have a scrolled outline with arched top and the face has foliage scrolling done in relief. Made of cast brass. *Plain type used ca. 1760–1800. Ornate type, ca. 1765–1775.*

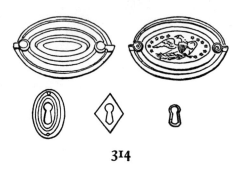

314

314. Hepplewhite Oval Mounts

Are found on all case pieces with French feet and on tables with characteristic square tapering legs. The plates are of *stamped* brass, have a classic oval outline, a molded rim with its center either a molded medallion or an embossed decoration. Designs for the latter include the patriotic spread eagle with thirteen stars, an acorn with oak leaves, a stylized thistle spray, a sheaf of wheat with sickle or a horn of plenty. Curve of the bail conforms to the plate oval. Plates range in size from three to four inches in width and two to two and a half inches in height. They are secured by posts with rosette heads.

Three kinds of keyhole escutcheons are used. They are the vertical oval or circular type with beaded rim like the foregoing, the inset cast-brass keyhole surround that is about an inch high, and the diamond-shaped inlay of satinwood veneer or sometimes of ivory, measuring about two inches high by an inch wide. Plates are of stamped brass; bails, posts and keyhole surrounds are of cast brass. *Used ca. 1785–1800.*

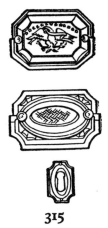

315

315. Sheraton Oblong Mounts

Are found on case pieces and tables with turned and reeded legs and some American Empire furniture with carved paw feet and columns or pilasters. The stamped-brass plate is oblong in shape with canted or incurved corners. It has a molded rim and the embossed design in the center is oval with a variety of motifs, including the patriotic spread eagle. The shape of the bail conforms to that of the plate and it is held in place by posts with rosette heads. Plates are from three to four inches wide and two to two and a half inches high.

Two types of keyhole escutcheons are used. They are oblong embossed plates with quarter-round incurved corners, a beaded rim and nail holes top and bottom and inset cast-brass keyhole surrounds. Plates and keyhole escutcheons are of stamped brass; bails, posts and surrounds are of cast brass. *Used ca. 1800–1830.*

316

316. Pendent Ring Handles

Are found on case pieces and tables inspired by the French Directoire. The plates are of two designs, a cast-brass lion's-head with ring held between its jaws or a stamped-brass rosette embossed with acanthus-leaf foliage with ring hanging from a central post. The lion's-head plates are about an inch and three quarters to two and a quarter inches high and from an inch and a half to an inch and three quarters wide. The rosette plates are from an inch and three quarters to two and a half inches in diameter. The pendent rings are from an inch and a quarter to two inches in diameter. The lion's-head and rings are of cast brass; the rosettes of stamped brass. *Used ca. 1805–1820.*

The escutcheons are either stamped ovals or inset key-hole surrounds like the foregoing.

317

317. Rosette Knobs

They are of two kinds, brass and pressed glass, and are found on Sheraton and American Empire case pieces and tables with turned and reeded legs or carved paw feet. The brass rosette knobs are made of two disks of stamped and embossed metal crimped together at the circumference and are mounted on threaded shanks which are inserted in holes bored in the drawer front. The face of the knobs is embossed in flower, leaf, geometric and other motifs. Each knob also has a rosette plate with beaded rim of the same diameter. These knobs are from an inch and a half to two and a quarter inches in diameter and project about two inches. *Used ca. 1800–1830.*

The pressed glass knobs are circular and are mounted by round-headed bolts that are inserted through a central hole. Designs vary from those resembling patterns of some of the early pressed glass cup plates to plain or swirled shapes. They are found in clear, opalescent, blue, green and yellow. Were made chiefly by the Boston and Sandwich Glass Company at Sandwich, Massachusetts, and by Bakewell, Pears & Company in Pittsburgh, Pennsylvania. *Used ca. 1820–1840.*

The escutcheons are chiefly inset brass keyhole surrounds.

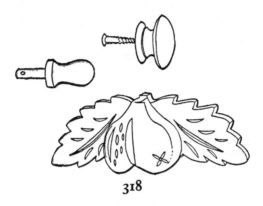

318

318. Wooden Knobs and Handles

Are of three kinds: the elongated turned knobs found on Puritan Span case pieces, William and Mary and Queen Anne tavern tables and desks-on-frame; the flat, mushroom-turned knobs of the late Sheraton and American Empire periods and the carved leaf and fruit handles found only on Early Victorian case pieces.

The elongated knob is a simple turning about an inch and a quarter in diameter by about three inches long and has a circular shank that fits into a hole bored in the drawer front. Is generally of maple and used with plain keyholes. *Used ca. 1650–1730.*

Mushroom-turned knobs are shaped like a mushroom button and are attached to the drawer front by screws. They are from an inch and a half to two and a half inches in diameter and project about an inch. Most frequently made of mahogany. Used with inset brass keyhole surround. *Ca. 1820–1840.*

Carved handles generally have a leaf background with pendent fruits at the center. The lower edge has finger-grip space behind the face. These vary in width from four to seven inches. Are attached to the drawer by screws. Most frequently carved of black walnut but some are of rosewood or cherry. Used with inset brass keyhole surrounds. *Ca. 1840–1875.*

319. H-Shaped Hinges and Scrolled Keyhole Escutcheons

Are found on doors of secretaries, corner cupboards, linen presses and dressers of Queen Anne and Chippendale periods. Hinges take name from similarity of shape to that of capital letter H. They have exposed narrow, tall leaves that are either plain or have a slightly scrolled outline. They are always mounted so leaves show and add to decorative trimming of the piece. They vary in size from two and a half to five inches in height. Usually made of cast brass but sometimes of wrought iron for corner cupboards and dressers. *Ca. 1720–1775.*

Scrolled keyhole escutcheons are found most often on the paneled doors of secretaries of the Queen Anne and Chippendale periods. They are of a variety of designs with scrolling that corresponds to that of other escutcheons on drawer fronts. Two of those most frequently used are illustrated, one with balancing right

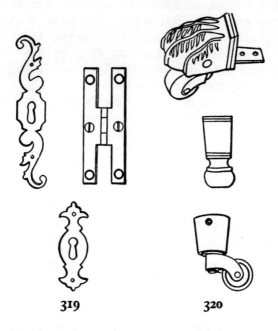

319   320

and left scrolls above and below a central oblong and
the other with matching triple-arched shaping above
and below a central oval. They vary in size from about
three to five inches in height. Made of cast brass. *Used
ca. 1720–1775.*

320. Brass Feet

Are found on tables, sofas and some chairs of the
Sheraton and American Empire periods. There are three
types — the paw foot, the cup caster and the ball leg
tip. All are of cast brass.

Paw Foot

Has a design like that of an animal's paw with fur and claws, probably that of a lion. It is hollow, fits over the end of the leg and is secured by four screws, one on each side and two below. It generally has a pivoted roller placed well to the back of the hollow shoe, which is about three inches long by two inches wide. Complete with roller, it measures from three to three and a half inches high. *Used ca. 1810–1830.*

Cup Caster

Is cup-shaped and fits over the end of a table or chair leg. Either circular or square, it is from an inch to an inch and a half high, from an inch and a quarter to an inch and three quarters across and has a pivot-mounted roller beneath. Total height varies from two to three inches. *Used ca. 1800–1840.*

Ball Leg Tip

Is found mostly on chairs and some tables and sofas. The lower end is ball shaped with a cup above which fits over the end of the leg. *Used ca. 1805–1820.*

321. Small Knobs and Pendent Loops

The knobs are chiefly found on pull brackets of desks and on various small drawers. They are of two kinds, those with a screw and those with a nail-like point. Measurements vary from half an inch to an inch and a quarter in diameter by an inch and a half to two and a quarter inches in length. *Used ca. 1690–1840.*

The pendent loop is attached to a small head and

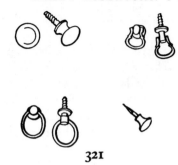

321

varies in width from three quarters of an inch to an inch and a half. Is also found as a ring. Used as handle for small drawers and sometimes in larger size for secretary and cupboard doors. *Ca. 1740–1820.*

322. Wrought-Iron Hinges

(*a*) *Strap design.* From pin joints a long straplike leaf tapers to an arrow or spade shaping with either a spike tip or an enlarged circle. The anchor leaf is rectangular and at right angles to the strap leaf, giving the entire hinge a T-shape. The strap is from six to 12 inches long and about two inches wide. The anchor leaf is from three to seven inches long by an inch and a half to two inches wide. Strap hinges are attached with hand-wrought nails clinched on the inside and mostly found on cupboards and dressers, mounted on the outside, and on chests where they are generally attached to the underside of the lid. *Used ca. 1700–1825.*

(*b*) *Butterfly design.* Has flaring leaves that somewhat resemble butterfly wings. Outer edges are slightly concave and curve is repeated at top and bottom when leaves are open. They are from three to five inches across

and from two and a half to three inches wide at the pin
joining. Generally found on small chests and slant-top
desks, some cupboards where they are exposed for
decorative effect, and on undersides of gate-leg, butter-

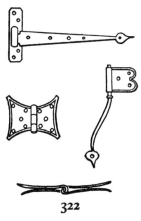

322

fly and other contemporary table tops with drop leaves.
Attached with hand-wrought nails, frequently clinched.
Used ca. 1700–1750.

(*c*) *Rat-tail design.* Shape of supporting bracket is
similar to a rat's tail, is from five to seven inches long
and terminates in arrow or spade shaping with spikelike
point. A leaf with outer edge scalloped or rounded fits
over the upper end of this bracket. The leaf is about
two and a half inches high and three inches wide. Rat-
tail hinges are mounted exposed and are found chiefly
on cupboards and dressers of Pennsylvania Dutch origin.
Used ca. 1725–1775.

(*d*) *Snipe design.* Is not ornamental and never exposed. It is made of two lengths of wirelike wrought

iron, bent double, with an eye at one end, the other tapering to a point. One part is slipped over the other so that the eyes are interlocking. The pointed ends are inserted in bored holes, turned over as with a modern cotter and clinched. Found only on chests and blanket chests. *Used ca. 1750–1825.*

(*e*) *Butt design.* Is more frequently used than the shaped types. Leaves are rectangular, made of two thicknesses of iron, bent double around the pin and then riveted together. With later examples and replacements, the leaves are stamped of one thickness of metal with one edge rolled for the pin joint. They are mounted with screws with only the pin joints exposed. Majority are of wrought iron but may be of cast brass on some of the finer pieces. This type of hinge antedates American furniture making and is still in use.

Nails and Screws

Nails are found on backboards of case pieces and mirror frames and are sometimes countersunk for applied moldings and the like. They are of two kinds, handmade and cut. A handmade nail has a square shank tapering to a sharp point and a slightly cresting top that is about square and shows the marks of the hammer blows with which it was forged. The irregularities of handwork are the distinguishing marks of these nails. Sizes vary from one to six inches. They are the original nails found on furniture made before 1815. The cut nail is the earliest form of machine-made nails and came into use about 1815. As the name indicates the nail was produced by a simple cutting machine from strips of sheet iron, an eighth to a sixteenth of an inch thick. This machine also shaped the flat square head. Traces of the cutting can be seen along the edges of the shank. Those used in cabinetwork vary in size from small brads to those that are almost spikelike and in length from one to six inches. Wire nails are all replacements when found on pieces of antique furniture since these modern machine-made nails did not come into use until about 1875.

All original screws found on furniture made before 1815 are handmade. Whether of iron or brass, such a screw has a slightly irregular hand-filed worm, a blunt end and the slot in the head is apt to be a little off center. The early type of machine-made screw dates between 1815 and 1860. Its worm and slot are regular as to cutting but the end is blunt. Both handmade and early machine-made screws used in cabinetwork vary in size from a quarter inch to three inches or longer. They are used to attach hinges, brass cup and paw casters, corner blocks of chairs, seat braces of sofas and the like.

Furniture Woods

American cabinetmakers used a variety of twenty-six different woods of which eighteen were hard and eight were soft. Except for mahogany and rosewood, hardwoods used for entire pieces were all native to the country. Native also were the softwoods, equally essential for cabinetwork since they were the materials for concealed structural parts and the base for veneered pieces. Softwoods were also used for much of the less expensive country furniture, often finished with New England red filler paint.

Because knowing wood can be of material assistance in placing a piece as to period and provenance, the characteristics of the twenty-six woods are briefly summarized:

Amboina

Very hard wood, generally with small bird's-eye knots. Imported from the Dutch East Indies in the late eighteenth century. Finished, it varies from reddish brown to orange in color. Used for inlay details and as inset veneer panels.

Applewood

Very hard and close-grained. Color ranges from light brown to amber when finished. Difficult to distinguish from yellow birch. Used by country cabinetmakers for

case pieces, particularly corner cupboards, and sometimes for tables and chests of drawers from 1750 to 1825.
Pieces made of it are more unusual than those of cherry
or birch.

Ash

A heavy wood of great strength with grain and texture similar to oak. Finished color, a light cream. In
the mid-seventeenth century it was frequently used for
turned chairs but was replaced by maple about 1700 because of its tendency to split when worked on a lathe.
Its use thereafter was chiefly for bows, arms and other
bent parts of Windsor chairs.

Basswood

A light, straight-grained softwood. In unfinished state
it acquires a brownish-yellow tone with age. Chiefly used
for interior parts, such as drawer bottoms and backs and
backboards of case pieces. During the eighteenth century
a few painted chests of drawers, highboys, desks and the
like were made entirely of it by country cabinetmakers.
These pieces were sometimes grained or finished with
New England red filler.

Birch (Yellow)

Very hard and as close fibered as maple but with
more pattern of grain. Takes a high polish. Finished
color ranges from light brown to amber. Sometimes
found with curly grain and used decoratively for table
tops, skirts and drawer fronts of all-birch pieces. Some
slat-back chairs and four-post beds are found with turned
birch uprights. Chiefly used from 1750 to 1825 by coun-

try cabinetmakers of New Hampshire and Maine. Turned parts of Hitchcock chairs are sometimes of birch. Entire pieces made of it include chests of drawers, tables and slant-top desks. Weight is heavier than that of similar pieces made of maple.

Boxwood

Hard, very close-grained wood of yellowish-orange color, used for inlay details in place of holly. Of West Indian provenance, it was sometimes dyed green or other colors when vivid contrast was desired for elaborate inlay designs.

Butternut

Hard and close-grained, it takes excellent polish. Color when finished is a very light brown. Sometimes called white walnut but is finer in texture. Both trees are of same botanical family. Not widely used but some eighteenth-century case pieces of it are known, notably Queen Anne highboys. Was also used by early nineteenth-century cabinetmakers of Middle West for chests of drawers, tables, desks, cupboards and similar case pieces.

Cherry (Black)

Very hard and close-grained with visible but not pronounced pattern. Sometimes is finely flaked when quarter-sawed. Takes high polish. Has reddish-brown color when finished which approaches that of mahogany. Wide boards frequently have a yellowish streak of sapwood at one side. Sometimes found with curly grain but less pronounced than that of maple. Used by Connecticut cabinetmakers at beginning of eighteenth century for their butterfly tables, either for entire piece or for base. Was substituted for mahogany from about 1770 for tables, chairs, chests of drawers, highboys, lowboys, chests-on-chests and mirror frames. Also used during Hepplewhite, Sheraton and American Empire periods. For some of the fine pieces was combined with fancy-grain maple for decorative contrast. Tall clock cases were sometimes made of cherry, also posts for low-post beds until about 1830. Arms of Boston rockers were frequently of cherry, finished natural. Pieces are heavier in weight than those made of maple.

Chestnut

A medium-hard wood with large pores and distinct pattern of grain. Somewhat resembles oak. Takes a good polish. A warm, mellow brownish yellow when finished. Sometimes used in seventeenth century for bases of large stretcher tables. Also for a few large chests in early eighteenth century. Otherwise its use was mostly confined to backboards and concealed structural members of case pieces, tables, beds and sofa frames.

Ebony

A very hard close-grained black wood from India. Used for stringing and other inlay details, such as herringbone borders where it was combined with holly or boxwood for the black and white contrast.

Hickory

A heavy strong wood. Because of the tenacity of its fiber was widely used for Windsor and Boston rocker spindles. Not popular with cabinetmakers otherwise since it does not stand heat or moisture.

Holly

A hard white wood with slightly flecked grain. Used for inlay, especially stringing. Effective contrast to mahogany or other reddish wood. Dyed black was often used as a substitute for ebony. Most of the holly used by American cabinetmakers came from trees growing southward from New Jersey.

Mahogany

A tropical wood of great strength, hardness and firm texture with a variety of grain and figures, depending on location in tree and method of sawing. It takes a high polish. Color varies from deep reddish brown to red with brown undertone, according to the finishing materials used. Some pieces of American furniture were made of it early in the eighteenth century, but use was not general until about 1750. Majority of fine Chippendale pieces were made of mahogany. Continued as the top quality cabinet wood through Hepplewhite, Sheraton and American Empire periods.

Crotch-grain veneer, used for the decorative quality of its markings, comes from crotch of the two main branches. Used extensively during Chippendale, Hepplewhite and Sheraton periods. Veneering of entire pieces prevailed during American Empire years.

Mahogany tree measures as much as 10 feet in diameter. Therefore table leaves made of mahogany are practically always of one piece. Island of Haiti the chief source of the most desired variety, known as San Domingo mahogany. Is heavier, finer grained and of richer color than Central American or Amazon Valley mahogany.

Maple

Very hard, close-grained, with distinct fineness of fiber and pores. Takes a high polish. Color when finished varies from light brownish yellow to a rich amber. There are three varieties — straight-grained, curly and bird's-eye. The straight-grained has an even texture without distinctive markings, except for a fine flecking when so sawed as to present a cross-section cut of the annual growth rings. Curly markings vary from random twists to those that alternate so regularly as to be described as "tiger-striped." Bird's-eye markings consist of small, closely placed, knotlike whorls.

Straight-grained maple was used for American cabinet work by 1650 or earlier. Curly maple came into use about 1700 for decorative parts or for entire pieces. Was both turned and carved. Was also a substitute for satinwood veneer in Hepplewhite period. Bird's-eye maple was widely used for drawer fronts, crest rails of chairs, and so on, during the Sheraton and American Empire periods. Furniture all of bird's-eye belongs predominately to later factory-made period when it was used as veneer.

The wood of the hard or rock maple was chiefly used for furniture. That of the swamp or soft maple was sometimes used for structural parts and for painted chairs of the Hitchcock type. Curly and bird's-eye varieties do not occur with soft maple.

Oak (White)

A very strong hardwood with visible pores and distinct pattern of grain that can be intensified by quarter sawing. Takes a high polish. In antique furniture it is of a warm brown color with graining somewhat lighter, but not the very light shade of factory-made golden oak. Oak was used for seventeenth-century furniture, such as chests, court cupboards, wainscot chairs, Bible boxes, joined stools and bases of trestle tables. Rarely used after 1690 except for Hadley chests, which continued to be made until about 1720. Structural parts of some later pieces, such as chair and bed rails and table beds, were of oak. Where drawer sides, backs and bottoms are of oak, this indicates English or European provenance, as does the use of oak as the base for walnut or mahogany veneer.

Pear

The finest grain and hardest of the native American fruit woods. Takes a very high polish. When finished, its color is light tan tinged with brown. Understructure of a few early gate-leg tables were turned of pear wood. Also used sometimes for inlay before 1750.

Pine (Northern Yellow)

Nonexistent today except for scrub growth trees of the pine barrens of coastal Massachusetts, parts of Rhode Island, Long Island and New Jersey, but was plentiful during the seventeenth century. Relatively hard with a pronounced grain. Color, a light brown when finished.

Was used for lids of oak dower chests, for table tops from the large stretcher type to small "tuckaways," for seats of oak-joined stools and for some early cupboards.

Pine (Southern Hard)

Strong, relatively hard with a pronounced grain of alternating clear and pitch wood, it takes a fine polish. Finished, is a light brown with reddish pitch stripes. From about 1780 was used for much of the locally made furniture of Virginia, the Carolinas and Georgia.

Pine (White)

Sometimes called pumpkin pine. A straight-grained softwood available in wide knot-free boards. Finished, color can vary from a warm yellow to a light amber. Widely used for backboards, drawer sides, backs and bottom of case pieces, for unseen structural parts, tops of simple tables and headboards of four-post beds. In New York cabinetmakers of Dutch descent sometimes used it for painted kases. Cupboards and other simple country pieces were made of pine in New England as was much of the Pennsylvania Dutch painted furniture. It was the standard wood for Windsor chair and Boston rocker seats, for seats of painted benches and for those of late painted chairs of the Hitchcock type. In Chippendale and succeeding periods was used for carved and gilded mirror frames. It was the base wood for mahogany and rosewood veneered pieces during Hepplewhite, Sheraton, American Empire and Early Victorian periods.

Red Gum

Called *bilsted* by old cabinetmakers. A moderately strong, straight-grained wood but so soft of texture that it dents readily. Easy to work and takes good polish. In unfinished state color range is from reddish brown to dark chocolate brown. A favorite wood with New York cabinetmakers in the seventeenth century and until about 1750. Red gum was used for their kases, both painted and finished natural; for some of their chests, combined with oak; and for early William and Mary painted chests-on-frame and highboys. Toward the end, simple tables, chairs and chests of drawers were made but because of the softness of wood, few pieces have survived.

Rosewood

A very hard, brittle, fine-grained wood. Takes a high polish. Of a red-purplish color when finished. Sometimes has streaks that are a deep old ivory in color. Comes from forests of Brazil. When freshly cut, logs have a scent much like that of roses, hence the name. First used as veneer for inlay panels, banding and other inlay details on elaborate Hepplewhite mahogany pieces. More frequently used in same manner during Sheraton and American Empire periods. Furniture all of rosewood was made during late Empire and Early Victorian years, often elaborately carved, such as the laminated pieces by Belter of New York.

Satinwood

A hard fine-grained dense wood, quarter-sawed to accentuate the "fire" of its grain, which is often very curly. Takes a high polish, is satiny and lustrous. Of light honey-yellow tone when finished. So much satinwood was used for decorative inlays, veneer panels and banding on Hepplewhite and Sheraton furniture in America and England that the stands of such trees in Puerto Rico were exhausted. After that satinwood was obtained from Ceylon.

Spruce

A light but strong softwood with straight grain less pronounced than in southern hard pine. Unfinished wood was used for drawer sides and the like. Generally of a light brown color without yellow tinge. Sometimes simple utilitarian pieces, such as schoolmaster's desks, were made of spruce. Also used for table tops in northern New England from about 1800 to 1835. Often finished with red filler paint.

Sycamore

A hardwood with dense grain much like maple. Sometimes quarter-sawed to accentuate the flecks in its grain and used as a veneer for banding. Takes a high polish and when finished is a very light brown. Stained greenish yellow, it was known as *harewood* by English cabinetmakers, who used it frequently in the eighteenth century for inlay. Not as widely used in this manner by American cabinetmakers.

Walnut

A hard strong wood of fine texture and handsome grain. Sometimes has a pleasing curly grain. Color when finished varies from a warm reddish brown to a chocolate brown, depending on treatment. The "red" Virginia walnut of Queen Anne and Chippendale periods came from trees that grew from the Schuylkill Valley in Pennsylvania south into Virginia. Was plentiful and widely used. Victorian black walnut was achieved by treating the pieces with a stain or acid wash before varnishing. This killed the natural reddish tinge.

Whitewood or Tulip

Also known as *poplar* south of New York. A clear-grained but soft wood. Unfinished, it varies from yellow to gray in color, depending on exposure to sunlight. Chiefly used for backboards, drawer sides, backs and bottoms of case pieces and for unseen structural parts of tables, sofas and wing chairs. Also for Windsor chair seats. Some country-made blanket chests, cupboards, dressers and linen presses were entirely of whitewood from about 1770. These are usually of New England provenance. Also used for some Pennsylvania Dutch painted pieces. Very rare are early eighteenth-century William and Mary or Queen Anne highboys of whitewood. They are painted and grained to simulate walnut.

Suggested Books on American Antique Furniture

American Antique Furniture, Edgar G. Miller, Jr.

American Antiques in Words and Pictures, Alice Winchester

An Encyclopedia of Antiques, Harold Lewis Bond

Blue Book, Philadelphia Furniture, William Penn to George Washington, William Macpherson Horner, Jr.

Colonial Furniture in America, Luke Vincent Lockwood

Colonial Furniture of New England, Irving W. Lyon

Early American Furniture, Charles Over Cornelius

Early American Furniture Makers, Thomas Hamilton Ormsbee

The Encyclopedia of Furniture, Joseph Aronson

The Furniture Designs of Chippendale, Hepplewhite and Sheraton, Arranged by J. Munro Bell with introduction by Arthur Hayden and essay by Charles Messer Stow

Furniture Masterpieces of Duncan Phyfe, Charles Over Cornelius

Furniture Treasury, Wallace Nutting

Shaker Furniture, Edward D. and Faith Andrews

The Hadley Chest, Clair Franklin Luther

The Homes of Our Ancestors, R. T. H. Halsey and Elizabeth Tower

The Pine Furniture of Early New England, Russell H. Kettell

The Practical Book of Period Furniture, H. D. Eberlein and A. McClure

The Primer of American Antiques, Carl W. Drepperd

The Story of American Furniture, Thomas Hamilton Ormsbee